This book is part of the Critical Pedag

DIO Press International Editorial Board

Anijar-Appleton, Karen, University of Arizona, USA, Emerita

Brock, Rochelle, University of North Carolina, Greensboro, USA In memorium

Carley, Robert F., Texas A & M University, USA

Down, Barry, Murdoch University, Australia

Echeverri Sucerquia, Paula Andrea, Universidad de Antioquia, Colombia

Evans-Winters, Venus, African American Policy Forum, Planet Venus Institute, USA

Giroux, Henry McMaster, University, Canada

Goodson, Ivor, University of Brighton, UK, Emeritus

Holder, Winthrop, New York City Department of Education, USA, Retired

Ibrahim, Awad, University of Ottawa, Canada

Kim, Myunghee, Soonchunhyang University, Korea

McLaren, Peter, Chapman University, USA

Milne, Ann, Kia Aroha College Community, New Zealand

Soler-Gallart, Marta, University of Barcelona, Spain

Souranta, Juha, Tampere University, Finland

Vega Villareal, Sandra, Instituto de Pedagogia Critica, Mexico

Zalmanson Levi, Galia, Ben Gurion University & Hakibbutzim College, Israel

These 41 stories were part of an autoethnographic study for my doctoral dissertation, which explored the therapeutic value of storytelling on bereavement. Italics emphasize the introspection and self-reflection that occurs when immersing in evocative autoethnography, written to evoke emotion in the reader while examining the sociocultural interactions of a phenomenon. Longer sentences that begin with a lowercase letter reflect my internal processing, while longer sentences with an uppercase letter indicate a character's spoken dialogue. The larger italicized sections, separated by three asterisks, are my memories with my father, retrieved throughout my life, interspersed and connected to each story. From my analysis of all 41 vignettes, the following themes emerged: the art of storytelling (structure, language, drafting, revising) and the four cornerstones of grief stories (relationship building, designing a blueprint of grief, strengthening spiritual health, and leaving a lasting footprint). Therefore, the writing style is crafted and intentional.

*"If we're going to heal, let it be glorious."*

—Warsan Shire

A story carved in the palm of our Creator,

translated by the human hand—

written not for the praises of people,

but for the praises of God.

This book is the companion to:

*Life: To Be Given Back Again to Whence It Came:*
*A Pilgrimage Through Prolonged Grief,*
*Confronting Grief Illiteracy and Healing Loss Using the Art of Storytelling*

# DEDICATION

In the beginning, you breathed life into me.

In the end, I hope to breathe life back into you.

For my first teacher…

*As always, for my father, the light of my life.*

Eapen Mathew

January 5, 1946 – January 14, 2017

*I speak of a love that brings sight to the blind.*
*Of a love stronger than fear.*
*I speak of a love that breathes meaning into life,*
*that defies the natural laws of deterioration,*
*that causes us to flourish, that knows no bounds.*
*I speak of the triumph of the human spirit over selfishness and death.*

—Jan-Philipp Sendker

# ACKNOWLEDGMENTS

*I will not forget you.*

*Behold, I have engraved you on the palm of my hand.*

—Isaiah 49:15–16

*For my father, Eapen Mathew, who sacrificed the world and stayed home to alter the course of my destiny, may you know you succeeded.*

*For my mother, Mary Mathew, who sacrificed staying home and braved the world to secure a good life for her children, may you know you succeeded.*

*In honor and loving memory of my grandparents: Dr. M.J. Mathew and Mariamma Mathew (paternal) and Mr. Korah Kurian and Annamma Korah (maternal).*

\*\*\*

*For my brother, Lincy Mathew, who taught me more about grief than any other person, brought forward the genuine shades of life, and loved and cared for our parents wholeheartedly.*

*For Kripa Sabastian, who embodied the meaning of true friendship, lent me a second set of eyes for these stories, and stayed still when everyone else scattered.*

*For Riya Tharayil, who is a beacon of light in this world, occupying a child's place in my heart, and a grandchild's place in my father's.*

*For Thu Whalen, who personified the strength and resiliency of spirit, came into my life precisely, and saw me through to my core.*

*For Dr. Ian Winchester, who guided me unparallel, pushed me to step out of my comfort zone, and stepped into my father's shoes without knowing it.*

*For Dr. Thomas Attig, Dr. Reinekke Lengelle, and Dr. Robert Neimeyer, who willingly encouraged the work I have set out to do and graciously contributed to my books.*

\*\*\*

*For my family in Kerala, who sheltered me through the dark night of grief, carried my sorrow carefully on their shoulders, and communally grieves with me still.*

*~Thank You~*

# Table of Contents

Foreword — xvii

Introduction — xxv

**Prologue** — xxxi

The Last Request — 1

**~In the Beginning~** — 3

The Last Fall — 5

The Last Observation — 9

The Last Question — 13

The Last Fight — 17

The Last Return Home — 23

The Last Prophesy — 29

The Last Time in the Emergency — 37

**~In the Middle~** — 41

The Last Argument — 43

The Last Touch — 49

## Table of Contents

| | |
|---|---:|
| The Last Supper | 55 |
| The Last Praise From a Father | 61 |
| The Last Hope | 67 |
| The Last Touch of Reality | 73 |
| The Last Christmas | 77 |
| The Last Link | 83 |
| The Last Apology | 89 |
| The Last Conversation | 95 |
| The Last Act of Kindness | 105 |
| **~In the End~** | 111 |
| The Last Smile | 113 |
| The Last New Year | 117 |
| The Last Birthday | 123 |
| The Last Look | 129 |
| The Last Family Meeting | 135 |
| The Last Verdict | 145 |
| The Last Moment Between Father and Daughter | 153 |
| The Last Day | 161 |
| The Last Night | 165 |
| The Last Breath | 169 |

## ~A Year of Firsts~ 173

The First Night 175

The First Day 183

The First Confrontation of Changing Family Dynamics 191

The First Funeral and the First Burial 199

The First Trip to India 215

The First Time Back in the Classroom 229

The First Time on Social Media 245

The First Birthday 253

The First Wedding 259

The First Support Group 271

The First Year of Mourning 287

## Epilogue 299

The First Request: Continuing Bonds With My Father 303

References 315

About the Author 317

# Foreword

**We are all children, we are all sages**

Grief is as terrible as you fear

that is what you believe when the surprising and the inevitable has happened

your beloved has gone

fully grown, you are a child ravaged by death's unwelcome taking

You will always be the daughter, the son, the wife, the husband, the parent—the Beloved

That is why you will wrestle with the shadows and vanities and the control you never had but insist on with the clenched fists of loss

But there will be coconut trees again; there will be a hand resembling theirs; there will be a place where you can heal

even in the social exile and the killing platitudes of those you never thought would be strangers,

there will be the unforeseen right companion for your pain

who lands in the chair beside you

and always the "invisible hand" of guidance

Eventually your crying eyes will shine with compassion for all that lives and dies

your light will be a shower for the suffering

including your own

by and by the child becomes a sage

—Reinekke Lengelle, 10 May 2021 (*for Linita*)

Linita Eapen Mathew, adored and adoring daughter, tells the story of how the loss of her father flattened her. It did so by shattering her assumptive world and taking away the flesh-and-blood bond that nurtured her and steadied her physiology through deeply felt attachment loops. Death put an end to a shared world that, in her case, was filled with daily caring, meaningful dialogue, and respectful devotion. Her relationship with her father was central to her life, and her grief was monstrous, overwhelming her and leading her step by step to encounter her healing through a spiritual journal of experiencing and writing.

When mourning is prolonged and complicated, as it was in Linita's case, it can steal our sleep, appetite, ability to work, and even our will to live. But Linita's story shows us that in its very magnitude, we are invited by an "invisible hand" to our liberation and maturity. The way, however, can be difficult and raw, particularly in a society that is grief-illiterate, which she argues convincingly. She shares the experience of so many who are bereaved, including myself, who find that those we believe will support us won't or don't know how. Moreover, many—however well-intentioned—dull their expression of empathy with platitudes, and very few people can cope and stay present with the raw emotions that are a part of loss.

Why, Linita asks, in our hour and day of need, are there so few who know how to be present for us as we encounter our sorrow and anger? Who can sit and not judge or push us to "get over it"? How can we learn grief literacy and imagine a society ready to shift along with the erratic ways of grief? This is the question this book asks and responds to, and it does so with poignant and humane clarity.

The encounter with this potent story of love and loss impressed me deeply by its unique combination of profound self-insight and the expression of love for a father, which is at once mature and childlike. Like all of us, Linita is both child and sage. But unlike most of us, she dares to reveal both without reservation. To combine both agency and vulnerable innocence is courageous for a scholar, a professional, a woman in academia, and a person with a unique heritage who will be read by those from myriad cultures and spiritual backgrounds.

Some may be tempted to judge or psychoanalyze the close bond she had with her father, or perhaps they may even envy it. Still, the request to readers is to park their possible reservations and open to the perennial vulnerability that lives in us all. This book is an invitation to surrender to innocence and, in this way, to enter the process of trusting life, which is perpetually precarious, fragile, and marked by the end that awaits us all.

The questions this story brought up as I read, and perhaps will do so for other readers, is: Where have I allowed myself such closeness? Where can I remember the tenderness of my parents, even if they are no longer alive? It behooves us to let ourselves be touched and remain open, and thus draw ourselves out of the lonely tendencies of our individualistic notion of grief in western culture. This book shows us the what and the how, and supports it with the latest research on bereavement. Linita teaches us what we might know about grief to help prepare us and make us more supportive of others; she does so primarily through her vital personal narrative.

Linita describes her father's death as a birth of (her) new identity; she is reborn, realizing not that she must internalize all he has given her but rather that he is a part of her, in the most literal sense—she was created from his DNA. After his death, she is overwrought and tortured. Her bereavement journey is not simple, predictable, tidy, or even considered socially acceptable as it spans several years. Others have "given up" within months or in the first year, while Linita needs more time and support to develop a new equilibrium.

Linita ultimately develops a healthy continuing bond with her father; she is also cognizant of how she lives out a part of his lifelong dream by pursuing her doctorate. Such dynamics are well-known in the psychological literature; as Carl Jung observed, "the greatest influence on a child is the unlived life of the parent". Our career choices are influenced by where we have been wounded and seen our parents be wounded, "we are always trying to actively master, what we passively suffered," says Mark Savickas, career researcher and counselor. As a child, Linita sees her father's suffering when his career potential remains unfulfilled after arriving in Canada with educational credentials that aren't recognized and racism, which prevents him from being hired. She responds by defending him, shining a light on the inequities, and pursuing her education and work relentlessly. Her devotion to fulfilling his dream matches his devotion to raising his children as a stay-at-home father.

Though grief is a journey we must take alone, it is equally true that we are better off held by the love of those who remain and even those who we are losing or have already lost to death and draw strength from the bond. As Linita shows, the lifelong conversation with her father is also internal and is therefore abiding. In life, she hears his voice aloud; she also hears it internally; hence, in death, his voice remains with her. In a touching scene where she describes how he took along a wagon to transport her as a child while trick-or-treating at Halloween in Calgary, where she was born and grew up—she explains how he always showed her how she deserved to be treated: with care

## Foreword

and consideration. Now, by writing, it is her turn to honor him. She offers the reader her wisdom about how parents should be treated: with reverence for all they have given. Although it may seem from the story that she was a "Daddy's girl," she shows her mother's equal value and devotion to the family and does justice to the innate wholeness in the family, even as they adjust to the loss of their Eapen.

By her own example and through her stories, Linita teaches the reader not only about grief but about our refusal to engage with its visceral, painful, and unpredictable ways. Grief is a fierce dance partner for any human who has had the privilege of deep attachment. As Linita says poignantly, the sorrow was a reflection of her love, and she learned to welcome even the awful visitor we dread:

> When death finally stops and knocks on the door, we have no choice but to open it; we have no choice but to allow the unwelcomed guest inside. In Indian culture, guests are treated and cared for as though we are taking care of God. And the presence of God entered my father's room long before the doctor told me it was time. When I leaned into this knowledge of death, the wisdom of life unfolded. By now, I had learned I could carry hope and acceptance at the same time. (Revelation 26)

Linita goes back in time to show us her childhood while simultaneously telling a chronological story. She invites the reader along to face the daily joys of a family that is close-knit, dependent on each other in their chosen country, Canada, with rich traditions rooted in India. She writes about the value of gaining depth when facing transitions and maintaining a life guided by spiritual principles. In a culture overly obsessed with happiness and positive outcomes, which is death-denying, her story says, "look here—dare to be present to this." Grief well-lived, in fact, and faced squarely makes us more whole and, in the end, happier, too.

Another strength of this book is that Linita does not eschew the imperfections of her actions and thoughts as her father grows sicker and she has to face life without him. She tells of her struggles to eat as her father grows more gravely ill with an unknown diagnosis. She notices her temper, her moments of pettiness and jealously, her inclination to maintain and emphasize the special bond with her father (even when her mother rightly expresses some pained envy over this special connection). In other words, she does not avoid the valuable insight an author can share when they uncover the less beautiful parts of their desire for love, attention, and specialness.

What this book can do for every reader is remind them that to face grief is to be transformed. To turn away from it is to deny our humanity and the opportunity to mature into ourselves. Grief literacy is not only about alleviating suffering; however, it is a route to our conscious unfolding. As I say in my own book on the topic after the loss of my spouse around the same time as Linita lost her father, one must not miss the experience of grief; one must find a way through, day by day. Death is a birth of another kind. It births a new identity if we are not insistent on avoiding its contractions and the frequent reminders that we cannot shift reality with wishful thinking. Linita, and we as her readers, must continually give up hope of (her father's) recovery while maintaining dignity for everyone touched by the tragedy.

Linita's work is written with the hand of an experienced writer; she brings great clarity to her thought processes. She is intentional with her language and does not aim to impress or complicate her stories. Her work is a gift for those who wish to end the invisibility of grief and to consider that the words we put to it change the way we also feel about it. We are also called to be more authentic in our speech when others experience loss in our close circle. All of us fall short as we approach those whose worlds are falling apart. Well-meaning, we say things like "I am sorry for your loss..."; "Stay strong..."; "Be grateful for what you had..." and "He's in a better place...". In the rawness of the loss, Linita shows clearly how these platitudes are hollow and frequently increase the emptiness and pain of the bereaved. If we slowed down to feel our hearts first, better words might follow or even no words but our heartfelt presence.

This book shows that grief is both an individual journey and one best experienced as a social, culturally, and spiritually enriched occurrence. It is a social process, a soul journey, even when it feels like a sole journey. In describing her mixed cultural background (Anglican-Canadian steeped in Indian traditions from Kerala), Linita provides us with a perfect example of how one's approach to grief must be interdisciplinary: we can tailor-make our response one step at a time. It is our responsibility as counselors in grief or teachers of grief and mourning to show those we are present that all of it is welcome and can be combined in a way that is congruent for that person. In my own more agnostic approach, I relied heavily on psychology, my no-nonsense Dutch soberness, and a deeply poetic soul. That said, I revealed my interest in engaging with videos on near-death experiences and noted that this form of spiritual connection brought me comfort, even as an academic who tends to relegate anything "spiritual" to the realm of secular meaning-making.

The key question here is not: what is true about life and death in the religious sense, but what restores us, literally and symbolically? What uplifts and what does not? What serves and what does not. What "restores" us—a term that already contains the hint of "re-story"?

In reading this book, I see again how writing is key for engaging and articulating the most profound moments of our lives. To make meaning by writing our way through bereavement is not (only) a product but an idiosyncratic process that leads us into places in ourselves that we have not examined fully. We can also draw strength from other grievers who are willing to articulate their pain, like a nurse's aide who stops Linita in the hospital hallway and talks about losing her own father. Linita writes, "Grievers are not strangers; they are part of a community that understands the deep-seated pain of loss," and such knowledge gives us hope.

Linita does not avoid the difficulties and so-called ugly realities of illness and loss. Indeed, we can only be wise if we acknowledge our humanity in every step of grief; to do anything else would be cheap. Her father is deathly ill; in the photos shared along with the 41 stories, we as readers can see this in a glance, and yet she writes with such wisdom about how those nearest and dearest will still want to deny what they see. That reality dawns on us slowly, and, as grief researcher George Bonnano writes, sadness and tears help us to get real, and out of our wishful thinking. "Wake up, daughter," Linita hears her father's voice calling her as she prepares for his death. "He's dying. I know that he is dying, and I'm trying to accept that. If you want to support me, then let me step into this truth."

Reinekke Lengelle, Ph.D.

Author of *Writing the Self in Bereavement: A story of love, spousal loss, and resilience* (Routledge, 2021), Associate Professor of Interdisciplinary Studies, Athabasca University, Canada.

# Stories

## The Heart of the Matter

The stories we tell of loss and grief are love stories. We tell of our loved ones' lives, their ending, and our living in the aftermath. No one can take from us our memories and the times we shared with them. Among their most precious legacies, most of us are eager to share our stories with willing listeners. We also tell of life and love interrupted and transformed. When someone we love dies, we *react* as brokenness and sorrow come over us. We tell of our shattered life patterns, our stories careening off course, longing for the impossible return of those we love, broken hearts, defeated egos, homesick souls, and grounded spirits. We also *respond* as we engage with our losses and reactions and strive to relearn how to live in the world without our loved one's physical presence. We tell of learning to carry sorrow; reviving our souls and spirits; struggling to feel at home again in our physical surroundings, with fellow survivors, and in the greater scheme of things; reshaping our daily lives; redirecting our life stories; changing ourselves; and wrestling with the great mysteries of life, death, suffering, and love. In all of these efforts, nothing is more important, difficult, or rewarding than moving from loving in presence to loving in separation. We will always miss, and we will always love our loved ones after they die.

For years, I have urged that "stories are the heart of the matter" in understanding the nature of grieving, finding meaning while living in grief, and responding to and supporting the bereaved. Personal stories of love, loss, and grieving are *the heart of the matter in developing general understandings of these experiences.* They comprise the foundational evidence base in which all plausible thinking about love, loss, and grief must take root, the data that such telling captures a distinctive range of human experiences. We must learn all we can from those who have had the experiences and can talk about them if we are to think in any serious way, scientific or otherwise, about grief.

Remembering and telling personal stories of love, loss, and grieving *is the heart of the matter for grievers as they seek value and meaning in relearning how to live in a world transformed by loss and in loving in separation.* We continue to love and cherish the stories of lives now ended. No two of us have known and loved or been known and loved by the same person in the same way. We each have our own stories to tell. Together the stories we hold comprise a unique and precious legacy that no one can take from us, and legacies are gifts from those who have gone before us. The lives of those who have died and the meanings lived in them are not erased when death comes. Memory sustains our connection with them. Just as perception connects us across spatial distance with the physical reality of others who live with us, memory connects us across time with the full and rich realities of the lives now lost. Remembering and telling our stories sustains ties with our loved ones and fulfills their desires not to be forgotten.

In writing and telling the stories of their own experiences and the lives of their loved ones, grievers can grow in self-understanding and reach for understanding from others. Simply naming and finding the words to describe their experiences can be orienting and clarifying. Telling their stories sets the stage for reflecting, teasing out new details, interpreting their significance, reinterpreting them in the light of new experiences, and discerning new values and meanings they hold. Grievers can harvest meanings, recognize legacies, appreciate inner strengths, and begin to imagine hopeful paths in relearning the world and loving in separation. Finally, telling their stories can be one of the most effective ways for grievers to reach out for understanding, comfort, and support from receptive listeners, be they family members, friends, fellow grievers in support groups, or counselors.

Listening to and understanding the stories they have to tell is *the heart of the matter in caring for grievers.* It also affords insight into the characters of the storytellers: the driving forces in their lives and what matters most to them. Compassionate and effective caregiving is simply not possible without the courage and sensitivity to engage in heart-to-heart dialogue with grievers about what they are experiencing: listening and responding. Listening enables care for and about whole persons rather than treating "symptoms" or the like. It permits setting aside abstract theories and expectations and attuning to the particulars of the experiences and the uniqueness of the persons having them. Caregivers must know as much as possible about the particulars of the storyteller's experiences and the uniqueness of the character of the griever to offer appropriate psychological, behavioral, social, or spiritual support. Listening to and having a dialogue with grievers enables caregivers to build alliances with them as they seek hopeful paths toward living meaningfully again in a world where their loved ones are no longer present. We can, as a community, understand loving in separation after our loved ones have died as a lifelong exchange of love and gratitude.

Linita Eapen Mathew's *The Revelations of Eapen* is a superb telling of a loss, grief, and love story. She writes beautifully, vividly, candidly, and courageously about her love for her father, her grieving in anticipation of his dying (in twenty-nine brief and intimate reflections on "last" experiences), and the first year of her contending with the challenges of learning to live without his physical presence (in twelve more expansive reflections on "first" experiences). She is introspectively gifted—a keen observer, interpreter, and assessor of the significance of her own experiences. She harvests hard-won lessons about carrying her sorrows and meeting the challenges of relearning how to live in a world profoundly changed by devastating loss: within herself, in her family and community ties, in her spiritual tradition, and especially in finding continuing love in separation from her father. She grows in understanding of what she has lost and what she has not lost—how she has been shaped by and is different for having known and loved and having been known and loved by her father. Hers is an incomplete story as she will no doubt carry sorrow for her father and love him still as she continues to remember him and embrace his legacies in gratitude for the rest of her life.

I will place this book on the shelf next to C.S. Lewis's *A Grief Observed* as one of the finest memoirs of grief I know. *The Revelations of Eapen* deserves to be read by many for years to come.

—Thomas Attig, Ph.D., philosopher, and author of *How We Grieve: Relearning the world.*

**Vidyāraṃbham.** *Vidya* "knowledge"; *arambham* "beginning"

*The traditional ceremony in Kerala, India, where one's guru or teacher initiates a young child into the vast universe of knowledge.*

At age three, I sat in my father's lap as he inducted me into the cosmic world of letters, the gatekeeper to an education. A writing board was prepared and placed in front of us; a candle illuminated a picture of Jesus beside us. My legs twisted in lotus, and my fist scrunched down to a single digit. Invoking blessings from our Maker, my father took my hand in his and glided my index finger seamlessly between the grains of brown rice spread across the metallic plate. First, we made the sign of the cross, then composed the word: *Amma*, mother. Soon, we enticed the rest of the alphabet to appear like magicians waving wands. When all the letters were in our midst, served on a silver platter, my father placed his hand on my head, prayed, and blessed me. Banishing the ego, he asked God for blessings of prosperity—for my words to multiply and be fruitful, extracting the maternal essence of my first written word. The writing, woven as fine as silk throughout these stories, results from his effort. My father, my guru, auspiciously sought Divine blessings for me that anointed my gift to write, passing his artistry onto me.

# Prologue

*Not I, not any one else can travel that road for you,*

*You must travel it for yourself.*

*It is not far, it is within reach,*

*Perhaps you have been on it since you were born and did not know,*

*Perhaps it is everywhere on water and land.*

—Walt Whitman, *Leaves of Grass*, "Song of Myself, 46"

**Figure 1**
*Eapen Mathew (my father)*

# 1

## The Last Request

He sat in his usual seat on the left-hand side of the church, at the right end of the bench, three rows from the altar. This Anglican home had housed his faith for the past thirty-five years. Resting his head balanced between his index finger and thumb, propped up by his elbow, he leaned against the side rail of the pew and dreamed of a place that felt *warm* and *familiar*. All at once, he jolted awake. Not knowing how long he drifted off for this time but knowing it was happening more frequently now, an uneasiness emerged. The spaces between these occurrences stretched thin and blurred together, but his mind sharpened around his unusual circumstances.

The protruding golden cross hung slightly above his line of sight, drawing his face to tilt upward, locking in his steady gaze, communicating—*It's time*. A surge of sadness washed over him as he sifted through the mental pictures, memories of loved ones flooding his thoughts. A vivid portrayal of his life as *Eapen Mathew* materialized, moving through his mind. Stuck on a family portrait of four, he paused, briefly resisting the intrusive messenger who had arrived like an unwelcome guest entering a wedding banquet. Still, he understood the fragility of time that remained, and he did not want his final hours consumed by human resistance.

Reaching deep into his spiritual reserve, seizing the supply stored for this exact moment, he manifested the strength and tenacity necessary to move forward. He reminded himself that every transition is an equal cause for celebration. And he was not worried. He knew his faith would lead him. That, even at the eleventh hour, God would carry him over the threshold.

Now, he truly awoke.

Gently, he rose from his place in the pews and walked toward a place more deserving of him. A rainbow of light streamed through the stained-glass windows designing the back wall, calling upon the rays of angels to enrobe him as he slowly exited the church. The service had not yet ended; however, this was not out of the ordinary. But instead of heading to the upper hall and reaching for his usual cup of black coffee, he spun left and entered the small chapel where two chaplains sat eagerly stationed, waiting for him.

Here, on this holy ground, he unknowingly initiated his last rites himself, seeking prayers, shepherding his final days. Confident in the Lord's guidance, humbly, he sat down and surrendered.

*"Shall we begin?"*

*"Yes."*

*"What are you seeking prayers for?"*

*"Something is wrong—but I don't know what."*

*"Okay…let us pray."*

# ~In the Beginning~

*Two roads diverged in a yellow wood,*

*And sorry I could not travel both*

*And be one traveler, long I stood*

*And looked down one as far as I could*

*To where it bent in the undergrowth;*

*…*

*I shall be telling this with a sigh*

*Somewhere ages and ages hence:*

*Two roads diverged in a wood, and I—*

*I took the one less traveled by,*

*And that has made all the difference.*

—Robert Frost, "The Road Not Taken"

**Figure 2**
*A Fatal Fall*

# 2

## The Last Fall

Hearing a loud commotion rise from the main level, my brother ran downstairs to see what had happened. He found our father lying face down on the kitchen floor. Rushing to his aid, he grabbed Dad's arms and lifted him to his feet. And as my father stood upright, the evidence grew to suggest that this was no ordinary fall; this was not one of those typical clumsy shuffles we were used to. The aftermath was all over his body—his glasses had bent out of shape, his arms were scratched and torn, and a small bump was already forming on the right side of his forehead. Alarmingly, he fell while cooking a meal on the stove. But out of all the eccentricities that transpired, the most worrying was yet to be revealed. When questioned in the moment and interrogated later on, my father's explanation for the collapse remained consistent: *I can't remember what happened.*

Over my father's senior years, he had experienced many unexpected falls—sometimes at home, sometimes at the mall where he walked daily, or sometimes in the parking lot with strangers coming to his rescue. Being a heart patient, severe diabetic, and elderly man whose sight and sound capabilities were deteriorating, he was prone to stumbling now and then. Although these were all contributing factors to the likelihood of his instability, this time, something felt different. A feeling emerged through the understanding that, in the past, he always knew exactly why or how he fell. Usually, he tripped on objects that missed his line of sight, or his eyes had not adjusted to the outdoor light in time, unsteadying his balance. The reasons never pushed past these boundaries, which is why I knew that this fall, *the last fall,* was communicating something different. Instigating a sudden drop, his illness stood up and disclosed itself to the rest of us.

*\*\*\**

*By the time I was eighteen, my father was an avid member of Calgary Toastmasters. One evening, after staying later than the rest, he accidentally got locked out of the building, trapping himself in a fenced-off area. Because he was helpless, alone, and without a phone, he made the unwise decision to "jump the fence". The result would end in shredded clothes, ripped and bruised skin, and the wrath of an unhappy daughter. My heart dropped at the sight of his gashes. My grandmother, his mother, had lost a limb to diabetes, and the severe outcome of infected wounds terrified me. Scolding him for his daredevil moves, I applied an extra amount of Dettol disinfectant while I cleaned and mended his cuts—one of the rare times the child punished the parent for upsetting behavior. Yet, his diabetes did not stir from this incident. Instead, he suffered a heart attack a week later. After the coronary artery bypass, he relied heavily on the three of us. And from this age onward, my overactive mind would not stop imagining the possibility of his death. As a result, I called my father multiple times a day, every day, to ease my fears and reassure myself he was still alive.*

*\*\*\**

The day after his unsettling fall, I took my parents to an Indian engagement ceremony. While waiting downstairs, my father's struggles were obvious. Leaning into me for support, he took fifteen minutes to walk from the front porch to the car. And, fully supported by myself and others, he took double the time trekking from the car to the church. We missed the service. As the revelation of my father's sickness slowly crept on us, I became clouded with denial, blind to the seriousness of his situation. I could see it, but I did not believe it.

My mother and I persuaded him to attend the evening reception for the sole reason that our hearts would not go without him. In the end, he conceded to our request, but the expression on his face was pained. Once the formal events wrapped up, our family friends were ready to leave the party and offered my parents a ride home, allowing me to stay and enjoy the festivities. My father left, but I did not enjoy my time. From the minute he was gone, I was *there* but *not there*—a pattern that drifted well into the later stages of my grief. My celebratory mood had diminished, and so I sat at a table, giving company to an aunty who looked as lonely and lost as I was. Sitting still like a statue, the severity of his state swept over me. *Why didn't I go with him?* This night would later solidify into one of those remorseful memories that taunt the griever, encircling my mind, using repetitive, rhetorical questions that no longer held a satisfactory answer. However, purpose is always in the eye of the beholder. This small amount of remorse was necessary, fueling the fire that kick-started my adrenaline for the bigger battle that ensued. And the regret of leaving him that one night—forced me to stay glued to his side every night thereafter.

The puzzle as to why my father fell took a permanent seat in the back of my mind, and I can pinpoint the exact moment my curiosity fell away. During his regular rounds, one doctor offered a probable explanation: *It is more likely he fainted rather than fell.* Upon hearing his medical interpretation, my mind stopped and then slowly spiraled. The thought of him fainting proved much more difficult to reconcile. Emotionally, I was forced to accept my dad's dwindling condition, and my guilty conscience found further ammunition. Muddled by meddling thoughts, my mind searched for reasons to hold myself accountable. *How could I have not known he fainted? Why wasn't I paying closer attention to him? Why didn't I realize something was wrong? Why didn't I take him to the hospital sooner?* The rising actions that were thickening the plot led me to form a climactic realization—that, *it's my fault he died.*

The last fall was that moment, the conclusive evidence my subconscious needed to rationalize what it was seeking all along, a need to take responsibility for my father's death. Examining my innermost thoughts and unmasked guilt only revealed the raw nature of my distractibility—a belief I held firmly in my heart for all of these years—the impression that, truly, *he is going to be okay because he is going to live forever.*

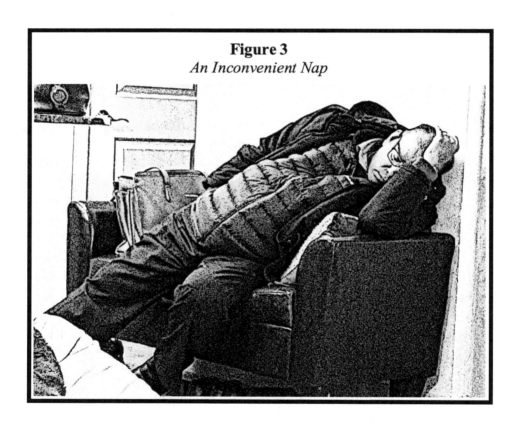

**Figure 3**
*An Inconvenient Nap*

# 3

## The Last Observation

*I finished brushing my teeth and jumped into bed, eagerly awaiting my parents. I was four years old, and we lived in a tiny, two-bedroom apartment. They occupied the master bedroom, and my brother, who was five years older than me, hogged our bedroom to himself. Happily, I slept in between my parents, always leaning into Dad a little more. On this particular night, Mom took her place on the bed, but the rest of the room fell silent. Noticing my father had not yet joined us, I could feel the tension rising. Patiently, I waited for him, but the longer I waited, the more restless I grew. I tossed right, I tossed left, I tossed right again. Growing annoyed at my uncontrollable movements, my mother retorted, "If you're looking for your dad, he's sleeping on the sofa either lie still or get up and go to him." Without hesitation, I scrambled from the bed and bolted into the next room. I found my father lying on the couch, pensive, probably contemplating an earlier fight with my mom. Breaking him out of his sullen spell, I pounced on him and hugged him. Bear-like, Dad wrapped his arms around me and said, "You're my best friend in the whole world." I placed my head on his chest, felt his relief, and fell asleep.*

*His warmness is the first token in my treasure chest of memories. Vividly, I can recall this feeling in an instant. A phrase that has shaped every decision I made from this day forward.*

\*\*\*

I noticed. *How could I have not?* Later, this would be both a blessing—and a curse—that I noticed first. The possibility of my father dying was not a topic I willingly discussed; my mind would not concede to this universal truth. Yet, even though I refused to acknowledge the inevitability of this tragedy, intuitively, I knew time was closing in on us. Far before any other sign or physical recognition of his illness appeared, indicating possible danger ahead, my soul cautioned me to tread lightly. An innate knowing surfaced in a multitude of unintentional ways: through a metaphorical image I painted, symbolically portraying his ascension; through more frequent conversations I initiated, acknowledging my inability to let him go; and, through journal entries I wrote, alluding to a foreboding feeling of despair and resistance. *I could feel the tension rising.* Accordingly, a few weeks before my father's fall, I spontaneously sat down with him and informed him I was ready to apply for the doctorate program—a journey I had earlier postponed to my middle years. But, all at once, I was prepared to fulfill his lifelong dream. And a few short weeks later, we applied together as I read my Statement of Intent over the phone to him while lying in a hospital bed. *It's perfect, Linita, send it!* Granted, he would not stay to hear the outcome; I am grateful he knew one would result. His expression of pure joy could have passed me by had I not been wise enough to slow down and listen. In hindsight—my father and I—our stars aligned.

While contemplating the matter more deeply, I could have filled pages with omens suggesting his life was nearing its end. We can sense danger, the destructive kind—a relationship, a job, a life, *ending*. Instead, I insisted on wiping the slate clean like a child firmly gripping an Etch A Sketch, eager to create a more desirable outcome. That's what I was before he died, a child. At last, a crucial observation caught my eye and shook me awake. It was not when he fell asleep while we watched *that* movie, read *that* book, or discussed *that* ideology—although those were all times. It was a more unusual instance, handpicked specifically for me.

Dad had walked into my apartment and sat on the bench, intending to unlace his shoes. Assisting him with this task was my humble duty, and so it was a natural, automated response that caused me to check and see if he needed my help—not my mother, not my brother, but *me*. And what I looked to find stopped my soul in its tracks. To my surprise, he had fallen asleep *mid-shoelace*. With his strings half-loosened, he sat hunched to the left as though knocked out by a tranquilizer dart. In the nanosecond I had taken my eyes off him, my father was sleeping soundly. My muscles froze as bewilderment, panic, and disbelief glued me in place. *This isn't normal*, I thought. I knew my father well, and I knew this was not him. Involuntarily, I grabbed my phone and snapped a picture. My actions did not stem from wanting to savor his usual amusing antics or procure a keepsake of the incident. I took the photo because, in an instant, my father's fleeting final days flashed before me. And I began bargaining. By collecting proof of his illness in images, I gathered evidence to take to the doctor and mediate on his behalf. *Here is what happened, can you help him? I'm begging you, please!*

Over the next three months, I took picture after picture, tracking and monitoring his progress through visuals. As much as I wanted to believe I was compiling photos that would lead to the road to recovery, I knew one does not compile photos leading to a recovery. All of the odd and irregular captures led to my father's decline and eventual demise. Without even realizing it, without ever admitting it, I was the first to know that something was wrong, and this *last observation* solidifies that. He was my father, my guru, my beloved—and I was his daughter, his disciple, his best friend. If not me, *then who?*

**Figure 4**
*A Teacher and His Student*

# 4

## The Last Question

Something was off that night—*me*. I should have picked up on his energy, but *I didn't*. With a spiritual self-defense mechanism in place, my intuition was purposely shut off. But my mother, who cared for my father meticulously, a supernatural intuitive, she knew. That night, she argued with him relentlessly to let her call an ambulance. Still, he would not concede. This was his last attempt to control his fate, and though his willpower was strong, his pulse was not. Eventually, with coercion, he surrendered to the words already written on the page.

Instantly, my fight or flight took over, and when it comes to my father, *I fight*. Yet, ironically, I was the one who grabbed his boots, not knowing I was initiating the final steps of his journey. For the last decade, as he aged and endured rising health complications, he could no longer reach his feet without a solid struggle. And so, for the last decade, I gladly reached them for him. For the last three decades, I did most things for him. I liked how much he relied on me; it was integral to my identity and taught me how to embody love. Our relationship was simple—he was my teacher, and I was his student.

Slowly, I put on his socks, then his boots, and then I zipped the fastenings. I have carried out this service innumerable times, on countless occasions, but this time with slight unease. A sliver of intuition snuck in, a knowing that this would be the last time. I froze on my heels with my hands still resting on my father's feet, organically taking his blessings. Before the unwanted thoughts could form, I noticed Dad's eyes staring down at me, patiently waiting for me to catch his gaze.

## The Revelations of Eapen

***

*I was nineteen, and my dad had just gone under the knife—an open-heart surgery, performing a quadruple bypass plus the clearing of two additional blocks. The surgery itself went well; however, his diabetes interfered with his recovery. And as the postoperative complications rose, so did the water level in my father's lungs. During a pivotal prognosis, I was the only family member in the room. I stood stock-still, watching him gasp for air with eyes that begged me for help. I was mortified. Soon, the nurse turned to me and asked, "Do you have any other family here?" My throat closed tight like my father's, barely letting out a cracked "no." Then, she delivered unimaginable news, a destructive phrase I would have to hear twice in this lifetime, "I think you should let your family back home know. I don't think he is going to make it." My eyes widened to accompany the tears that came bouldering out. In the heat of this moment, I radically forged a path toward education, switching my career from pursuing medicine like my grandfather to becoming an English teacher like my father. Because of him, my chosen purpose finally aligned with my vocational calling. Luckily, the nurse was wrong—my father survived and recovered. My mother, a senior nurse, saved his life. But moving forward, I would never fully accept the statement—"he's not going to make it"—again.*

***

Softly, in Malayalam, a question brewing in the back of my father's mind spilled, *Njan marichu pokuvodi? Am I going to die, daughter?*

Panic overpowered me, shutting down the sincerity of his question; I exploded, *No, Dad! What are you talking about? You are going to be fine!* My heart sank, knowing he drew from mental telepathy.

Those words, both his and mine, still breathe air, raw and at the bottom.

My father gave me a wry smile—the grin that means he is checking to see if I love him as much as he loves me. For now, he was satisfied with my answer, but he knew I was wrong. And, unlike the other times in my life, he did not correct me. This time, he let me come to the realization on my own, as he knew it had to be. During my last Christmas with him, this was my father's final gift to me, completing my transformation from student to teacher.

**Figure 5**
*An Arranged Marriage Type of Love*

# 5

## The Last Fight

Watching my mother take care of my father day in and day out was a blessing. Their love story may not have been the Hollywood romance existing in fairy tales and movies, but theirs was a deeper version I have come to understand as greater than that. The nature of their relationship was not sugar-coated, abused, or concealed from others; it was a raw, real, work-hard-at-it love. Truth be told, they were exactly and most definitely the opposite of one another—two people who met for the first time on their engagement day. My father's uncle brought the proposal to my mother's side, and after a short conversation between the two, engagement rings were exchanged. Later, Mom divulged that Dad was not her first proposal; she had rejected seven offers before him.

My curiosity piqued, and I questioned, *What made you say yes to Dad?*

Frankly, she revealed,

> *A month before, I had a dream that a dark-skinned man with long sideburns, wearing an off-white, half-sleeved shirt, was walking down the street. I saw that I would be happy with him. The day your dad came to meet me, he looked like the man in my dream, and I recognized him. So, I said yes, and my dream came true.*

In 1978, a year after their engagement, my parents reunited in St. Anthony, Newfoundland, where my mother had worked as a nurse for three years. Her boss refused to let her resign, so my father, eager to earn his doctorate from a North American institute, followed her to Canada. They had a traditional Indian Christian wedding in St.

Anthony's United Church. Dad explained our eastern customs to the priest, who happily embedded our matrimonial rituals and ceremonies into the service. A year later, they moved to Halifax, Nova Scotia, where my brother was born, and a short while after that, in search of work for my father, they fell in love with and permanently settled in Calgary, Alberta, where Mom gave birth to me. The landscape of their marriage not only journeyed across continents and countries, but their union also traversed peaks and valleys, mounting the hurdles that came from leaving their families behind and settling in a foreign land. Undoubtedly, for most of their lives, they only had each other. Consequently, the depth of their love was equally bold and courageous; hence, no one or nothing could come between them. And when they fought, the same rules applied.

Due to their personality traits—introvert meets extrovert—my parents clashed. Moreover, they had a different and uncommon dynamic than most married couples in our community; my mother was the breadwinner, and my father was the stay-at-home parent. At times, arguments stemmed from this reason alone. But as they grew together, they understood their reliance and cooperation cemented our family system. And as they aged, little pitter-patters about misplaced items or dishes left in the sink too long never amounted to much more. I always referred to it as *old-people fighting*—arguments that appeared for no rhyme or reason, could not be contained, stopped, or explained by outsiders. The type of quarrel that always ended in smiles and laughter, keeping their love fresh and vibrant. Unless their squabble erupted into something bigger, such as a rash or hurtful comment, a slip of the tongue—in which case, my father, the introvert, would go steel silent for days, exuding Gandhi's *passive resistance* against my mother who had the *slip*. Because Dad raised us, Mom always accused me of siding with him, and because of my overprotectiveness of him, she was usually right. Yet, despite the refereeing from their children, they always found their way back to one another. My mother claims a quick pinch of my father's nose always cracked a smile across his face. And, whether he exercised his right to remain silent or not, Dad would not sleep until Mom returned home from her evening shift, and she would not go to bed without drinking the tea he left out for her. This was their shared understanding—through all of the challenges and curveballs life threw us, they were always a team, balancing the scoresheet evenly.

# The Last Fight

The context of their last fight was simple. My father was scheduled to undergo an MRI to determine if lesions in his brain were responsible for causing his deep, exhaustive sleeps. Even though this was a painless procedure, he did not like small, closed spaces; they brought on anxiety and shortness of breath. Knowing this, my mother requested he be given a calmative to soothe his nerves. She accompanied him to the hospital basement where the scanning room was, and before he entered the lab on his own, she reassured him that she would be *right here* waiting for him. The sedative worked, and my father escaped the process with minimal repercussions. After the scan, he was taken out the back door and returned to his hospital room. However, when I joined them after work, my mother was nowhere in sight and noticing my arrival, my father bombarded me with questions:

*Where is your mom? Have you talked to her? She never came back after the MRI, and I don't know where she is. Do you think something happened to her? Can you call her?*

My brother, who had already tried calling Mom several times, jokingly suggested, *Maybe she went for lunch with one of the other visitors?*

Dad's face drooped to a visible frown. All at once, he moved to rip out his IV and go in search of his wife, crying out in desperation, *If you won't go and find her, I will!*

In an attempt to keep him calm, I reassured him that I would track her down. But after a few unsuccessful attempts, I informed him that the calls went straight to her voicemail. *Maybe she did go out for lunch?* I thought. Although out of character for Mom to leave Dad hanging, leaving to eat seemed like a probable explanation at the time.

Hours flew by, and still no sign of my mother, causing my father's irritation to grow. Finally, around six P.M., visibly flustered, she scurried into the room. *Where were you?* My brother and I inquired. Blatantly ignoring us, she rushed to Dad's side, and with her hands flailing in the air, let out a long-winded explanation. She drew an image of her sitting in the MRI waiting room for the past three hours, expecting my father to return, refusing to leave her base without him. Listening to her version of the events, Dad stayed steel silent, but hearing her narrative unfold, my concern turned to confusion.

Astounded, I spoke, *Let me get this straight, you waited down there, for three hours? Why didn't you call one of us?*

Her response was simple, *I didn't have any reception in the basement, and I didn't want to go anywhere until your dad came out.*

I paused in awe as I realized why the calls kept going to her voicemail. Continuing, I asked, *Okay, why didn't you ask the clerk at the desk?*

She stammered, *I did; that's when they told me he had gone back to his room.*

Carefully, I proceeded, *You waited three hours to ask them?*

It was not out of the ordinary for my mother to complicate a situation. Nevertheless, she justified her stance, *Every other patient that went in through those doors came out through the same ones! How was I supposed to know they wheeled him out through the back?*

Finally, my father chimed in, *Do you know how worried I've been? I thought something happened to you! Or maybe you went out to have lunch with your friends.*

Dad had been clinging to that one possibility since my brother mentioned it. And now, the other shoe dropped; the swelling volcano brewing between the two erupted. My father guilt-tripped my mother, protesting abandonment and accusing her of purposely not returning to the room on time. My mother listed off every caretaking duty she undertook, declaring her sacrifices had gone unappreciated. The cascading arguments between my two senior parents were nothing short of amusing but also showed no clear end in sight. The war of words went back and forth between them for **no less than two** hours. I tried my best to play peacemaker, but after being tossed aside multiple times, I left to pick up our neighbor who wanted to visit my dad.

***

*Dad was turning sixty! Since this was his first birthday after the operation, we planned an extravagant surprise party. We booked a hall, catered the food, and invited 150 of his closest family and friends to the event. Because it was a small gesture for the man I owed so much to, I worked tirelessly to ensure every detail was perfect. And when the night finally arrived, everything went smoothly. The food was on time, and so were the guests—the only person missing was him. I called home, warning my brother to hurry. Unbeknownst to me, as a ploy to get our father to the hall more quickly, my brother misinformed him that Mom had fainted in the kitchen. A short while later, I assembled the crowd accordingly. But the visual of my dad entering the hall was not quite what I had imagined. Darting up the stairs, he hurriedly made his way to the cooking area, and instead of seeing the anticipated face of joy, he donned an expression of dread, worry, and panic. He was so determined to reach my mother that even our collective screams of "Surprise!" did not stop him. Blocking his path, I halted his tracks and almost received a scolding for doing so. Luckily, Mom appeared from around the corner and shocked him. Beaming her wide smile at him, she was clapping and laughing. Relieved at her sight, yet still unsure of what was happening, my father's tension eased. Not realizing my mother was clapping for him, he followed her lead and began clapping himself, bringing laughter throughout the room. In a few unplanned actions, Dad demonstrated why we had thrown him a party in the first place.*

***

During the drive, when I contemplated the whole scenario, I realized how beautiful their tussle was. My mother, concerned for my father, stationed herself like a soldier outside the MRI lab for over three hours simply because he did not return from the same doors. My father, concerned for my mother, did not shut his eyes once over that interval, even though he was a victim of uncontrollable sleep for days. *They really loved each other.* Dawning that understanding, I dropped the situation. But returning to the room, to my amazement, the row had not settled. And, my parents brought our neighbor into the spat, justifying their respective, stubborn positions. Frustration arose as they both continued talking over me, and finally, I scolded them. *Enough is enough, you have a visitor, and she did not come all this way to hear the two of you fight!* At last, they were silent.

With a small but sizeable chuckle, Dad proceeded to dip his toe in the water. Matter-of-factly, he looked at our neighbor and stated, *Do you know what the real problem is? The real problem is she loves me too much.* With laughter rising from the neighbor, myself, and my father, the tension had no choice but to leave the room. Although the sharp cut of my mother's eyes did not fade with the comment, hearing his giggles, they softened. She settled on ending the argument by smirking out her usual retort, *You will only appreciate me after I'm gone.* As always, my father's deeper grasp of my mother's love weakened her stance.

**Figure 6**
*A Picture for My Son*

# 6

# The Last Return Home

Families have distinct patterns, symbols stored in spiritual archives that surface in the form of omens. My father was admitted to the hospital on his father's death anniversary—November 21, *a bad omen*. He returned home a day before my parents' wedding anniversary—December 2, *a good omen*. Our Christmas miracle arrived a few weeks early when Dad's pulse steadied, permitting him to be discharged and sent home. And as soon as his right foot hit the hardwood floors, the four of us breathed a sigh of relief. But the alleviation noted on my father's face differed. After removing his boots, I stood back and watched him briskly scatter to and fro. Generally, my father moved slowly, so to see him operate at this pace was unusual. My eyes followed him as he traveled to every nook and cranny of our house, rushing to organize his affairs. *He really wants to put his things back in their proper places*, I decided. But later, when he could no longer walk, I realized I had it all wrong. He was not rushing to put things in order; he was rushing to get things in order. My father did precisely that throughout the nine days of his *last return home*—he got things in order.

After Dad died, I turned detective, trying to gather the missing pieces of the puzzle that would help me make sense of his death. Upon investigating further, subtle clues slowly came to light, and I became aware of his mannerisms, matching those of a person who knew his time was ending. For instance, when I met with the priest to discuss the details of his funeral, she informed me that the last time he attended church, he sought prayers from the chaplains, stating: *Something is wrong, but I don't know what.* I learned from my mother that during his last week at home, he requested she sleep in their bed beside him, even though sometimes they slept separately due to her work hours. She also told me a few nights before his readmittance, my father called and spoke with all eight of his siblings. Later, while in India, my uncle elaborated on their conversation, how the two of them talked for over an hour, Dad asking his younger brother question after question. Eventually, when my uncle inquired into the intention behind his interrogation, my father responded: *I think this will be our last conversation. We won't get another chance to talk after this.* His words crashed down on my ears, blanketing my mind. The constant swirl of thoughts, forming my reasonings and imaginings of the untimely nature of his death, were brought to an abrupt halt. Only two words managed to survive my shock—*he knew.*

If my father had died in a hospital in India, the body still would have come home to be among the gathered community, praying for his soul's repose. Once the ritualistic prayers were performed, a procession of people would have led him from our house to the church, crossing spiritual landmarks along the way. Since we cannot practice this tradition in Canada, the good omen of him returning home this week was not attached to his survival. Instead, it was the week *God gave back to him* so he could finalize his responsibilities, shower love on his family, and lead the procession himself. Symbolically, my father came home and headed toward his final destination, and metaphorically, we trailed behind him.

\*\*\*

*Ready for school, I ran downstairs and found Dad engulfed in his routine. As per usual, he was an early riser and was sitting in his rocking chair, reading the newspaper. To my surprise, I caught him carefully scanning the Sports section. My dad was more of a philosophy, religion, politics kind of guy.*

*I commented on the change of scenery, "I didn't know you were interested in reading hockey stats, Dad."*

*Sporting a sly grin, he peeked around the corners of the paper, "I'm not."*

*Confused, I asked, "Then why are you reading that?"*

*Putting the paper down, my father looked me square in the eyes and explained, "Your brother loves sports. I wake up early and read the Sports section before he comes down so that we have something to talk about and I* can show him I care about his interests."

Silence washed over me as an important truth sunk in. As much as I like to pretend that I am Dad's favorite child, I'm not. Our dad loved us equally and exactly the same.

*** 

My brother is the Christmas decorator of the household. Every year he goes bigger and brighter to put an expression of awe on the faces of others. Since the joyous day was nearing, he made sure to have the house illuminated before Dad's grand return home. Our place looked bright and vibrant, and our father appreciated his efforts. Usually, due to his shyness, we were the ones asking him to stand and take a picture with us—but seeing the beauty of this year's tree, Dad initiated the asking. With a planned objective in mind, he planted himself firmly in front of the artificial pine and said, *Come take a picture with me.* One by one, he called on each of us to stand beside him in front of the well-lit festive decorations.

I jumped at the opportunity and went first. Dressed in matching attire, we smiled widely, full of glee. Next, my mother joined him, and then my best friend and her daughter followed suit. My father stood in front of the Christmas tree for as long as our hearts delighted, waiting for each of us to get our fill of stills with him. Noticing my brother had not yet taken a picture, Dad called for him a second time, *Son, come down, I want a picture with you.* My brother, exhausted from the previous week in the hospital, put off the chance to take this photo. A foreboding feeling grew in the pit of my stomach.

I went upstairs and asked him once more, *Dad really wants a picture with you. I think you should come down and take one.*

Brushing me off, my brother sternly repeated his initial response, *I'll take a picture later.*

But later never came.

For the remainder of our father's days in the hospital, my brother's guilt grew heavier. Each of us had something to feel guilty about, and this remorse was his. As Dad's health deteriorated, resentment festered between us, and I had trouble making sense of his actions. My grief would not permit me to forgive his misjudgment. But, upon further contemplation, a fresh perspective emerged through the planning and writing of these stories. I brought forward the understanding that we each did our part. Each family member did the best we could with the knowledge and information we had during those final months, not knowing they were *his final months*. My brother's part was not to come down for a few minutes and take a picture. His part was putting in the endless hours of work to raise and decorate the tree in the first place. I realized had it not been for him, Dad's *aha!* to take advantage of a golden opportunity for his family would not have materialized. I would not have had one last merry Christmas memory with my father. When it comes to fulfilling a person's last wishes—we all play our parts.

> *And, for Dad, your efforts have always been more than enough. The pictures he took that day were for us, not him. Nevertheless, he knew you would hold onto your regret—and so, he left one just for you.*

**Figure 7**
*A Prophetic Painting*
*October 29, 2016*

# 7

## The Last Prophesy

I sat at the table, eerily calm. The phone call had not come through yet, but a part of me knew it was coming. Wrapping up a twelve-hour workday, I rose from the chair, packed my belongings, and headed out the door. As I stepped into the darkness, the voicemail notification appeared: *Mom wanted me home.*

Using the speed dial function in my car, I returned her call and connected to a troubled tone, *Daddy's not feeling well. I think you should come home.*

Worn out from the day, I missed the intonation of her words and rejected her request, *I just finished parent–teacher interviews, Mom. It's late. I'll come by tomorrow.*

Rearranging her words from suggestion to adamancy, she repeated herself, *No, you need to come home now. He's not well.*

The trill of fear in her voice brought my second wind; I shifted lanes and drove straight home.

Growing up, our family was poor; genuinely, we struggled. We relied heavily on one another for different forms of security. My mother carried the four of us on her back using a nurse's salary, which in the eighties, barely made ends meet. She often worked double shifts at multiple jobs to feed us. A remorseful memory I still harbor today is, as a child, asking her if I *had* to eat the *same* boxed macaroni and cheese *again* for the fourth time that week. My mother's face, which typically stood brave, enticing me, ruptured. I never asked that question again. Although Mom was not always present to soothe us directly, her physical, emotional, and mental endurance nurtured us. Her endless vitality funneled into our growing systems. Painfully, she sacrificed the time a mother craves to cradle her children. On some days, still, she holds us too tightly; on most days, *still*, she is stuck in survival mode. Yet, the scars on her heart bore for no one. Radiant, her laughter spreads through any room she enters. I have seen the grace of God descend in the form of a woman, and that woman is my mother. Her loss is one my mind cannot even begin to formulate.

My father's education—a Bachelor of Arts in English, a Bachelor of Education, and a double-major Master's degree in English and Economics—did not follow him here. To disguise the nonacceptance of foreign degrees, the school system declared him overqualified for a job he had already been doing back home. On their insistence, he enrolled in the same Canadian university courses once more and attempted to start over but pursuing that level of education twice was not financially feasible. So, when they shifted to Calgary, he completed training for various trades, obtaining diplomas in computer programming and banking. Mom recalls paying one thousand dollars, *money we didn't have*, for Dad to become a banker, a course he excelled in. Yet, when applying for jobs and facing rejection after rejection, he learned his intelligence was invisible, that prejudices would not penetrate his skin barrier. The rough and weary soles of my grandfather's feet, trekking many miles in the middle of the night to pay and sustain my father's education, would not be repaired on Canadian soil.

I grew up witnessing my dad try everything. He traveled twice from coast to coast, *A Mari usque ad Mare*,[1] searching for a steady income. With persistence, he applied for job after job and even started his own business venture, *EPM Computer Consulting*. At the height of our devastation, he was offered a position that was rescinded by the time we came home from a celebratory dinner. After this last defeat, my father surrendered to his fate, or as he put it, *God's will*. He accepted his role as a full-time househusband and channeled all of his energy into raising his children. And though Mom was placed on a pedestal for her ability to support us financially, Dad was put down regularly for stepping into the role of our primary caregiver—an ignorance that lingered past his death, reviving ghosts rumbling in whis-

---

[1] Canada's official motto: "*From Sea to Sea.*" The Canadian Encyclopedia Online. (2021).

pers. Yet, through all the criticisms, insults, and hurtful accusations, he stayed silent, turning the other cheek, teaching my brother and me to defy social constructs: *Who fulfills which role is not important, a job well done is.* As far back as I can remember, Dad was always at home with me. I followed him around everywhere, attaching myself to his hip. Naturally, I developed a deep and affectionate bond with him, more than anyone else in my life. And as my mother continued to work full time, I continued to view my father as my security blanket well into my adult life.

Reaching the house, I got out of the car and stopped at the door, pondering the situation ahead of me. Normally, I would head inside, scream for my dad, run past the others, and go directly to his room, where I knew I would find him. However, this time, I slowed my steps. Steadily, I walked into our home and found my mother waiting for me, her face dejected, riddled with unsettling concern.

*Where's Dad?* I asked.

*He's upstairs sleeping*, came her dispirited reply.

I broke my regime, staying a few minutes longer with her as she explained the events that unfolded that evening. Her sad, shaken voice made me uneasy. This time, choosing not to run, I walked up the stairs slowly.

***

*"Dad! Dad, where are you?" Returning home from school, I ran swiftly up the stairs in search of my father. He followed a set routine, so I knew he would be napping. Standing in the doorway of his bedroom, I watched him as he slept in his regular position, curled and facing left. Before moving any closer, I stopped to perform my regular check—his belly rose, his belly fell. Good, he's still breathing. Next, I inched toward him and napped down beside him. The natural rhythms of our bodies were in sync, and lying beside him always rejuvenated and recharged me, especially after a long day. Sensing my presence, my father startled awake.*

*Capturing me in his Goldilocks bear hug, he chuckled and inquired, "Who's this sleeping in my bed?"*

*We exploded with laughter.*

*"It's me, Dad!"*

*Holding me tight, he closed his eyes again and softly said, "Good, I was waiting for you."*

\*\*\*

Stopping at each step, I reminded myself of the countless times I had climbed these stairs and gone in search of my father. Reaching the summit, I turned left and quietly crept to his room. I found him as I always had—in the exact room, in the exact bed, in the exact position—sleeping, *not exactly* as before. With heavy feet, fearfully, I entered. The room was pitch black, save a blue hue that shone on his face, descending from a lit picture of Jesus hanging above his bedframe. This small flicker in the shadows made it possible to see the serenity my father wore. Lost in his tranquility, an ambiance appeared. An *invisible hand*, whose palm I had been engraved on, opened a window to my sixth sense, asking me to stand guard and be ready. I took the anointing to heart and wholeheartedly accepted the shifting responsibility that came with being my *father's keeper*—a role that would influence the depth and breadth of my grief later on. Carefully, gently, I went and took my spot on the bed beside him.

I placed my body next to his in our usual arrangement. However, this time, I went unnoticed. He gave no startle, no chuckle, no soft-spoken words. He was in such a deep state of unconsciousness that nothing could get a rise out of him. I tried my usual tricks—I nudged, I squirmed, I poked—but still, no movement came from his side. He had slipped into another world, a place so far from us that he lay unreachable. Realizing my father would not even respond to *my* touch, a deep, unrelenting sadness washed over me. A shadow had entered the room and cast a feeling over us that I had never felt before. Now, I was the one slipping into a new layer of consciousness, one that forced me to pay attention to everything. My body emanated heat as divine energy flowed through me, preparing us both for the journey ahead. Lying still, I soaked every ounce. Then, when I was ready, I turned to my father and shook him.

With little to no energy left, he spoke softly, *Who's this sleeping in my bed?*

Even softer, I replied, *It's me, Dad, it's me.*

Nodding, he acknowledged a final time, *Good, I was waiting for you.*

Lifting my father from the bed, I assisted him to the washroom. His body, stiff, as though jilted by his spirit, leaned heavily on me for support. Grabbing onto my arm with one hand, he pressed firmly down on his cane with the other, and together, we shuffled forward in small movements. I propped his body in an upright position and left him alone after insisting he would be okay on his own. Waiting outside the door, I blocked intrusive thoughts from flooding my mind and stood patiently, listening for his call. Five minutes went by without a word. Suddenly, a *crashing* sound broke the silence. I ran back into the washroom and found my father standing as I left him, but now, he was fast asleep with his cane collapsed on the floor.

His crutch, I helped balance my father down the flight of stairs and sat him in his rocking chair. Turning to my mother, I spoke, *He has no energy. He needs to eat.* Then, walking him from the rocking chair to the kitchen table, a mere four-meter distance, took my dad a full ten minutes. Because of his lack of appetite, we had to coerce him to eat, and after eating a few handfuls, he complained he was full and slowly shut his eyes once more. My mother wobbled him awake.

Finally, she asked the question for all three of us, *Do you want to go to the hospital?*

Unsurprisingly, my father responded with a weak, *No.*

Due to his numerous health issues and the many complications that arose from the treatments, typically, my father actively resisted going to the hospital. *And I didn't blame him.* But I was also unsure why we surrendered to his protests that night, as clearly, he was ill. Perhaps we had hoped so badly that he would sleep it off and be fine. Nevertheless, having seen the whole picture now, I am glad we listened to his wishes. Because we gave in, Dad had one last night of sleep in his own bed. Before I left, I tucked him in, kissed him on the forehead, and reassured him, *Don't worry, Dad, get some sleep. You're going to be okay.*

On the drive home, the events of the evening and my interactions with my father sent shockwaves through my system. I needed to be still and silent, as this was the only way to gain mental clarity and find spiritual sustenance. Dad was the one who taught me how to pray, using a Christian acronym he had once learned, ACTS: *Adoration, Confession, Thanksgiving,* and *Supplication.* It was an easy-to-follow template that stayed with me as I grew. But as I aged and my discernment narrowed, so did my list of supplications, dwindling to two specific requests: *Please make sure my dad is here when I get married*, and *please make sure my dad is here when I have children*. Encountering so many obstacles with his health had taught me that these two needs were all that mattered. Slowly, I stopped asking for so many things, and humbly, I began listening for what was asked of me.

Apart from being a middle school teacher, I am a trained, intuitive Reiki healer. When heat surges through my body—as it did just then with my father—I know spontaneous wisdom, nudges, inklings, or messages have come through. And this time, a line of communication opened solely for me. An acceptance of an inevitable truth would soon rush forward, sought from me. Back in the privacy of my apartment, I distracted myself with menial tasks and began washing the dishes—yet within the menial, the meditative state is the highest. Coupled with the connection of warm, flowing water, my mind became still, and my voice became silent. The stream trickled off the edges of my palms, relaxing me, leaving me in a tranquil state, ready to receive. Instantaneously, a voice greater than my own took over, asking me only two questions: *Are you okay if he's not here when you get married? Are you okay if he's not here when you have children?* Stunned, I froze. Then, torpedoed by emotion, I collapsed onto the sink. My wailing was so severe that I consider this moment a pre-release of my grief, shedding an enormous agony from my body into the drain. After allowing myself to suffer, permitting the pain to release, I stood straight and decided to move forward with grace. From this point onward, I agreed to focus my attention solely on my father, paving the way for a peaceful transition.

By sheer coincidence, a flash of fate, or because the words were written, my best friend called just as I wiped the last tear from my eyes.

Sensing my melancholy, she inquired, *Linita, what's wrong?*

I paused to regain my composure and then invited her into my newly birthed premonition, *I think I will have to say goodbye to my dad soon.*

Over the span of our thirty-year friendship, those words had never left my mouth, leaving her shocked at my statement. Immediately, she jumped to reassure me, *What do you mean? He's going to be fine, Linita. He's only falling asleep, and he's back home.*

Now I was the one who needed to repeat myself. Keeping a calm but firm tone, I reinforced what I originally stated, *I need you to listen to what I'm telling you. I'm going to have to say goodbye to my dad soon.*

Noting the sternness in my voice, she acknowledged what I knew. Emphatically, compassionately, she advanced the conversation, *Okay, why do you think that? Did something happen?*

For the rest of the evening, she stayed on the phone with me, listening to my experiences, mindful observations, and the spiritual knowingness that came through my body.

Alas, the revelation of *the last prophesy* materialized the very next morning. On December 9, 2016, in an unexpected turn of events, my father initiated his final journey himself, requesting my mother—*for the first time*—to call him an ambulance and take him to the hospital.

**Figure 8**
*Keep Calm and Breathe On*

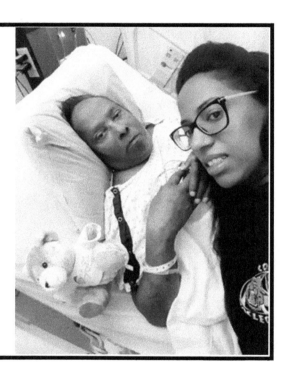

# 8

## The Last Time in the Emergency

The call came through in the middle of the school day—a rare time I answered my cell phone in class. Stepping out of the room, I learned that my father had been readmitted to the hospital. Time slowed down; each second dragged, preventing me from rushing to his side. And when the last bell sounded, I got my affairs in order and quickly left the building. Maneuvering down the long strip of road to the hospital, my mind twisted and turned with tormented thoughts, a routine that would last for the next thirty-six days. He had never been admitted two times in a row before, and even though, on some level, I knew what was happening, I still needed time to grasp and comprehend. In my car, I was quiet and alone, and every day during this stretch of driving, I cried. This was my time to process the pain and let the emotion out before reaching him. I was not one to repeat past mistakes twice.

***

*I was a first-year university student studying with my friends on campus when I received a life-altering call. I was on edge all day because I knew my father was awaiting results. My mother, to protect us, said it was a routine visit, monitoring his diabetes. But I knew she was lying; I had heard the doctor's tone on the answering machine the night before.*

*I called home throughout the day, but no one picked up. One o'clock, two o'clock, three o'clock—no answer. Then, suddenly, a call from the hospital came through; I recognized the number since it was my mother's place of employment. Grasping the seriousness of the situation, I stepped out of the room and answered my phone. Hidden behind her calm voice, my fears were realized, as my mother instructed me to get to the hospital.*

*Cautiously, I shuffled into his room. My eyes widened as my father's condition struck me: lying in a hospital bed, dressed in a hospital gown, attached to all sorts of unfamiliar machines. Seeing me enter, he swiftly reached for the magazine on his stomach and pretended to read the print, albeit upside down. I sat beside him on the bed; he glanced upward and smiled into my fearful eyes, trying to ease my anxieties.*

*"Dad, what happened?"*

*"Oh nothing, I'm just reading a magazine."*

*"It's upside down, Dad!" I retorted, unamused by his antics, attempting to change the subject.*

*Taken aback by his inadvertent actions, he let out a chuckle and matter-of-factly stated, "I know, that's how I like reading them."*

*Within seconds, he reversed the magazine and his ability to suppress his emotions. Looking at me, he knew there was no use. His eyes softened as one visible tear streamed down his face. No one had yet disclosed the news of his heart attack, but his sentiments spoke for them. Frightened by the thought of losing him, I sobbed on his chest and ran out of the room, ashamed of my inability to stay strong for him.*

\*\*\*

I rounded the steep hill of the parking lot and was brought to a standstill, observing the giant *H* that marked the building. My mother was a nurse at this hospital for nearly thirty-five years. The protruding H, the old-fashioned hallways, and the scent of her unit had long since imprinted my memory. Visions of my father and me driving her to work late in the afternoons and picking her up later in the evenings—day after day, year after year—surfaced and spun. Traveling inward, I remembered how these walls had sheltered us many times before, whether through our sicknesses, celebrating my mom's pinnacle anniversaries, or my dad's open-heart surgery. This building was a part of us and partly responsible for shaping my upbringing. The essence that fluttered through the hallways, felt the minute you enter, intertwined with many aspects of my life and on multiple occasions. And now, the most significant was yet to come.

## The Last Time in the Emergency

I walked through the emergency doors, gave the attendant my father's information, and waited to be escorted onto the unit. The ward was packed with people, sporting all sorts of conditions and illnesses. Attentively, I moved through the roundabout and finally located my parents in a small cubby off to the side. Pulling back the curtain, I made myself visible to him. The complications from the previous night were still in effect; however, now, Dad was hyperventilating his way through a series of anxious fits. Usually, my father did not show his distress; his suffering stayed hidden, away from the limelight. But as I observed what was happening, possibly for the first time, it clicked—a probable source of my own anxiety was inherited from him. We both experience common symptoms generated by the same environmental stressors: *closed spaces, loud noises, surprise attacks,* or *unexpected fright*. All of which resulted in chest pains, increased heart rate, and difficulty breathing. Dad was experiencing the all too familiar fight-or-flight.

Noticing the small space of the room and the dread of being in the hospital had created angst for my father, I tried calming his tremoring body as he had entered a state of hyperarousal. Holding his face in-between my hands, I instructed him to make eye contact with me. Then, locking in his gaze, I initiated a deep breathing technique that I kept in my toolkit. *Okay, Dad, let's breathe, let's breathe together: in for four, hold for seven, out for eight.*[2] The fear in his eyes eased as he focused on the security found in mine. With his face gently resting in my palms, we practiced several successions of breathwork together. He inhaled deeply, held it effectively, and exhaled as instructed, letting out a slight whistle on the way out. A smile formed on my face. *Dad really was the cutest old man.* Even though these exercises stabilized him, his panic attacks continued to spike by the hour—whenever he cycled through suddenly sleeping and waking. And, every single time, we breathed through them together. Watching us, the nurse mentioned, *We gave him medication, but your touch seems to do the trick*. My father did always call me the girl with the golden touch.

Dad endured all sorts of tests and trials in the emergency ward to figure out why his pulse was so low, and his sleep was so deep, but the results always came back empty-handed. Soon, the doctors suspected leukemia as the culprit, and he had enlarged bruises on his body to support this, but thankfully, that too, came back negative. Feelings of

---

[2] *Three Breathing Exercises and Techniques.* A. Weil, M.D. (2016). DrWeil.Com.

relief and uneasiness merged into one. As our gratitude grew for the negatives, our turmoil surrounding that one positive also grew.

By the end of the third day, my father became despondent; his face filled with a visible gloom, and his mood declined.

Sensing this, I asked, *What's wrong, Dad?*

Child-like, in Malayalam, he informed me, *Eniku vishakunnu—I'm hungry.*

Knowing he was starving on his liquid diet and having no control over satiating his hunger, I became disheartened. The situation was moving further away from me, and I tried to control the outcome. But as Dad continued to battle his unknown illness, I markedly struggled with surrendering the process. I complained to my mother, *He's hungry, Mom. When will he be able to eat?*

She responded the best way she knew how, *When all the tests are done.*

But what she did not know then was that we were waiting for a diagnosis that would never come. And once my father moved to a proper bed on a dedicated unit, these three grueling days in the emergency ward turned out to be a walk in the park.

# ~In the Middle~

*Love is patient, love is kind.*

*It does not envy, it does not boast, it is not proud.*

*It does not dishonor others, it is not self-seeking,*

*it is not easily angered, it keeps no record of wrongs.*

*Love does not delight in evil but rejoices with the truth.*

*It always protects,*

*always trusts,*

*always hopes,*

*always perseveres.*

*Love never fails.*

*—NIV, 1 Corinthians 13:4–8*

**Figure 9**
*2 x 2 = 4*

# 9

# The Last Argument

Ever since I can remember, our small family of four divided into two: the *father and the daughter*, and the *mother and the son*. As a family, we held a united front. But when it came to personalities, likes, dislikes, hobbies, interests, careers, blood group, and overprotectiveness—it was in this division we operated. Perhaps this is why when a deep knowing arose that my counterpart was weakening, I lashed out at the other half, specifically, my mother. Mothers and daughters have that unique ability—to love fiercely and to fight in the same way.

How the dichotomies split never bothered me; my mother and brother have always had a special bond, secured by the fact that he was her *firstborn* child. I was younger, spoiled in my own way, and well-known as the *apple* of my father's eye. Because he showered me with all of his love, attention, and affection, I paid no heed to the strength of the alliance of the other two. Prior to his final days, aloneness was a mirage; I had never encountered true loneliness until I had to face the loss of my father. Now, slowly, this overwhelming sensation of feeling left out started to spike. And as his condition dwindled, jealousy landed directly on the tip of my tongue. In other words, my reactions and responses to grief, aimed at my mother, sharpened, as the image of my father planted firmly beside me did the opposite.

The dynamic between the three of us—my mother, brother, and me—was in limbo. And I challenged them. At first, tiny incidents unnerved me, like our mother preparing food the way *he likes it* or serving him at the table first. I reverted to an immature state of mind, throwing temper tantrums and refusing to eat, behavior that was out of character for me. Coincidentally, this followed the first round of my father's hospitalization. Soon after, my bursts of anger deepened, becoming more irrational and uncontrollable. By chance again, this occurred during the second round of his hospitalization. Crystal-clear now, at the time, I could not see how anticipatory grief moved through my body. That, I had regressed to childlike mannerisms to cope with the loss of my primary parent. And, as my awareness grew around my dad's impending death, my grief-fueled, green-colored face spared no one.

Dad's second and final hospitalization triggered my generalized anxiety disorder, causing my unreasonable thoughts to spiral. As a proactive person, I upped my ammunition, performing more breathing, more yoga, more meditation, and more one-on-one counseling. I fit in appointments with my psychologist in between leaving work and heading to the hospital. I grounded myself as much as possible, filling my cup so I could fill his. One evening after my session, I came into the room to find my mother watching my father, who was, once again, hypnotized by sleep. We started making small talk that turned into light bickering at the drop of a hat. I do not remember why the conversation took a drastic turn; I only remember that it did. Honestly, at this point, I doubt anything she could have said or done would have been right—I was insistent on making mountains out of molehills. Before I knew it, I blew up in the middle of the hospital room. All of this anger and bitterness and frustration that accompanied my father's unknown illness bubbled and boiled over, creating a sharp *I'm ready to go* whistle for those around me to hear. *You didn't even ask me how my session went*—was code for—*he's leaving me, and you aren't being vigilant*. The only person who took notice of my struggles would soon be gone, and I was crushed by the fact that she would not be able to divide her attention. Veritably, it was not her fault—it was, after all, our family's predisposition.

Privy to the knowledge that my grief had crept in, my mother stayed quiet, hoping this would diffuse my bullheaded behavior. The nurse who came in to assess my father's vitals wore a facial expression that did not hide her displeasure with me. *I didn't care; her father wasn't the one dying.* I left the room to compose myself, to get some space and air to ease my choking heart. When I was far enough away from prying ears, I dropped my head into my hands and cried. *What is happening to me?* I did not know why I was acting this way; I just knew he was not allowed to die. My sweet, sweet father who loved me wholeheartedly, fought for me consistently, and understood me fully—if he left, *who else did I have?* I was not ready to let my kindred spirit go. No matter the intuitions, no matter the warnings, no matter the extra time, no matter nothing. I tried pleading to a higher power for understanding, *how do I live the rest of my life without him, especially when we both have so many years yet to live?* At the time, a response was withheld from me—later on, a rebuttal rushed forward as a renewed sense of purpose.

Out of the fifty-four days of Dad's illness, I can count three instances when my behavior was nonsensical, and this was one of them. Even though the medical staff told us my father would not be able to hear us while absorbed in his coma-like sleep, he always proved otherwise. Cognizant of my struggle to squeeze a square into a triangle, he would later converse with me during a beautiful, private moment—a father–daughter one. Using his telepathic ability, he communicated my combativeness back to me and guided me through my predicament,

> *Linita, don't fight with your mother and brother. Take care of them and protect them. Who else do you have after I'm gone? They are your tribe now.*

Even while dying, he recognized my internal battle. He knew each of ours. And before he left, he dissected all three in front of me and found the element of healing that would soothe our wounds. Knowing he would soon be gone, he passed on to me the glue that held our family together, entrusting I would take care of what he loved most—his beloved tribe.

Throughout my first year of bereavement, I tried my best to live up to my father's expectations. But the turbulence of grief, and the loss of a pivotal member, brought instability to our family as we set out to learn and navigate a new normal. Whenever the sorrow of missing him was too heavy and crippling to bear, we took turns taking the ache out on each other. We attack those we feel safest. When the brunt end of the storm passed, we understood more clearly that *that's what family is for.* Family holds up a mirror in times of deep grieving to reflect our pain and difficulties, to remind each other that *it's okay, I understand,*

*I miss him too*, and *I am here.* The anger, the rage, the frustration, and the unsettling hurt were merely the stained portions of the glass where the blood, sweat, and tears of our loss accumulated. And as we worked harder to cleanse the tarnish of grief from our spirits, the only element that sustained long enough to stare back at us was the pure and unconditional love each of us held for him.

*\*\*\**

*Culturally, the darker shade of my skin is considered unattractive. From the moment pregnancies are announced in the Indian community, mothers-to-be are bombarded with home remedies that increase the likelihood of a beautiful light-skinned baby. Then, when the baby is born, their first compliment depends on their melanin production. Indeed, the stars of our films are cast according to their complexion, as even in our imagination, the rich color of Indians is devalued and underrepresented. Thus, ever since I can remember, I was told by my community that girls shouldn't be as dark as me; that I didn't wash my skin hard enough; that being dark was equivalent to being ugly; and that when I grew up, no one would marry me.*

*As a child, I felt helpless looking at myself in the mirror. I could not understand how my skin defined my spirit. I started wishing I was lighter, "How do I change it so that they like me?" I stretched, scratched, pinched, pulled, and scrubbed. I even experimented with well-known skin bleaching creams. I tried everything to change how they saw me—to convince my own community that I was pretty. But no matter how hard I tried, nothing worked; I was stuck in the sheath of my skin. And as I got older, the comments and criticisms only worsened, reaching a much broader audience.*

*When I was twelve, my father and I went to India. This trip would be the first time I had visited my relatives since I was a baby. I remember sitting on the plane whispering, "they will look like me." After an extremely long flight, we finally reached my father's home. I entered, nervous and excited to meet my grandparents, uncles, aunts, and cousins. I was quietly standing in the hall smiling when suddenly an older relative blurted out, "She's too dark. I don't want to talk to her." My heart dropped to the floor and smashed into a million pieces. Even in India, the color of my skin demeaned my value.*

*I ran to my father, buried my head in his chest, and cried.*

*"Linita, what's wrong? What happened?"*

*"They don't want to talk to me because I'm too dark."*

*My father paused; he knew I had been struggling with this issue for a long time. After waiting for me to finish crying, he continued, "Linita, look at me. What color is my skin? Light or dark?"*

*"It's dark."*

*"That's right; I'm dark. And you are dark because I am dark. Mom and your brother are lighter, and they look like each other. But you—you look like me. Everything that is mine belongs to you, even my skin color! If you are ashamed of your skin, then that means you are ashamed of me. Are you ashamed of me?"*

*"No, Dad, I'm never ashamed of you!" My chest rose as I responded.*

*Dad smiled. "Good. From now on, I don't want you to let anyone discourage you because of the color of your skin. Think of me and feel proud—it means you are a part of me, and I am a part of you."*

*After hearing my father's wisdom, I never questioned the quality of my skin color again. I knew it was handed down from a king.*

*That evening, I heard my father scolding the family member for what she said to me. Then, a short while later, she found me and apologized, "I was only joking."*

**Figure 10**
*Memorizing Memories*

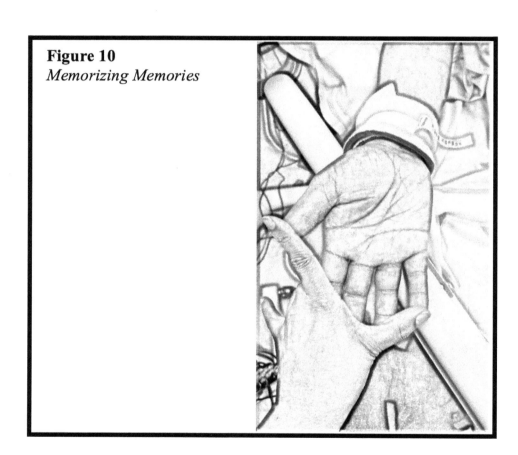

# 10

## The Last Touch

The days and nights amalgamated into one. Thinking back now, I have no idea how I did what I did, how I lived through those terrifying trials without breaking down. Our family's world had collided with tragedy, and I froze in place—my thoughts, words, and deeds were stuck on repeat. Somehow, I managed to run on minimal sleep, little food, long days at school, and longer evenings in the hospital. I suppose that is what happens when the fate of a loved one is uncertain. Shadowing the medical staff, I moved alongside them to assist with my father's recovery; my actions were automatic, fueled by our common goal to get him home. Whenever the situation required someone to physically handle Dad—to move, to bathe, to feed—I swooped in and offered to help, knowing the familiarity of my touch would soothe him. That, our touch communicated to one another. Eventually, a conscious effort was no longer needed, as positioning myself to calm him was standard. Most days, time progressed without my knowledge. But it stood completely still for specific seconds—during my time alone with him.

Every night, shortly after five, I arrived at the hospital and switched places with my mother and brother covering the day shift. We never left my father alone. Before leaving, Mom informed me that Dad's pulse was still weak, sitting at a meager thirty-four. In an attempt to raise his vitals, the medical staff administered allopathic medicine, but thus far, their efforts had failed. Contemplating the situation from a different, eastern perspective, I wondered, *could I help?* A year ago, a spiritual teacher advised me to learn the art of Reiki:

*Linita, there is healing in your hands, harness this energy. Reiki healing is directly tied to helping your father.*

That was reason enough. Before the year ended, I found a teacher and learned the modality, completing all three degrees and becoming a Reiki Master a few months before his hospitalization. The opportunity to help him had perfectly aligned. Yet, I was apprehensive in the hospital; I did not want to interfere with the ongoing medical treatments. After consulting with my teacher, who reminded me, *no harm can come from this form of healing*, I decided to move forward and give it a try. I knew my father would welcome my efforts; he loved receiving energy healing from me. Our previous sessions benefitted him greatly, relieving the discomfort in his legs. He even went as far as asking if he could write a testimonial for my website:

*I had swelling and pain in my legs. First, I tried traditional treatments. It didn't work. Then, I had a couple of Reiki sessions with Linita. During the session, I felt a warm feeling under my feet and legs. The next day the swelling and pain in my legs went down, and now I am able to walk without any problem. I strongly recommend Linita's line of treatment for those who have similar problems.*
–Eapen Mathew

Honored, Dad's testimonial sits at the top of my website still. Now, in his hospital room, I stepped into his line of sight and sought his permission once more, *Dad, would you like some Reiki?* Peacefully, he nodded.

Beginning at the crown, I started with the opening ceremony, which prepares the body for receiving treatment. Slowly, I moved down his chakras with the palms of my hands and rested on his heart and pulse centers. Steadying my hands, a heating sensation warmed the affected areas. The heat communicated to me that healing was occurring, and so I stayed put in those places a while longer. When the energy cooled, I closed the session, and simultaneously, my father opened his eyes. He acknowledged an alleviation, and I sat back down in the chair beside him. A short while later, the nurse arrived to check his vitals.

Holding his wrist in one hand and glancing at her watch on the other, she strangely noted, *Hmm, that's weird.*

Nervously, I inquired, *Is everything okay?*

Keeping her focus on my father, she replied, *Everything is great.*

*His pulse has gone up to seventy-five, and that's the highest it's been since he was admitted. Did something change while I was gone?*

Timidly, not knowing how she would react, I responded, *I did Reiki on him.*

Smiling, she looked at me and said, *Well, whatever you did seems to be working. I would keep it up if I were you.*

Letting out a sigh of relief, I relaxed and reflected on my new level of awareness as a healer. Once again, my father was responsible for raising my confidence in my abilities. And from this day forward, I gladly gave him treatments daily, as Reiki became a new part of our routine. At times, onlookers observed our sessions, quickly noticing our coinciding rhythms—as soon as I opened, he fell fast asleep, and as soon as I closed, he awoke. The visitors could not help but comment on what they saw, *Wow, he really responds to what you are doing.* I often questioned whether it was the Reiki or the practitioner, but in the end, I settled the matter as a combination of the two. I was satisfied knowing my spiritual understanding of life had once again allowed me to do something good for my dad.

Physical touch was a vital aspect of our father–daughter duo. We were wired the same—shy, introverted, and highly sensitive—and had a unique ability to comfort each other without using words. I never gave this paranormal power much thought. I assumed the experience was universal, *a person who felt like home.* However, as our true nature revealed itself to others in the hospital, and from the subsequent responses that arose because of it, I realized our connection was unparalleled. We went beyond close fathers and daughters and soulmates; we matched in the arena of *twin flames.*

Another aspect of touch that was pertinent to my father's healing also stemmed from the use of my hands. Traditionally, in a Malayalee household, it is common for youngsters to massage oil or lotion into the arms and legs of the elderly. This task was a way for the child to give back to their parents or grandparents and was essentially considered a form of blessing. My dad had trained me to carry this out from a young age, and as far back as I can remember, this was a part of my daughterly duties. For him, it was not merely a traditional custom; he needed me to apply a special lotion to his skin to soften the effects of diabetic dermopathy. As a small child, the task often irritated me, a chore one tends to avoid, but as I grew older it became a bonding element for us. And here, in his final days, the blessing aspect materialized. Willingly, I initiated the job myself and sincerely took pleasure in doing this for him. I was worried about the condition of his legs, now that his limbs were not getting enough circulation. So, whenever we were alone in the room, I nudged him awake and asked the question I knew he wanted to hear, *Dad, want me to massage your legs for you?* Without hesitation, he lifted into my arms as I moved him from the hospital bed to the reclining chair.

Seated upright and across from each other, I placed his legs firmly on my lap. The second my hands touched his skin, Dad relaxed. I applied the lotion to his legs and pushed hard against his muscles and joints, ensuring his blood flowed. Kneading from his thighs to his feet, I watched as my father journeyed deeper into his sleep. He trusted me. I treasured these moments, wanting them to last as long as possible. Even when my fingers throbbed or pain seared my arms, I continued to move them. I had witnessed his anguish directly—the stiffness in his arms and legs, the unending pokes and prods of needles drawing and pushing in fluids, and the blood-soaked bandage on his back from the lumbar puncture. My pain went unnoticed because my pain was irrelevant. This knowing allowed a continuous surge of energy to fill my veins, reminding me not to stop. If I did, our time together would follow suit. And prolonging our time together, for as long as I could, was what I intended to do.

A silent melody serenaded us as an ethereal sense filled the room—we were alone, but not alone. Consciously, I smoothed his skin beneath my fingers, knowing that soon it might not be so readily available. Gently, I stretched, examined, and analyzed each spot, trying to imprint the features of his casing into my memory. Before I knew it, an alchemy stirred my circulation as painful tears fell freely down my face. My thoughts could not form the reasoning behind my actions, but my spirit knew. A profound awareness had reached the peak of a steep mountain; our story was nearing its climax. I could see the stage of life my father had reached and, slowly, I tried to embrace it. Alongside us, the *peace of God that passes all understanding*[3] flowed through him, which then flowed through me. The intensity of this peace is what stopped the clock in the room. God was present, watching us, weeping

---

3   *Philippines 4:7*. King James Bible. (1611). King James Bible Online.

with the same pain and consistency as me. Now, the blessing came from Him in the form of these rich experiences and the cessation of time. This was our time to be together, to heal together, and to eventually learn how to leave each other. The days and nights amalgamated into one—every second, every minute, every moment—except those.

***

*At seventeen, I was physically attacked when the restaurant I worked at encountered a robbery. It was eleven o'clock at night, and two large, middle-aged men rushed me as I opened the door to take out the garbage. I was closing alone, but luckily a friend of mine was waiting to drive me home. Hearing me scream, she ran across the parking lot to another store and called the police, preventing a life-altering outcome from transpiring. I do not remember much of what happened afterward, as the two men punched my head numerous times. I vaguely recall their masked faces, the police interrogation, my friend's expression, and my mom's over-the-top reaction. Yet, the one image that stayed solid in my mind after all these years was my father's helpless demeanor and the accompanied grave silence.*

*That night, I stayed awake, petrified. I thought of the men, who now had my wallet and home address; I thought of the probable circumstances behind their actions and their reasons for targeting me; and I thought of the numerous knives that had been hanging on the wall to the left of me. Narrowly, I escaped a tragic situation. The events repetitively played through my mind, preventing me from falling asleep. Finally, around two A.M., I noticed a light on downstairs. Slowly, I walked toward the glow. I saw my father sitting in his chair with his head buried in his hands. The thoughts darting through my mind were also racing through his. I sat on his lap, pressed my face into his chest, and cried. He held me here for a long time, gently patting my back. We spoke not a word between us. Within seconds, I was sound asleep.*

**Figure 11**
*One Last Sweater for the Road*

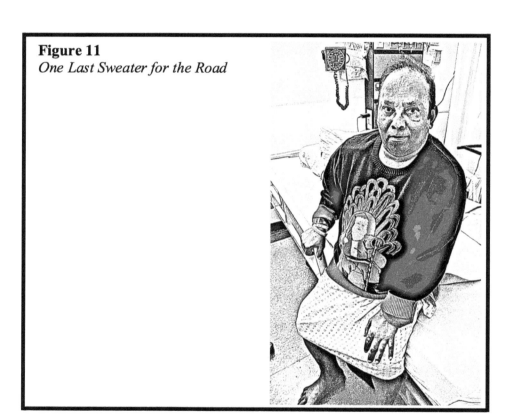

# 11

# The Last Supper

Dad set his sights on me as soon as I walked in the room. As predicted, my sweater caught his attention. Our father loved Christmas sweaters; my brother and I bought them for him regularly. Grabbing my arm, he pulled at the threads, trying to get a feel for the material. *This seems thick. It must be warm*, he commented. Warmth was always the deciding factor, as ever since he started taking the heart medication, my father was always cold.

Knowing the question would spring forward, I went ahead and asked it myself, *Would you like me to buy you one?*

Without swaying from the fabric, he concurred, *Yes*.

Laughing at my father's simple demands of life, I reassured him, *Sure thing, Dad. I'll buy the sweater and bring it here for you, that way you can wear it home.*

That evening, I did as promised and ordered the sweater online. I was so excited for our matching gear that an immediate plan brewed; we could wear the sweaters together and have a mini father–daughter photo shoot. Taking pictures with Dad was my favorite pastime.

When the sweater finally arrived, I sprinted to show him. But in the days leading up to the delivery, the strength of his health wavered, leaving the cotton hanging in his hospital room closet for longer than I had anticipated. And when the day came for him to try the threads on, I had left my twinning attire at home. Nevertheless, I encouraged him to wear it, *Should we see if the sweater fits, Dad?* In retrospect, he was probably too exhausted to do much of anything, but he tried the clothing on for me anyway. Even though I did not get a picture of us together, I did get one of him proudly sporting the last Christmas present I would gift him. It was the first and last time he wore that sweater. Now, it sits in my closet, resting on top of mine.

After this, the *first of the lasts* lined up quickly, one right after the other. Dad's physical state grew weary, showing a steady decline in his capabilities. His sight and sound were weak before entering the hospital, but now they diminished almost entirely. I did my best to be his eyes and ears for him, to try and soften the blow—I repeated what I said, what others said, and drew attention to his visitors: *Do you know who this is, Dad?* Sometimes, the overemphasis on that last question frustrated him, as I learned that he, too, needed to come to terms with his deterioration. In the evenings, I took him for short walks, pointing out the lights and decorations on the unit. Initially, he made it to the Christmas tree and back, but eventually, he barely passed the edge of his bed frame. Quickly, his stages went from walking into the hospital on his own to leaning on one of us for support, to using a four-footed walker, to not being able to walk at all, permanently confined within the rails of his bed. Although I observed the slow decay of his health directly, it was not until he stopped eating that I finally connected the dots.

***

*Per our family's custom, the four of us went for lunch to celebrate a special occasion after the Sunday service. I sat down and took a look at the menu alongside my mother and brother. Glancing upward, Mom noticed Dad sitting motionless, his folder on the table untouched. Impatient to order, she asked him why he was not picking it up.*

*Without batting an eye, he informed her, "She knows what I want. She will order for me."*

*Mom shot us her usual irritated look, then released her go-to sarcastic phrase, "Inghane oru appanum mollum"—loosely translated as such is this father and daughter.*

*Dad and I smiled, sensing her jealousy. Little did they know, I regularly brought my father to this restaurant for our own lunches. I stayed quiet so as not to add salt to her wounds, but by now, she had caught on to our game. Although she teased us, our closeness brought her more happiness than she let on, flashing memories of her and her father scolded by her mom.*

*Rolling her eyes, she gave in, "Order for him then."*
*Smugly, my response followed, "I will."*

\*\*\*

I always kept a close eye on my father's diet; his various sicknesses allotted me this entitlement. Using a multifaceted approach that enforced healthy eating habits, I helped him follow strict guidelines. Daily, I called to make sure he ate on time; weekly, I cooked lean meals and brought them to him; and often, for a change, I picked him up and treated him to his favorite foods at our restaurant. I was so used to cutting his serving into small, manageable pieces that the first time I did this for myself after he died, I broke down and wept in public. Genuinely, I loved taking care of my father, whether it was sizing his suspenders when he could not get free, adjusting his glasses when he could not see, or reaching his feet when he could not reach—no greater joy in life existed for me. Therefore, *secondary losses* were a strange battle, as everything I was fond of doing for him was taken from me all at once.

When my father's eating patterns started to change in the hospital, I instantly took notice. Mimicking his other senses, his nutritional intake conformed to a clear, visible line of reduction. First, he moved from solids to soft solids and liquids only, and then, he began pocketing his food. The first transition seemed normal since the multiple tests he endured required him not to consume solids. But when my father began holding food to the bottom of his cheek, my tension rose. My mother scolded him for doing this, but I knew it was not in his control, nor was he merely being difficult. Dad does not do things to garner attention. Thus, only two options were plausible: either he was unable to chew and swallow his food, or *he forgot how to*. Desperately, I prayed we were tackling the first out of the two; most likely, it was the second. Eventually, his desire to eat diminished altogether, leaving both of us unable to stomach anything.

Our bodies were nourished by Dad's home-cooked meals, my portions strategically hidden from my brother in the corner of the stove. Satisfying and savory, no matter how hard I tried to replicate his dishes, the scent of his soul food was irreplicable, a medicine fading in the distance. Now, watching him struggle to eat, my own body became defiant. My cells refused to keep growing without him; they were in open rebellion. I had to exert myself to eat the same soup from the same coffee shop at least once a day—but mirroring him, often, the food was rejected. That shop, a symbol of his suffering, is still loudly avoided. Naturally, I clung to coffee for comfort, my father's preferred beverage, his scent lingering in the cup calmed me. Morning, noon, and night this was my staple—a cup of black coffee.

I fed my father his last supper. Slowly, he managed to swallow small mouthfuls of the softened dinner made from gravy and mashed potatoes. When I was sure the first few bites traveled down his esophagus and were not pocketed, I alternated the food with sips of thickened juice, added to his liquid diet. Slightly increasing the pace, Dad continued to eat his meal, gaining a little more stamina with each bite. When this also went down smoothly, I thought, *well, this is a good sign*. But right then, all of a sudden, the direction reversed. Halfway through the meal, just as I brought one last, promised spoonful to his mouth, without warning—he vomited. Quickly, I grabbed the pail leaning against the side of his bed and encouraged him to use it. Running behind him, I moved my hand in circular motions across his back, *It's okay, Dad, it's okay. Don't worry, you're okay.* After everything he ingested was fed to the pail, I cleaned both of us and put him back to sleep.

    I sat back, surveying my father closely, remembering the times he fed me as a child, the cold winters when he walked my brother and me to the local corner store and let us pick out treats, or when he tried to feed me with his hands as an adult, missing the mark due to his failing sight. Feeding one another with our hands is a signature aspect of our culture, something I took pride in doing for him. Hence, knowing I was the last person to feed my father was a bestowed and valuable gift—his version of a warm, comfortable sweater. Yet, the state of surrender I conceded to because of witnessing his deteriorating abilities was equally a sign of grace.

**Figure 12**
*A Father's Pride*

# 12

## The Last Praise From a Father

This day already felt like a good day. A lighter sensation lingered in the air, and only my father and I were around to feel its cooling breeze. He was asleep, and I was in a meditative state watching him. We had this ability to communicate through our joined calmness; a cord traveling through us transmitted waves of energy from heart to heart. Perhaps this was why he allowed me to make decisions for him—*she knows what I want*; or, why he handed me his to-do list when I walked in the door—*she knows what I'm thinking*. Since our connection was otherworldly, whenever the two of us were in the room, like today, an unearthly, dreamlike presence joined us.

    Daydreaming about the night before, I went over the events in my mind. Overwhelmed from teaching two new grades and starting my first year at a new school, I became overstressed with managing my workload and spending most of my time at the hospital. I needed one evening to catch up on all of my planning, preparing, and marking, and then I would be able to dominate both my teacher and daughterly duties until the designated winter break. I called my father from my classroom and explained my dilemma to him, *Is it okay if I stay home tonight and work, Dad? I will come to the hospital every day after*. Without even considering the option, his response was a hard no. Normally, he did not interfere with my schoolwork, and since this was equally unexpected and unlike him, I did not question his decision and made my way to the unit.

    Dad greeted me with a smile when he saw me. Relieving my mom and brother from their bedside stations, I sat down and took a seat next to him. My father watched the door closely, waiting for them to slip out of the room to grab a bite to eat. Then, when the coast was clear, he turned to me and broke his silence,

> *I'm sorry I stopped you from doing your work. I know you have a lot of work to do. It's just that when you are here, I feel at peace. You never get angry or upset with me. If I can't hear something, I repeat it for me over and over again, without getting frustrated or mad at me. As long as you are somewhere in the room, then only do I feel at peace. That's why I told you to come.*

Marveled by him, my heart swelled ten times in size, the way it always does whenever he expresses his love for me. His shining quality—others rarely communicate how they feel about me, whereas my father's warmth was soul-stunning. After this display of affection, missing a day never crossed my mind again.

Dad began to stir, and I came back to the present moment. He had not fully awoken, so I picked up the book in front of me and started reading, stumbling upon this passage:

> *How will you know how strong you are*
> *unless your strength is tested?*
>
> *How will you know how deep you are*
> *unless turmoil breaks your surface*
> *and forces you to dive?*
>
> *How will you know what sleeps inside*
> *until the whole of you is challenged to wake*
>    *up?*
>
> *Then you'll turn inside to gather your*
>    *resources*
> *your untapped reserves of strength and skill*
> *then rise like a sun, amazed by your own*
>    *brightness,*
> *stronger than you ever suspected*
> *deeper than you ever dreamed.*[4]

---

4  *The Calm Center: Reflections and Meditations for Spiritual Awakening.* S. Taylor. (2015). New World Library.

For three years, I ran a Spiritual Book Club to support those seeking spiritual counsel. And for December, I just so happened to choose Steve Taylor's, *The Calm Center*. The bounded meditations and pages of inspiration were precisely what I needed to rise above the obstacles we were facing in the hospital—a reminder my father would have given me to see the bigger picture. Absorbed in my reading material, I did not immediately notice the visitors who had walked in the room, nor that my father's eyes had opened. Broken out of my spell, I stood from my chair, offering them a place to sit near him.

The uncle turned toward me and inquired, *You have so many books with you. Which one are you reading?*

Before I could let out a proper response, my father interrupted, exploding into a fit of excitement, overpowering the conversation:

> *Linita is always reading! She always has a book in her hand, and she reads multiple books at a time. Did you know she runs a book club that raises money for charities? Did you know she has her own Reiki company? She does Reiki for me in the hospital, and it helps me. Did you know she's a writer? Her articles are published in a magazine, so many of them! I have the copies. She wrote them while finishing her Master's degree! She became a teacher, like me.*

Never in my life had I seen my father gloat. He was bursting at the seams as the profound love he carried for me in the most intimate parts of his heart overflowed and expelled, listing every accomplishment he could. And even though we had decided not to announce the next bit of information because I had just finished applying, I saw the twinkle in his eye that told me he was about to let the cat out of the bag. *She is going to do her doctorate!* That was supposed to be a secret. But my father was no longer able to keep our aspirations to himself. To achieve the highest level of education was, first and foremost, his dream come true.

\*\*\*

*I sat in the middle row of the riser, listening intently to my teacher, who, one by one, called out the names of students. Dad was in the audience, attentively keeping an eye on me. I could feel his disappointment at the vacancy of my name. I could also feel my blood pressure rising, thinking of the consequences awaiting me back home. In my father's hierarchy of strict-*

ness, academic achievement was at the top. Hiding from his gaze, I sunk lower and lower as student after student rose to receive their award. Time was running out, and I had not moved an inch. Luckily for me, before the ceremony closed, a plot twist appeared.

The teacher stopped the roll call and paused, transitioning into a small speech: "The last award of the night is the Student of the Year. This award goes to a student who worked tirelessly from September to June. Not only is she an avid reader, but she wrote and submitted over three hundred stories within the school year." Oh my God, I thought, she is talking about me. The last quality tipped off the rest of the class as well, now stomping their feet and chanting my name like in a movie. Then, my teacher confirmed their suspicions, "Linita Mathew, please come up and receive the Grade 3 Student of the Year Award!" Thrilled, I went to the podium and obtained my certificate, smiling widely.

Afterward, I ran to my father and screamed with uncontainable excitement, "Dad! Look what I got! I'm the Student of the Year!" My father stayed cool, calm, and collected, giving me a stern look that conveyed I should do the same. Later, in the car, he gave me advice that would shape the acknowledgment of my achievements from that day forward, "Linita, when you win something, you must stay humble. Don't show so much excitement in front of others. Accept it and be humble." Saddened, I sat back in my seat, confused by the lack of congratulatory remarks. *All I ever wanted was for him to be proud of me.*

That night, when my mother returned home from work, I woke up and listened in on their private conversation from over the railing. My father, in his own reserved way, told her how proud he was of me. Satisfied, I smiled and went back to sleep.

***

Dad wanted to make sure my achievements did not go unnoticed. So, he stacked them up one on top of the other and commended me for everything all at once. The couple nodded and smiled at me, allowing my father's pride to spill. *All I ever wanted was for him to be proud of me.* And, here, he made sure I knew he was. The magnitude of love I felt in this moment was somewhat surreal, hearing everything I needed to hear before the time lapsed. Frankly, the whole situation made me nervous and uncomfortable. I stood still and silent, staring at the floor, unable to make eye contact with them, waiting for the adulation to pass. A tiny voice in the back of my head prodded at his motives: *Why is he saying all of this now? Is he planning on going somewhere?* The fear of him leaving crept in and overshadowed the last praise my father showered on me, revealing a passioned truth he wanted me to know—that our time together is ending, and *this is how I feel about you.*

**Figure 13**
*A Daughter's Pride*

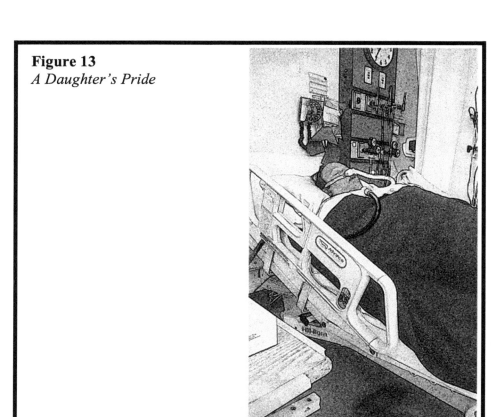

# 13

## The Last Hope

My father fluctuated in and out of consciousness—but mostly, out of it. The opportunity to see him awake was sparse, and when he was, I made sure to confirm he was not in any pain. Watching him drift in and out of sleep was one ordeal; to know he was suffering physically, emotionally, or mentally was another. So, every time he woke, he reassured me that he had no recollection of experiencing discomfort. This need for reassurance traveled both ways, as he often inquired if the doctors had any new leads on his condition.

He even questioned his role in the illness, *It's not my fault, is it? Did I do something to cause this?*

Since no discovery or resolution had materialized, I shook my head and responded, *No, Dad, it's not your fault. They don't know what the problem is.*

Feeling satisfied that he was not responsible for his sickness, he whispered, *Okay*, and fell back asleep.

His demeanor during these slumber sessions resembled a person who had fallen into a coma; his body showed no movement or response to the outside world. Because I once read that people who enter these deep states of unconsciousness can still hear and understand the words spoken in their surroundings, I was adamant about speaking carefully around my father at all times, using positive and uplifting language only. This was my way of taking care of him when he was not fully present. This was my way of protecting him still.

Unfortunately, some of the medical staff tending to his needs were not as courteous. Even though most doctors were a beacon of light, asking us to hold on and persevere through the dark days, a select few spoke of his condition in a depressing, deflating, and demeaning manner. One physician repeatedly bludgeoned us with her words—*Sometimes, there's just nothing that can be done*—in the early stages of his illness as if we were burdening them to try. A few times, I became an interruption for a nurse who was busy on her phone instead of watching my dad. And once, I caught a nurse's aide commenting how heavy my father was, ridiculing him under their breath. Yet here I was with half the strength, sliding him up and down and lifting him in and out of bed, time after time, day after day, without uttering a word. I suppose that's the difference between medical care and family care. All that aside, the most horrendous and heartless experience we encountered was when my brother overheard a conversation taking place outside my father's room. Two medical professionals, who were unaware family members could hear them, were disputing the need to find a proper diagnosis: *Why are resources being wasted on a seventy-year-old man with heart problems?*

    Disgusted, I sat in the hospital room, trying to make sense of the discourse between those two physicians. Perhaps working in this kind of environment for long periods led to desensitization. However, *is this not what you signed up for?* To treat the ill and dying with persistence, showering them with every last bit of hope. My father was not just another corpse taking up a bed, wasting precious resources—he was a husband, father, brother, and beloved friend. His loss would devastate us. Still, one doctor kept pushing us to take the initiative over his final directives while he slept on the bed beside her, brazenly stating, *It is better to expect the worst and accept the end result.* Eventually, my mother, a woman who, for many years, worked as a palliative nurse, had had enough. She stood tall and fought back, making it known that, *Intimate decisions are best left in the hands of the family members. We will decide what's best for him, not you.* With her firm hand, the discussion closed. Death is the result for all of us; that does not mean you let tragedy fall without a good, solid fight. And we were not a family to let any harm come to our loved one without *a good, solid fight.*

    Soon enough, I, too, became vocal about the dispassionate behavior we endured in the hospital. After again witnessing negative conversations take place in front of my father, I pulled the nurse aside and shared my concerns with her. I explained to her that I knew he was conscious, though unconscious. He could hear every word, phrase, and morsel of advice the doctors discussed in front of his sleeping body. Bluntly, I informed her that I did not want staff members talking about his death in front of him because I knew he was listening. And with no confirmed prognosis, self-fulfilling prophecies were not welcomed at his bedside. I described our family dynamic to her—we were not a family with realistic ideologies. We are unrealistic, brimming incessantly with hope, wholeheartedly believing in miracles. Last, I pleaded with her:

> *Please tell them to let us at least believe there is a chance he will make it. Besides, this wouldn't be the first time my dad beat all odds and came home. He was declared a lost cause once before and fully recovered.*

It was too early for our family to make funeral arrangements for a person still alive. The nurse saw my eyes fill with tears and pour out through the genuine nature of my words. She agreed and left the room, assuring me that she would handle the situation—and she did. A few minutes later, my anxiety steadied. And minutes after that, I felt the stiffness in my father's body ease.

***

*In 2007, Mom finally purchased the house of her dreams. This buy was a monumental milestone for her; decades of hard work led to this moment. Today, my parents were picking out the furniture, and I could feel my mother's excitement through the phone. So, after finishing my classes at the university, I decided to join them on their shopping spree. I walked into the store and found them moving from showroom to showroom, debating over the items they liked. My mom, who tends to change her mind often, took a little longer than usual to make firm decisions. As I stood back, I noticed the salesperson growing annoyed. She was huffing and puffing, rolling her eyes, and making suggestions in a sarcastic tone. Although she was acting unprofessional, my parents stayed calm. Over the years, they had trained themselves to diffuse conflict created by ignorant people. I, on the other hand, had not.*

*Driving home, the treatment they endured ate away at me. Sitting in the driveway, I called the manager and made a formal complaint. Staying reasonable, I stated, "I know my parents are older, they take a long time to make decisions, and my mother can be indecisive—trust me, I know this. But the way the salesperson behaved with them was completely unacceptable. My mother spent a lot of money at your store, and this woman is paid to help them. It's her job to tolerate the process no matter how long it takes."* The manager apologized immediately and sided with my position. He assured me our needs, as well as the commission, would be transferred to another salesperson. Relieved, I walked into our new home and told my parents what had happened. Mom was a little surprised by my actions, but she agreed with them. Dad was not shocked at all. Casually he mentioned, "She is a force to be reckoned with."

***

When the last hope diminished for others, mine grew stronger. I sat at my father's bedside, holding his hand firmly, sending rays of reassurance from my heart to his. Slowly, he came to, looking fragile and meek. Confirming my intuitions, meeting my eyes, he earnestly asked, *The doctors have already pronounced me dead, isn't it?* Heart-shattered, I stayed silent, unable to muster the words to combat their cruelty. *They cannot find out what's wrong with me, isn't it?* I nodded. Without hesitation, my father brought forward the moral of the story, *So you see, Linita, in the ongoing battle between God and science, God always wins.* This time he gave the nod, agreeing to the wisdom of his statement. Then, his body relaxed, and he closed his eyes, rejoining his distant dreams once more.

Unable to erase the heartache created by my father's question and the hurtful actions that instigated it from my mind, I later took it upon myself to write a carefully crafted complaint to the hospital. The words emphasized his human value and contested the despicable actions of the physician, and my letter received a sincere, apologetic reaction. When I questioned if I should take further action, the reviewer commented, *I think your letter speaks volumes. It is very well-written.* I did not demand an apology; I never wanted to speak to that person again. But I did request sensitivity training in hopes that no other family would share our experience—that no other daughter would have to carry the unbearable weight of my father's question.

During the initial stages of his illness, we were exposed to varying degrees of insensitivity, and my faith in the healthcare system crumbled. When I should have been focusing on my father, the unnecessary distraction of moral questioning inundated my mind:

> *Are we not supposed to treat the sick and elderly? Are we not supposed to care for the ill with the utmost compassion, respect, and attention? Are seniors thrown to the wayside when there's no diagnosis? Are resources reserved by social status?*

Our experience was exasperating and not reflective of my understanding of the Canadian healthcare system. But sadly, after the loss of my father, I would hear of many similar stories where apathetic, aggressive medical staff were encountered, and basic compassion and bedside manners were lacking. I learned that we were not an exception; we were part of a commonly felt rule—one where saving time and money outweighed the desire to save a life.

When my father was first admitted, I saw my friend's photo hanging on a wall outside his room, another omen. Younger than me, my friend mistakenly died in this hospital because of a preventable medical mishap. Now, I hoped my father would not suffer the same fate.

**Figure 14**
*The Road Not Taken*

# 14

## The Last Touch of Reality

Days short of Christmas, the seriousness of Dad's illness became more apparent. Due to *possible* encephalitis caused by *possible* pneumonia, my father became delirious. The initial stages of his incoherence were subtle confusions that appeared as illogical questions or exaggerated identities of the people seated around him, turning them into celebrities. Often, these confused gestures brought smiles and laughter to the visitors who could not see the depth of his sickness or were in denial that he was dying. Yet, as the delirium intensified and, bit by bit, drowned my father's mind, I knew his condition was severe. I retaliated by doubling down, paying closer attention to his words and actions, as making sense of my father's dialogue became crucial.

First, I honed in on his discussions, listening closely to the upkeep of conversations he was having with the doctors, attempting to pinpoint the source of his issues. Gradually, my father's comments struck me as odd. For instance, during one of the rounds, he told the doctor that all of his problems started after he came to Canada and that he would have been much better off staying in India. Having had many intimate talks with my father, fleshing out the fine details of his life, I knew this was not the case. He was a proud Canadian who lived in Canada for over forty years, a man who insisted on dying on Canadian soil. Because of this, I understood his personality was fading into the background. That perhaps he reverted to a simpler time for his own safety. And judging by the doctor's reaction, this was not only normal but expected. *At least he's safe*, I decided, not knowing the brunt of the delirium was still on its way.

The conversation that sounded an alarm, sending my autonomic nervous system into disarray, did not take place with others—they were words he divulged to me.

By late afternoon, visitors huddled around as my father clutched onto my hand and spoke to me with urgency, *We need to go to the basement. Will you take me down there?* The somberness of his voice cut through the illusion, permitting me to grasp he was no longer in the hospital with the rest of us; he had drifted back home.

Carefully, I proceeded, *Why do you need to go to the basement, Dad?*

His tone spiked as his eyes, locked with mine, shifted back and forth, showing deep concern. *Achende body thazhe undu. Athu adakan ready akanam—Father's body is downstairs. We have to ready it for the burial.*

Baffled, my eyes widened as I held his stare. For a fleeting moment, my father embodied the role of a grieving son, determined to fulfill the duties he was forced to relinquish in his lifetime. A seed of regret planted twenty years prior emerged through a psychic wound, revealing itself to everyone. Slowly, quiet laughter arose from the crowd around us; they could not look past the absurdity of his comment and soak the spiritual meaning behind his words. But I could. And the sincerity that softened his eyes, begging me for help, broke me.

Feeling the emotion ascend from my heart to my throat, I jolted upward and ran out of the room, his gaze trailing behind me. For the first time, out in the open, but away from him, I cried. The few friends who joined to offer support could not understand my reaction and pain; an intimate bond with the patient was not present to guide them. *He sees my grandfather; he sees his father.* As the grip on my father's existing reality loosened and unraveled, the grip on my upcoming reality tightened and became clearer. A profound spiritual truth emerged, hidden in the visitation from a deceased loved one. I allowed the consequence of his revelation to overpower me, sink in, and spill through me, regardless of who was watching. Then, I wiped my tears, stood straight, and went back inside to care for my father—to take him to the basement of his house in India. To take him wherever he wanted to go. To speak to him softly and to reassure him, *I will go with you*—wherever you want to go, *I will go with you.*

\*\*\*

## The Last Touch of Reality

"Do you ever regret coming to Canada, Dad?"

"Why do you ask that?"

"Well, if you stayed in India, you would have completed your Ph.D., you would have had a good job and not struggled for employment the way you did here. Your life would have been so different."

"Yes, but so would yours."

"What do you mean?"

"Your life, Linita—not your mother's or your brother's—specifically, yours. Your path would have had restrictions. You wouldn't have had the same opportunities you have now to create the life meant for you." He paused to let that sink in, then continued, "And, if I had to do it all over again, I wouldn't change anything."

"Do you want to go back to India?"

"My parents have died and my reason to go left with them. Now, I want to live out the rest of my days here. This is my home. I want to die on Canadian soil."

"Okay, Dad."

I sat back and stared at my father—the man who sacrificed everything for me.

**Figure 15**
*Merry Christmas, Dad*

# 15

## The Last Christmas

*I could not sing a tune to save my life, but my father insisted I join the choir; he thought singing was an important skill to learn. As a result, I was an involuntary member of the school's choral class well beyond my formative years. And because I did not like my singing voice, I often stood in concerts lip-synching the words, saving myself and the audience from the embarrassment.*

*My grade six choir teacher signed us up to sing for the Calgary Carol Festival, a prestigious affair. When I told my father about the showcase, he found the address and planned our route. We parked at the station, rode the train downtown, and walked what felt like forever to reach the venue. The obsidian night coupled with the frigid winter air, made my knees clack together the entire way to the church. Finally, we were inside the building, enveloped by warmth. I went and found my place in the choir while Dad found the nearest spot he could in the congregation. When it came time to get up and sing, as always, I searched for my father's face in the crowd. And as expected, he was seated right in front of me. For his sake, I decided to give the songs my best shot, and I gave a performance that was a little more than just mouthing the words. The whole festival was rendered beautifully.*

*Now, we just had to make our way back home. Calgary winters were not for the faint of heart, and my thin skin, though bundled nicely, could not bear the bitter cold. The only heat I could feel was generated by the friction of my father's grasp, holding on tightly, trying to raise my persistence to reach our destination more quickly. By the time we made it back to our car, our bodies were numb. I looked up at my father, shivering and rubbing his hands together, patiently waiting for the car's heat to kick in. The realization dawned on me that he had not uttered a single complaint all night—that he would do anything for me.*

\*\*\*

Since Dad would not make it home for Christmas, we brought Christmas to him. My brother brought a miniature tree which he lit on the top of his cart, a place where he knew he would see it; my mother brought prayers and carols to his bedside, singing where she knew he could hear it; and I brought my hope for a Christmas miracle, hugging him so tight I knew he would feel it. Banding together, the week leading to our family's favorite holiday overflowed with as much love and joy as we could muster. And now that Dad had moved to a different unit, the rotated hospital staff brought an uplifting change of scenery as well. The nurses catered to my father's medical and festive needs, sprucing up his room, and displaying yuletide cheer. They acted on the knowledge that, for some, these holidays were neither easy nor merry. For us, this could be our *last* Christmas together.

As the days to December 25th dwindled, so did my father's condition. His health took a drastic but crucial turn, leading us to believe that this Christmas Eve announced the likelihood of death, not birth. Entering the room, I found my father incessantly patting down his arms, retrieving imaginary items, and keeping them safe in the side pocket of his gown. *What are you doing, Dad?* I inquired, trying to persuade him to communicate with me, knowing he had not responded to anyone for the past few hours. But the more I persisted, the more he resisted and remained mute. Dad would not engage with any of us; he had entered a world of his own, foreshadowing what was to come. Childlike, immersed in a game of hide-and-seek, he grabbed a white towel from his bed and covered his face, refusing to be seen. A part of me wondered if subconsciously he was preventing us from witnessing his deterioration. Either way, these behaviors were severe enough that a specialized physician from the neurology department came by to observe him. After examining Dad and receiving the same denied entry into his imagination, the stern expression on the doctor's face softened. Looking at me, he spoke straight, *I need you to know that his condition is serious. What you are witnessing here is severe. I need you to understand that.* I bent my head in agreement. My internal state was teeter-tottering; as tension rose from the doctor's words, relief also depressed my fluttering. Finally, the physicians in charge of my father's care saw his illness for what it was, a serious matter. At last, the rest of the world aligned with what I had been feeling all along, that something was seriously wrong.

The neurologist left to discuss his findings with the rest of the medical team, ordering the commencement of a rare IV-infused treatment plan. The name of the medication has long since left me, but one nurse's reaction to the drug has not, *Wow, I've never even administered this before. They sure are bringing out the big guns for your dad.* My internal seesawing continued. Resisting the emotional vortex, I fixated on my father's uncontrollable movements, deflated by his irregular fidgeting. *Where has he gone?* I wondered. Before I could contemplate an answer, my mother entered the room, and as if on script, my father started *convulsing.* Within seconds, a full-blown fit ensued. Mom instructed me to help her hold him firmly in place, limiting self-injury. The seizure could not have lasted longer than sixty seconds, but it was the most frightening minute of my life. The other nurses rushed into the room and injected him with an anti-seizure medication that prevented a second round from developing. Now, the severity of his situation was disclosed to everyone; he was no longer a patient simply suffering from heavy sleep and a critically low pulse. Officially, his cover was blown—too bad it only took episodic hallucinations and a seizure to confirm my inkling.

Christmas Day had dawned, and I arrived bright and early in the morning to greet my father, carefully hiding the sadness accompanying our circumstances. I did not realize then that the last time I would wrap him in warm wishes—*Merry Christmas, Dad*—would be within the four walls of a hospital. That the joy and merriment had not only vanished for this year, but these season's greetings would never stop and knock on our family's door again. Instead, my father's raw illness over the holidays would imprint our minds forever. And no matter how many years rotated since, my body would remember and relive the trauma we endured this Christmas, bringing forward a draining and exhaustive revival. Now, the days were exactly unpredictable. Dad's condition cycled through rapid peaks and valleys produced by an unknown disease, creating a roller coaster of emotions for his family members. This ride lasted from morning until night, ranging from extreme highs to severe lows by the hour. To stabilize our spirits, multiple families from our community visited him every day, spending time with him and bringing us food or gift cards, ensuring we took breaks and ate. As a community, the support leading to the death is solid; we excel in the rising action, climax, and resolution. It is in supporting the *dénouement* of loss that we need improvement.

Dad acknowledged his visitors even though he could not recognize most of them, mistakenly identifying some as well-known figures. One uncle was labeled our prime minister, while his wife transformed into the prime minister's wife; a priest who came to bless my dad was subjected to baseless, angry convictions; and a select few were identified and addressed appropriately. Overall, the eccentric behavior and unrelenting anger brought chuckles to those around him. Initially, we did find it funny. The shared laughter brought back an ounce of normalcy, a reassurance that convinced me none of this was real. Dad was merely passing through a phase, and soon *he would snap out of it*. However, the delirium transformed by Christmas evening into full-fledged outbursts proving otherwise. The earlier subtle misconceptions were now sharp, vivid scenarios conjured in my father's mind. Interestingly enough, within his fictional fantasy, he reinvented himself as a movie director—*he did love watching movies*.

Not everyone played a part in the figments of my father's imagination, but my mother did, his best friend did, and I definitely carried a unique role. Sadly, we were all villains who restricted his freedom, accused of taking videos of him without his permission. I was still his daughter but depicted as a careless editor who failed to revise his script as promised. Even though blatant humor existed in my portrayal, some of the dialogue was hard to digest: *I trusted you, Linita. How could you—of all people—betray me?* They were just words, but stiff words I never thought I would hear my father direct toward me. No matter how hard I tried to stuff my feelings down, a seed of sadness grew. Unfortunately, my villainization expanded over the next three days, and the hatred he felt for me fortified. For his sake, I played along. The realization dawned on me that *I would do anything for him.*

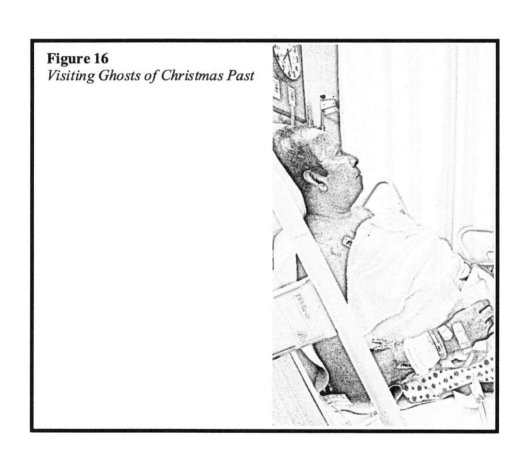

**Figure 16**
*Visiting Ghosts of Christmas Past*

# 16

## The Last Link

Christmas had come and gone, but my father's hallucinations had not. The anger he felt for my mother and me became more visible, manifesting through his words and eyes. Most of the interactions were bearable—but perhaps, not as funny. What added to my trials and tribulations was that the only family member my father could stand was my brother. In this dreamt-up version of life, he trusted him immensely, ordering him to clean and arrange the contents of his invisible living spaces. As siblings, we had always vied for Dad's attention—so I was out of sorts that, for the time being, *we had traded places*. However, deep down, I knew my father had an ally, and that was all that mattered.

As evening approached, a shift occurred, barring the rest of us from his imagination; he could no longer hear nor see us. Because we were of no use in the room, the nurse requested us to go home and rest. My mother and brother agreed and retired to the house while I stretched my stay longer. Clinging to my father's previous reasoning for needing me in the room, I was having a hard time leaving his side as if I would be abandoning him. I rationalized that even if he could not consciously grasp my presence, beneath the complex layers of his condition, he would join with my calmness.

Dad sat upright in the hospital bed with his eyes fixed on illusions far out in the distance; the atmosphere was ideal for mirages. I watched him talk to the thin night air, holding conversations with others that grew richer and deeper in context. Appearing before him were visitors from all angles of his life—familiar names of old friends and family members rolled off his tongue as he engaged in serious discussions with them. The words he spoke out loud were as honorable as his remarks in real life, instilling a sense of pride and comfort. Though he is not himself, *he remains himself.* Watching him, I became obsessed with his delusions—I wanted to see what he was seeing and understand his visions. I grew envious of those captivating his attention, forming new memories with him without me. And, from time to time, these exchanges ended in an uproar of laughter, enthralling me even more. My father's laugh was precious, one of his finest qualities. When I heard his contagious chuckle bubble and boil over, I could not help but join in and shake with laughter also. In the dark room, a light.

The dialogues continued through the night while I sat mute, knowing only a flimsy curtain separated him from his roommate. I was worried his pitch, which raised and lowered like a soundwave, prevented the other man from sleeping. But my father's actions were out of my hands; he would not respond to my requests even if I tried. Despite the commotion, the next day, I caught short, reassuring phrases while this patient conversed with his visitors:

> *Oh, I'm okay. I'm lucky, some people are so sick they stayed awake all night, and the doctors can't figure out what's wrong with them. That's worse than me.*

Easily, I was reminded that in dire times compassion and understanding bloom in unexpected places, sprouting out of the crevices of loss, rising to support us. Unfortunately, in the same circumstances, I also learned the opposite to be true.

*\*\*\**

*My parents always welcomed my friends with open arms. If you stepped foot inside our home, you were family. Their house was a haven, a place to watch movies, eat plenty of food, have open conversations, and laugh to our heart's content. I particularly enjoyed watching Dad interact with my female friends since his fatherly love ran deep for me and spilled over onto them. He listened to their problems, gave them advice, and supported their life choices. When they introduced him to their significant other, their partner received the third degree, ensuring the proper intentions were intact. And if heartache arose, he joined in their sadness and empathized with their pain.*

*After one of our regular visitors had left, I turned to my dad and questioned a patterned interaction I had observed for some time.*

"Dad, you're giving out a lot of compliments these days."

"Yes, she is going through a hard time. They were together for so long, and I noticed the breakup affected her self-esteem. So, whenever I see her, I make sure to compliment her a little extra so that she feels good about herself again."

*Without explaining his actions further, he left the room. We were all his daughters.*

\*\*\*

When the laughter faded and the fear of what was happening quietly crept back in, I froze. I sunk back, helplessly watching my father descend further into some form of madness. Gradually, my bright, intelligent, brilliant dad deteriorated in front of me, and the trepidation of it all struck me. Tears formed in the corners of my eyes, but I refused to let them bleed, reminding myself that these turning points were not about me. Breaking the flow, the nurse came back to check my father's vitals and attempted once more to relieve me of my daughterly duties, *Maybe he's not sleeping because he knows you are here. Try to get some rest and come back tomorrow.* I agreed to leave by eleven o'clock, assuming by then, I would feel ready to go. Underneath it all, I knew I could not leave because I could not bring him out of his delusions. My father always described me as his stubborn and persistent child; I had no choice but to live up to his expectations.

A short while later, I paused to check the time on my phone—one A.M. had come and gone. Desperate for a distraction, my eyes hung on the notifications that popped at the top of the screen. I should not have opened the messages; *I knew better than that.* But foolishly, as if by impulse, and on account of a poor automated decision, a group chat swiftly spread open before I could stop the tomfoolery. Instantaneously, pictures, messages, and emojis flooded my view, revealing a party that did not feel the need to conceal itself from me. Here I was, *silent* and *suffocating*, and there they were, my closest friends, running wild. Flung over the edge from everything I had already seen that night, my stomach twisted and churned into perfect double-crossed knots. Luckily, challenging times had parted the good from the bad in my life. And now, critical times were dividing the authentic from the reckless. My wounds were not salted because their lives kept turning freely without me—the knife turned on the notion that *his life* was at a standstill, omitted and disregarded by their actions. It was not that at the most harrowing and arduous juncture of my life, my closest friends were incapable of empathizing with me—it was that at the culminating stage of *his life*, they were incapable of empathizing *with him*. A man who welcomed them with open arms, loved them, fed them, consoled them, encouraged them, and treated them as his own for the past thirty years, lay here dying and was treated no different than a stranger. I stared at his frailty. I had come to accept that I was witnessing his slow demise. And, while he was dying—*they were out celebrating?* My lungs took a full, heavy breath of air. Then, snapping back to my father's side, I closed the chat and powered off my phone.

I bore witness to a lot that evening, but those messages did the most damage. My interpretation that *he's dying, and they don't care* stayed with me long after the funeral. Eventually, I ended up walking away from most of my friendships. I blamed myself that it took my father's death to disassemble and discard those relationships I had kept in my life for far too long, the false social constructs of who was reliable and who was not. *I was naïve.* I firmly believed that when the time came to be supported through his loss, they would step up to the plate. They did not. *Over* and *over* again, they did not. After his death, I could no longer justify their hurtful actions. I owed it to myself—*to my father*—to become a better version of myself, one who surrounds herself with people who equally reciprocate the true value of friendship. As I formed this realization, my father's words echoed in the distance: *Friends are good, Linita, and friends are important. But, in the end, your family is all that matters.* It took me thirty-one years to understand my father's wisdom. Blood is thicker than water; blood is blood. And my blood was about to diminish by one.

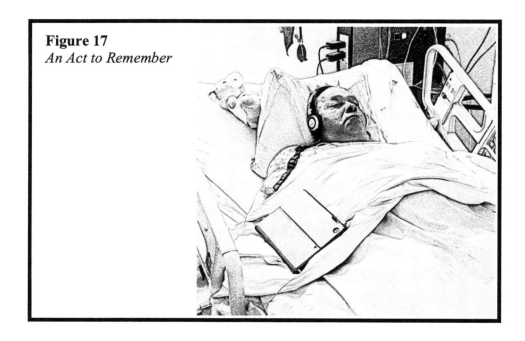

**Figure 17**
*An Act to Remember*

# 17

## The Last Apology

He hated me for three days, undeniably, a Biblical reference. The doctors had now confirmed the flooding in his lungs was responsible for creating pneumonia, which inflamed his brain, causing delirium. Each downfall was a step toward delivering his new outlook on life, where he loved my brother, was annoyed with my mom, and vehemently hated me. On the first day, I laughed, on the second felt fear, and on the third day, this day, *I descended into hell.* No amount of preparation prepared me for that.

Heading to the hospital, I reached for my phone and texted my brother first to recalibrate my mindset before arriving: *How's Dad today?* His response remained unchanged from the past two days: *He's still angry, be ready.* Grasping onto the knowledge that I could yet again act as a trigger for my father, I used the drive down to reinforce my mental capacity, envisioning what to expect and grounding myself in the probable scenarios. Yet, as I walked down the hall of the unit, my pensive mood was suddenly shaken when my father's laughter rumbled through the corridor, throwing my mental adjustments out the window. *He's laughing! Dad's back!* I mused, excitedly running the rest of the way to his room.

The second he saw me, the laughter stopped. The eyes that normally longed to see me glared back with bloodshot veins, zoning in on their target. Then, the unrestrainable screaming began. *You! What are you doing here? Get out of here! I don't want to see you! Get out of here right now!* I stopped dead in my tracks. A new sensation of pain seared through me. I should have understood this was not my father speaking to me harshly, but my intellect had vanished when my heart heard his laughter. His anger was so convincing that others pointed out his resentment funneling toward me: *What did you do to make him so angry?* The question trapped air in my lungs, causing me to stay silent against their absurd accusations. And though I stood courageously tall, resisting a response to their retaliatory remarks, my tears were swift to cower uncontrollably at his actions. The doctor, noting my terror, reassured me the delirium would subside, *He most likely will not remember what he said to you.* Remembering what he said was not my concern—remembering me was. I sank into the chair and closed my eyes, heartbroken. Dad closed his and fell back asleep.

***

*Kindergarten was my first real memory of trick-or-treating. My brother and I were dressed in our Halloween costumes, faces painted, and bundled in our winter gear. Before leaving the apartment, Dad disappeared around the corner and grabbed our toy wagon.*

*"Why do we need the wagon, Dad?" I asked out of curiosity.*

*"Because of all the candy we are going to get," my brother intrusively stammered back.*

*My father spoke only to lay down the ground rules.*

*With the wagon in hand, the three of us went off on an adventure. We circled the neighborhood, traveling from house to house, collecting our candy. My brother, who was more experienced than me, complained I was slowing him down and ran ahead on his own. But I was not slighted by this; I was utterly content holding my father's hand and walking with him.*

*As the sun went down, so did my energy.*

*I tugged at my father's jacket, "I'm tired. I don't want to walk anymore."*

*He nodded, waiting for my brother to return.*

*"Take your bag of candy," Dad instructed him.*

*"I'm not done trick-or-treating yet!" he whined.*

*"I know, but the wagon is not for your candy. It's for her."*

*My brother did as he was told and returned to his activities. Dad sat me in the wagon and pulled me the rest of the way until my brother eventually tired out.*

***

Alone in the room with my father, I stood from the chair and walked to the tall, ceiling-high windows. The sun shone brightly, mid-afternoon. Staring into the distance, I kept my back turned to my dad, wanting to hide my painful tears from him. I knew this morning's fiasco was not his fault. Looking out and upward, I noticed the clear, blue sky and acknowledged another possibility. I had no choice but to plead with God:

> *Three days of pure hatred in exchange for thirty-one years of pure love is nothing. I can take it. But You need to know that this is hurting me now. If knowing this, still he must hate me, then fine I will bear it. As long as You know, this is hurting me.*

When I was sure the tears gathered in the hollowness of my chest had released and emptied— that God had heard me—I sat back down and guarded my father while he slept.

Before the hour passed, he awoke. Cautiously, I walked toward him, trying not to agitate him further. I saw that his eyes were visibly softer, and I grew hopeful.

I spoke slowly, *Dad, do you know who I am?*

My father chuckled in disbelief, *Linita, how could I ever forget you?*

His shoulders shook as he snickered. In the blink of an eye, as *Allie* came back to *Noah*, my sweetheart had come back to me. Waves of relief resounded through my heart as I felt God's mercy pour down from head to toe. Then, remembering Dad had gone three days without water, I quickly grabbed a sponge stick and began swabbing his mouth.

Softly, two words came out, *I'm sorry.*

Caught off guard, I demanded an explanation, *Sorry? Sorry for what?* The turmoil stirred from his anger had erased from my mind.

My father's concerned eyes moved inward, *I'm sorry for the things I said to you while I was in emotion. Forget those things, don't keep them with you.*

In an instant, my life flashed before me—the countless apologies that overlooked me, avoided me, or refused to materialize, now towered in front of me. Here was my sweet, frail father, apologizing for something that was out of his control, and with his *last apology*, the tower of poor excuses from others reduced to rubble, never to hang over my head again. *You never have to say sorry to me, Dad*—my voice cracking, my eyes glistening. Lovingly, he looked on, conveying this was not the acknowledgment he wanted me to make. One last time, my father placed me in the wagon and showed me how I should be treated.

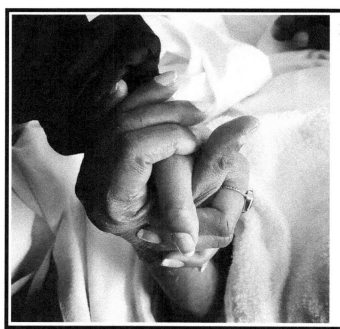

**Figure 18**
*The Greatest Gift*

# 18

## The Last Conversation

*After a long day at work, I decided to stop by the house and spend time with my family. My mother cooked in the kitchen, my brother watched television in the loft, and my father, barely visible, sat slumped in his rocking chair. Since his usual greeting went unsaid, I came around to confront him. But instead of feeling his natural warmth, I met with a sullen stare, a grouched face, and graying hair standing upright. His disheveled features spoke to me before he did, and I quickly realized he was battling a cold. Confirming my suspicions, he sneezed and sniffled on cue.*

"*What's wrong, Dad? Are you sick?*" *I sincerely inquired.*

"*What do you think?*" *he scowled back.*

*Sensing that my other family members had neglected the seriousness of his state, I knew what I needed to do. Gently, I continued, "Okay, go lie down on the couch. I'll take care of you."*

*My father's visage softened, remembering the depth with which his daughter loved him. Retracting his stubbornness, he quietly shifted to the couch and eased.*

*For the next hour, I gave Dad the complete spa treatment. I massaged his arms, legs, back, chest, and head, applying a balm to soothe his symptoms. Next, I placed a hot towel on his face and encouraged him to breathe in the steam to clear his sinuses. Last, I did some Reiki to bring down his stress. My mother often looked over at us and mumbled her two cents, "Appande ponara mol alle," calling me out as my father's precious daughter. But her envy did not shake us. Ignoring the hubbub, we remained firmly planted in our own world, and I continued my treatment until I left my father in better shape than I had found him.*

*Returning to my apartment, I called to check on him.*
*"How are you feeling now, Dad?"*
*"Much better"—he took a pensive breath—"you are the only person who really cares about me. Nee mathram ullu eniku oru ashwasam—Only you give me relief. Thank you for taking care of me tonight."*
*His sentiment caused my heart to glow, "No problem, Dad. I'll come back tomorrow."*

*For the next three days, I went back and took care of him in the same manner until his flu faded. Three weeks later, he was hospitalized. Even though I never hesitated to go above and beyond for my dad, I know now, that those three days of committed care were as vital for me as they were for him.*

***

Bouncing from unit to unit, my father traveled from the emergency to cardiology and finally landed in internal medicine. His illness was perplexing, a condition that stumped the doctors, chasing after an accurate prognosis. Although each transition increased the medical attention he received, the rite of passage became progressively harder to witness, decreasing my ability to keep my emotions hidden. Watching his physical state wither in front of my eyes enabled them to act on their own accord. As if the valve responsible for holding in my tears had burst, lines of water spontaneously streamed down my face without conscious knowledge, causing those around me to question my well-being. My brother approached me and informed me that a few of the patients were concerned *about me*, asking him if I was okay. I could not believe I had taken the attention off of my dad without openly expressing any words but the sights, sounds, and people in the distance meshed and melded into the background as the image of my dying father forced its way to the forefront. Boxed in by our circumstances, the wall I stood behind to suppress the intensity of my sorrow had crumbled, and I was left mortified. Here, the raw, vulnerable, and acute nature of my grief materialized, refusing to leave my side.

Spotting my unsettled spirit, a nurse's aide found me frantically pacing the halls, trying to make sense of my father's rapid decline. She placed her hand on my shoulder and attempted to console me, *I know how you are feeling. I lost my father too, and it was very painful*. I lifted my eyes to hers, the first person who voiced my fears and spoke of a daughter's loss, and saw that she was not much older than me. This was both comforting and distressing, but I earnestly listened as she spoke. She briefly shared her father's story back home, who succumbed to his illness and was recently laid to rest. My head hung lower, pulled down by the deadweight of fear that instantly spread across my face. A well-timed messenger, she reminded me to stay strong for him. She tightened her grip on my shoulder as I let my lamentations loose. This woman was unknown to me, and still, she approached me. She knew nothing of me—except that I was a daughter, and she sought me out to comfort me. Grievers are not strangers; they are part of a community that understands the deep-seated pain of loss, and they use this knowledge to sustain one another. She was my first lesson in *grief literacy*.

Every move my father made, my mother shadowed. Knowing this, the nurses arranged a cot for her to sleep in on each unit, where she slept every night with her arm extended over her husband. For the duration of my father's hospitalization, my mother managed to cover her stretches of work, securing this nightly routine for them—except for three shifts that lingered in the back of her mind. When these evenings crept up on her, my father encouraged her to go to work, insisting he would be fine. In the end, she agreed, as long as I stood in to replace her. For those three shifts, I stayed in the cot beside him. And for those three nights exactly, the events that unfolded were life-changing. On the first night, despite being extremely ill, Dad's needs were neglected; on the second night, he awoke to tell me what his future held in store for him; and, on the third night, I helped set the wheels in motion.

    The first evening on my watch, my father started violently convulsing as I stood witness to the terrifying account. When the ICU doctor finally arrived, he glanced at Dad's quaking body and informed us that *"he wasn't sick enough"* to be admitted. After a whirlwind of grandiose hand gestures, slowed speech, and exaggerated facial expressions that attempted to explain basic medical terminology to us—*an ethnic family*—the doctor noticed my mom's displeasure, stopped overemphasizing the chances of survival, and settled on the following reasoning: *Trust me, the ICU is the last place you want your dad to be*. The decision should not rest on our wants but his needs. Often, I think back to this farce and wonder if this doctor had done something differently, anything differently, *would Dad have survived?* In an attempt to restrict the use of money, beds, and medical equipment, we are risking the lives of those who need this care most.

Before the sun rose on the night of my second stay—on December 28, 2016, at 5:30 A.M.—I awoke to my father's soft-spoken voice calling out to me with calm urgency. A pervading presence permeated the mildly lit room, providing us with an unexpected interlude before raising the curtain on the final act. An emboldening warmth advised me to stay present, to listen to my father carefully—the magical elements of death and dying were materializing.[5] Awake, he sat straight in his bed, waiting for me. Dreamlike, he looked changed, a radiant aura of silver outlining him. The room was still, and the hustle and bustle of the hospital were swept into silence, gifting him the solemnity to deliver his final message, blessing me with the only conversation I will need in this lifetime.

    The spiritual knowledge my father shared with me in the early hours of this winter morning is imprinted in my mind, etched in my heart, and dwells in the core of my soul. His words will never fade. If I leave the world with one keepsake, I exit with this, which is enough. At times, I look back on these words and realize I was rewarded for every good deed I have done and paid in advance for the goodness yet to come—and still, I will be weighed, measured, and found wanting. The bulk of the blessing is here; the essence of his message remains intact, word for word, breath by breath. But due to its intimate nature, an ethereal fraction remains inexpressible and can only be revealed with time, decoded by one's faith.

    Divinity is harnessed in the palms of each individual. Some have a strong hold on a higher power, while others allow life's beauty to slip through their fingers. *I hold on to it*. A Needleworker's spoken thread, stitching our hearts eternally, was the only force pushing me to persevere past my father's death. *Fiercely, I hold on to it*. When the intensity of my grief is heartbreaking, I refer back to his sound. And

---

5  *Life: To Be Given Back Again to Whence It Came*. L. Mathew. (2022). DIO Press Inc.

when my heartache is unbearable, my father's words reappear, ringing through my ears, reminding me he has already *applied the balm to soothe my symptoms*. While battling the relentless torment of my prolonged grief, my father's counsel saved me. The words my father wove into his last conversation with me were the pearls of wisdom that kept me breathing, my heart beating, and my blood flowing past his death.

*Linita—Linita, are you awake?*

*Come here.*

*What is the date? What is the time?*

*Two years ago, you taught me the importance of water,*

*and now I really know.*

*Stay by my side today—*

*Today, do not go anywhere.*

*Do not neglect the words I am telling you.*

*If you neglect them, you will regret it.*

*What is today's date? What is the time?*

*Pay close attention to the date,*

*Carefully watch the time.*

*Linita, today, I am going to die.*

*God is the greatest teacher—Waah!*

*No one has seen the face of God, but I saw it.*

## The Revelations of Eapen

*I met with God.*

*He came dressed in a cloak,*

*And told me my time has come and I will not live.*

*God told me to go back and prepare the girl,*

*She is having a hard time—*

*If I don't prepare her, she will suffer.*


*Linita, I am going to die.*

*Why are you crying?*

*Don't cry, look at me, I am not worried.*

*I am sorry I cannot cry with you,*

*I have already lost my emotion.*

*It is not needed where I am going.*


*God showed me where I am going.*

*Linita, I want to go there!*

*You are the one keeping me here,*

*Let me go there.*

*I choose to be with God, I have no regrets.*

*Never worry for me daughter,*

*I am happy to be with God.*

## The Last Conversation

*Linita,*

*Everything is already planned accordingly.*

*Look how beautiful God is—*

*He gave my last moments to you.*

*That is how I wanted it to be.*

*Linita, the beauty of a daughter belongs to her father.*

*Even if I die physically,*

*Spiritually, I am always with you.*

*You are my daughter, give me a kiss.*


*Tell your mother and brother I love them.*

*Your brother, I worry for him—*

*Encourage him to keep studying.*

*Ignore the things he says when he is angry.*

*Ignore it and defend him.*

*Ignore the things your mother says and take care of her.*

*Never discuss family issues or bring them to light in front of others.*

*Who else do you have after I'm gone? Only them.*

*These are your people,*

*Take care of them and protect them.*

*They are your tribe now.*

## The Revelations of Eapen

*Keep climbing upward, Linita—*

*God has great heights waiting for you,*

*You must reach them.*

*Do not let my death deter you.*

*Finish your doctorate,*

*and work as a professor at a university.*

*Write a book, and call it—*

*The Revelations of Eapen.*

*When the time is right,*

*Tell others what I have told you.*

*It is not written for the praises of people,*

*But for the praises of God.*

*Because it is God's will for you to write it.*


*I am always with you, Linita.*

*Physically, I will no longer be here,*

*But spiritually, I am always with you.*

*The beauty of a daughter belongs to her father.*

*Give me another kiss, it is almost time.*


*Will you pray for me?*

## The Last Conversation

*Watch the date, watch the time.*

*Today, do not go anywhere.*

*Today, stay by my side.*

*I don't know when it will happen,*

*But I know it will happen.*

*Before the doctors ask their next question,*

*If there is no response—*

*Then, I have already died.*

**Figure 19**
*The Final Visitor*

# 19

## The Last Act of Kindness

I had not spoken. For the entire message, delivered through my father, enveloped by a halo of light, I had not uttered a word. I did not want to interrupt him. I did not want to miss one syllable of the climactic dialogue that drew the narrative arc of our story. And when he finished speaking, a mixture of panic, fear, and *awe* washed over me. Moving my eyes back and forth from the clock to the monitors to him, I noted nothing visible had changed. Yet, my loyalty toward my father prevented me from disregarding his disclosure as delusional. Replaying the conversation on a continuous loop, I used my powers of reason to rationalize the spiritual experience that had just taken place,

> *Dad does not make things up; he does not overreact or exaggerate. He speaks honestly and only brings attention to something when he is sure. The strength of his faith matches his experience. This is happening, Linita. This is a real spiritual experience. This is what you've been preparing for. The time is now, be ready.*

My mind was racing, trying to grasp the depth of his words and comprehend the meaning behind his actions, but my soul had already aligned with his truth. I moved back to my cot, grabbed my iPad, and scrambled to record my father's words exactly as he had just spoken them.

As I read over the lines, my human side battled with the denial of his death. Intuitively, I knew the end of his life was near, but my physical understanding reluctantly dragged behind, and neither a diagnosis nor prognosis had arrived to quicken my steps. Thankfully, my spiritual side took over, pointing out that the phrases my father chose to use were too specific and could not have stemmed from his recent phase of delusions when his personality was not intact. For instance, *two years ago, you taught me the importance of water*, which was an actual occurrence. Two years ago, I gave my father the book, *The Miracle of Water*, and we had a lengthy discussion on the potential effect of this work, which I had introduced to him. Now, due to the complications of pneumonia, he compared our earlier conversation to his dehydration and thirst, being prohibited liquids. With this statement, he laid out a concrete reference that I could go back to and revisit, reinforcing, *Linita, it is me. I am fully present. I am telling you the truth, listen.*

I kept my eyes on my father for the rest of the morning, observing his interactions and noting the meaningful conversations that bloomed between him and his visitors. Our family regularly rode the ride of his unstable health, but today, a transformation was evident. Ironically, the day of the 28th brought Dad *back to life*—he was alert, articulate, engaged, and did not fall asleep once. Entirely aware of the people around him, his personality stood to greet them, conveying the contents of his heart. A touching moment ensued when my father held onto an aunty's hand, a tear spilling from his eyes, as he thanked her for coming. Dad always made sure to give credit where credit was due, keeping this virtue consistent until the end. I listened closely to see if he would allude to what he told me this morning, but not a word of our conversation came forward. He was so tight-lipped on the matter that I questioned whether he remembered the interaction or not or if it even happened. To my astonishment, just then, as if catching the doubt creeping in my mind, my father turned to me and whispered, *Don't forget what I told you this morning. You don't go anywhere today.* Guarding Dad's secret with pride, I bobbed my head in agreement.

Now, grasping, absorbing, and taking his morning message to heart, the situation dawned on me to give my brother some time alone with our father. Since Dad seemed stable, I took the opportunity to step out for a short while, even though I knew he was adamant I should stay.

Finding a plausible solution to this dilemma, I sat on the edge of the bed and asked his permission to leave, *Dad, is it okay if I go home and shower? I slept here last night, and I need to change my clothes. I will come right back after.*

He cautioned, *Okay, but don't take too long.*

Before I left, an urgency in my chest that did not match my father's current state caused me to stop at the door and instruct my brother to call me at once if any change occurred. He agreed, and I walked out of the room, feeling my father's eyes follow me out the door.

Alone in the car, I reflected on the truth received at the break of dawn. A revelation, presented over a perfectly planned and most significant hour, left us with the impression that we were the *only* two people *awake* to hear it. No staff member entered the room or interrupted us; no break in the conversation was permitted. We were shielded until everything my father needed to say was heard, allotting my mind the time required to grab onto his words. Driving back and forth to the hospital concurrently became a vehicle for meditation, and today, our time together as father and daughter spun through my mind. I gripped the steering wheel firmly as I realized the rising actions of our relationship—when I cared for my father, defended my father, protected my father, cried for my father, and desperately prayed to be present with him *when he dies*—were all accounted for. As if, all along, an *invisible hand* recorded my actions and listened to my requests, taking special note of what went unsaid, drawing from each source to pen the lyrics of my fate. A sentiment I could not express aloud was then summed and delivered beautifully back to me in poetic prose, serenaded by my father's voice. With all the spiritual grappling I have faced and defeated over the course of my life, I, all at once, was given solid proof that a force larger than myself not only exists but knew the most intimate details of my heart—my deepest fears and desires, both revolving around the extension of my father's life. That *force*, on this morning, communicated its knowing to me, simultaneously bestowing upon me an enormous honor—the right to be my father's keeper until his dying breath.

***

*Although I lived in Canada, being a woman in our culture still came with restrictions. While Dad broke some of the cultural norms by encouraging me to get a higher education over solely focusing on marriage, he enforced others, such as monitoring my whereabouts at all times. Even late into my twenties, I had to call him periodically, informing him of where I was and who I was with, and be home at a reasonable hour—I succeeded at the first two demands, but the third not so much. Yet, no matter what time I came home, Dad was awake, patiently awaiting my return.*

*High school, in particular, was a strict stage in our household, and my nights out usually involved attending multicultural events with my parents. At one such 'Kerala Night' function, I stood off to the side, observing the crowds of people. Suddenly, I overheard a conversation brewing between a group of young men openly discussing a desired gender-biased mentality. Jokingly—but not really—they unwaveringly stated, "When I have a family, I'm only going to have sons." Not to their benefit, my father was walking by. To my surprise, he stopped in his tracks, turned toward the group of men, and firmly contradicted their prejudiced views, "You won't know the value of a daughter until you have one. She's the one who takes care of the father and looks after him in his old age. A daughter is invaluable in general, but especially to you, as a dad." Without waiting to hear their responses, he turned around and continued on his way. The men were stunned and silenced—and my heart filled to the brim.*

\*\*\*

I hopped in the shower and got ready for another night at the hospital. Intentionally, I waited a few hours before going back, leaving a window of privacy open for my mother and brother. Finally, around seven o'clock, my nerves got the best of me, and I picked up the phone to find out how my father was doing.

*He's fine, but he won't stop asking for you,* my brother informed me. *When are you coming back?*

Scurrying out the door, I replied, *Now.*

Sprinting to his room, I found him fully awake and in good health.

*How do you feel, Dad?* I asked, leaning in.

Acknowledging my return, he confirmed, *Okay, now stay here. We have to be ready, don't go anywhere else.*

Dad and I reveled in our own company for the next few hours. I suppose, in the past, if someone were to ask me what I would do with my father in his final stretch, I would have listed off a number of extravagant things. But here, in the now—*in real life*—I preferred this. I simply wanted to spend time with him and attend to his needs, completing menial tasks that brought back a sense of normalcy for both of us. We enjoyed sitting in quiet, peaceful, ordinary moments with each other; we never needed more than this. Besides, for the first time in weeks, he was conscious and capable of holding meaningful conversations with me. *What could be more perfect than that?*

At ten P.M., I watched my father grow restless, silently contemplating the remaining piece of his puzzle, ensuring the image of his life was whole before he left. I felt him sifting through his mind to find any trace or tie that prevented him from leaving, and patiently, I waited for the exact thought to appear. Soon enough, the *eureka* bulb lit his face aglow, and motioning his hand, he summoned me to his bedside. I already knew what he was going to ask. Nevertheless, I waited for him to instruct me, *Linita, I need you to pick out a Bible verse.* I sensed this would be the pinpointed matter, as days earlier, in the middle of his misconceptions, my cousin made the request: *Uncle, you can't go anywhere. You have to pick out the Bible verse for my wedding card.* Some argued his delusions would overpower his interactions, but I knew my father to be the exception, not the rule. And together, Dad and I carried out his final act of kindness.

Searching for the perfect passage on my phone, I had a selection in mind that I knew would meet his approval, and facing my father, I recited the verses out loud:

> *Love is patient, love is kind. It does not envy, it does not boast, it is not proud. It does not dishonor others, it is not self-seeking, it is not easily angered, it keeps no record of wrongs. Love does not delight in evil but rejoices with the truth. It always protects, always trusts, always hopes, always perseveres. Love never fails.*[6]

Dad's eyes softened as he gazed upward and affirmed, *You always know what I'm thinking. That's what I wanted, send it to him.* Within minutes of texts traveling back and forth, the verse was confirmed for the couple's wedding card. And upon informing my father of their decision, he concluded, *Okay, now I can go.*

My mother wrapped up her third evening shift in a row and joined us on Dad's floor. She entered the room, ready to reclaim her rightful spot beside him, announcing, *I finished my shifts, and I can stay here*

---

[6] *1 Corinthians 13:4–8.* New International Version Bible. (1973). New International Version Bible Online.

*with you tonight.* I kept quiet, allowing my father to take the lead on this one. Slyly, he evaded her offer, *It's okay, you are tired, go home and rest. Linita will stay with me tonight.* She insisted a time or two more, but repeatedly met with the same response. Disheartened, she conceded to his request. She did not know the extent of the responsibility my father entrusted me with—although finding out later did not help matters either. Sitting down beside him, Mom initiated their regular post-work routine. Every night after finishing her evening shift, she returned home to drink the tea he made for her, and the two of them would talk late into the night. I did not dare break their cycle now; respectfully, I sat off to the side and stayed silent. They chatted away until a little after one o'clock. Then, she reassured him that she would be back in the morning and left us. Tucking my father in, I kissed him goodnight, got under the blankets of my cot, and went to sleep myself.

Two hours later, I awoke to the sound of my father's voice, calling out for me in the middle of the night, *Linita—Linita, come here.*

I got up and rushed to his side, *What's wrong, Dad? Are you okay?*

His gaze was held by shadows in the distance, silk silhouettes that stayed transparent to me. *Linita, two people are here. They are here to take me. I'm going to go with them.*

The expression on his face convinced me he was not mistaken, but to keep him calm, I gently patted his chest and dispelled his fears, *Okay, Dad, it's okay. You are tired, and you are on a lot of medication, try to get some sleep and rest.*

Tenderly, he agreed, trusting my guidance. He closed his eyes once more and went back to sleep. I returned to my cot, unsettled, my grandparents' memory on my mind. As it would turn out, those words—*rejoining his loved ones who are here to take him*—were my father's last words.

# ~In the End~

Death is not extinguishing the light;

it is only putting out the lamp because

the dawn has come.

—Rabindranath Tagore

**Figure 20**
*A Smile to Die For*

# 20

## The Last Smile

I was startled awake to the sound of tremors running through my father's body. Scanning the room, I found two nurses pinning him down as he shook uncontrollably, convulsing against the metal bed frame. Using the arms of the bed to catapult in his direction, I sprang from my cot and landed beside him. Grabbing his forearms, I held him in place as the doctor held my stricken stare,

> *We need to take him to the ICU. If we don't put him on life support now, he will die. We need family consent to do this. Do I have your permission?*

Comprehending that I was the only family member in the room, I consented as the words, *he will die*, pulsed through my veins. My mind, gyrating, trapped the rest of the doctor's counsel in a revolving door, unable to reach me. I stepped out into the corridor while the staff shifted my father's rattling body onto a mobile bed. Adrenaline filled my fingertips as I attempted to find the contact *home* on my phone. Dazed and confused, my mother's voice quivered while she caught up to the words, *life support*. In a panic, she wailed out in her native tongue—*Ente kunju ithu ellam thanne enghaneya cheyyunne? How is my child doing this all by herself?* Then, as fast as her tension spiked, her scattered thoughts slowed down. Agreeing to the terms laid out in front of her to save her husband's life, she settled long enough to form the words, *I'm on my way*.

    Clutching my father's hand, we entered the elevator alongside the doctor and three other medical professionals. I resisted the urge to spiral into an anxious fit, but the large metal doors closed tight, adding to my suffocation. Silence engulfed the small space around us; all that could be heard were the sobs of tears helplessly spilling from my eyes. I tried to compose myself, but I could feel the sadness rising in the people standing next to me.

As we entered the long stretch of the hallway leading to the ICU, I begged them to wait, pleading, *My family is not here yet.*

The doctor reiterated, *The longer we wait, the worse it will be for him.* My heart split: the larger portion pulled in my father's direction.

Just as they started rolling him away from me, my mother appeared. Suddenly, in front of me was nothing short of a scene from an Indian movie, a plot twist that seemed far too stretched to resemble anything even close to reality. But here it was. My mother, with her arm overextended, ran toward my father screaming—*Mocha*—her lifelong term of endearment for him. As if on cue, synchronously, his convulsions stopped. Sitting up straight, following the sound of her voice, he zoned in on her. Tightening his fists, he fought to sit still and looked longingly at her. Then, joy, embodied in a smile, joined us. A smile, curving so far upward that his lips lit his eyes aglow. A smile so vibrant that I had never seen a man look at a woman like *that* before. A smile that told a story, *I was waiting for you. I needed to see you. I needed to hear your voice one last time before I go.* And so, their perfect ending was also written. He never said a word to her, but no words were needed after praise like that. As always, my father's heart spoke volumes; it was the purest form of love I had ever seen.

***

*In my early twenties, my mother and I clashed. Whether it was over the money I spent, the clothes I wore, or the time I wasted loitering around with my friends—our opinions always differed. Often, her position on things led me to create full-blown arguments. And whenever my irritation grew, I always sought refuge in my father.*

"Dad, I'm having a hard time wrapping my head around what Mom said to me. I'm going to say something to her about it."

*After a long, weighted pause, my father replied,*

Linita, your mother has worked tirelessly for all of us. She has taken on two jobs, worked double shifts, and picked up overtime whenever she can. She works so much that she doesn't get proper rest, which sometimes makes her say things she doesn't mean. But we are all indebted to her. If something were to happen to her, what would we do? Keep that in mind the next time you want to complain about insignificant things. Ignore her frustrations and stay silent. Make sure your words don't affect her health; this is the least you can do to repay her endless sacrifices.

*My father opened a window into the love he carried for my mother, and that breath of air permanently changed my actions and never left my system.*

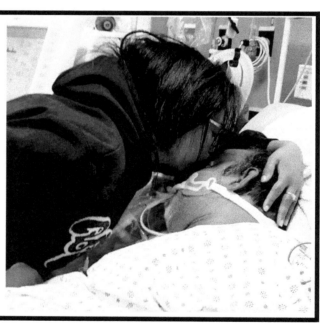

**Figure 21**
*Welcome to 2017, Dad…*

# 21

## The Last New Year

*Finally, after his endless attempts, my father received the call that heralded better times. Hanging up the phone, he exhaled a sentiment of relief and flashed a confident smile, "I got the job!" He was hired full-time as a computer programmer at a local company. And, for the first time, at the age of ten, I saw my dad don an expression of hopeful excitement, which suited him nicely.*

*To celebrate his victory, Mom took the family out for dinner, a privilege usually reserved for birthdays. We were allowed to order whatever we wanted, and the four of us ate to our heart's content. This day became one of those childhood memories where I can pinpoint the exact feeling of happiness. Even as children, my brother and I knew what this meant for us.*

*As we returned home, smiles and laughter crossed our doorstep alongside us. My father's happiness exuded freely from within, enabling us to do the same. Stopped by a blinking light on the answering machine, he pushed play and gave voice to a man filled with hesitation and regret,*

> Eapen, I'm sorry to inform you, but my earlier call came too soon. We looked at the numbers again, and unfortunately, the position we offered you has been terminated. Our sincerest apologies, but we will not be able to employ you at this time. We will be in touch if something else comes up.

*Before we could digest our food, our stomachs emptied. Dad's face dropped into a dismal gloom. I knew this expression well; he wore it often whenever others questioned his ability to take care of his family, when they challenged the gender stereotypes he did not adhere to. Without saying another word, he retreated from the rest of us and sat alone in a tiny corner of our home. Worried, I stuck my head around the edges of the wall and saw my father's face buried in his palms, crying. The image that drove my success was born.*

*For the next few days, Dad stayed silent in solitude, trying to come to terms with the hand life dealt him. He turned inward, found God's response, and from this day onward, he stopped incessantly applying for jobs. Instead, with my mother's encouragement, he focused all of his attention on his family, spending every ounce of energy raising his children—and raising us well.*

***

My brother did not make it in time to see our dad before the intubation. Completely caught off guard by the tragic turn of events, a burst of emotion exploded from within him, a reaction that was too heavy for me to carry. *It's okay you're reacting this way. I won't stop you, but I can't be around it right now.* Already submerged in sensory overload from transporting my father to the intensive care unit—like Dad—my nerves shook to my core. I stood up and left the room to stabilize myself, giving my brother time and space to do the same. For the next few hours, he raged through the understanding that our dad's death was now a likely possibility. He screamed, he shouted, he flung both his faith and a cross kept in the room against the wall. Onlookers, filled with good intentions, were unsuccessful at calming or consoling him. They did not know him the way I did—at this point, he just needed release.

The visitors always brought their *faith*, *hope*, and *love* into the ICU, thinking in these dire times, *hope* was the greatest. Hence, every minor victory for my father was a major cause for celebration, raising our expectations of his survival—*he smiled at us, he nodded his head, he moved his leg, he squeezed my hand, he recognized you, he blinked*. Each small step he took extended a bridge of hope meant to lead him to the other side of his illness, which in hindsight, was not a false analogy. The three of us were optimistic at every twist and turn, though the curve of our optimism was flattened by doctors, reminding us his consciousness was not consistent. When hope dwindles, one must turn inward;

one must turn to God and find the deeper layers of meaning that exist in our suffering. *My father taught me that.*

I removed myself from the crowds of people and sat alone in a secluded area, a protective measure I put in place at this same hospital a decade earlier during his heart surgery. Unlike my brother, much like my father, I needed solitude to dissect and dismantle my emotions; I needed silence to come to terms with the end of my father's life. Somberly, I sat, hands intertwined, fidgeting uncontrollably with his rings now placed on my fingers. Briefly, I flashed back to a time twenty years prior when I removed my grandfather's rings in a hospital in India, allowing the similarity to sink in. I made the call to put my dad on life support, and now I wrestle with the contrast between my actions and our last conversation. *He wanted to leave. Did I go against his wishes?* Sitting alone in these isolated rows, I cried. Even as strangers began filling the seats next to me, I cried. It is a hospital after all, *I'm sure they can predict the final result as much as I can.* Then, the image of my father appeared, the one I turned to whenever I needed the motivation to keep going, materialized. Second by second, I needed to relinquish my deep desire to save him from his unfair circumstances. Like him, I needed to accept his fate, already penned. And when I did, I noticed things I had not thought of before. I realized the extension of my father's life had little to do with me and everything to do with my brother. That, Dad, stayed a while longer for him to reach the same level of understanding as me.

In a heartbeat, 2017 arrived. Akin to Christmas, this was my first time ushering in a new year in a hospital. The ICU care team was tender with us, accommodating compassionately to our crisis. They interacted with my father gently and spoke to us reassuringly. And the doctor who took care of my father made sure to take care of his family members as well, frequently updating us on his condition and allowing us to stay in his room for extended hours. His genuine nature poured from his spirit, placing a comforting hand on our shoulders, gradually reviving my faith in the medical profession.

On New Year's Eve, the three of us were permitted to see Dad through midnight, but we had to leave once he met with the milestone. Ten minutes to twelve, we patiently gathered in the hall, waiting for the nurse to retrieve us. I paced myself, pondering this night in previous years, comparing past occasions to our current predicament. No matter where I was or who I was with, I always left the crowd a few minutes before the countdown and found a quiet place to call my dad. I was adamant to spend the exact minute to midnight with him. Now, my veins filled with the same urgency to reach him first, but in a much different setting, with a foreboding feeling attached to our circumstances. Briefly, I wondered, *How many people bring in their New Year in a hospital every year? Why has this not crossed my mind before?*

Outside *there*, people expended their energy in every possible way; however, inside *here*, every ounce was conserved. The ticking hand on the clock hypnotized me as my eyes refused to take their sights off of the time. Never had I been so fixated on the countdown before. Typically, I fixed on the event, the dress, or the company; naïveté prevented me from seeing outside the palace walls. But, just as *Siddhartha*'s veil of illusion fell after witnessing suffering for the first time, similarly, in these common areas, my eyes were forced open to see the fragility of life. Ringing in a new year, sitting in an ICU, made me aware of my ignorance, something I was thus far fortunate not to see. Here, beds upon beds of people were dying as families clung on to see their loved ones into a fresh start. Here, we counted upward, not down, as each second on the clock brought gratitude, not regret. In the end, Siddhartha could pinpoint the exact moment that put him on the path of enlightenment. Perhaps now, *I can too.*

We entered my father's room at five minutes to midnight. Bathed and newly clothed, Dad carried a feeling of utter peace into the new year. Later, the new year would gift him back the same. The three of us huddled around him, grabbing onto his arms and infusing our love and energy into his unconscious self. Clustering together, we formed a shield, protecting him from the inevitable truth that gripped him. Then, we waited. Silently, we watched the hand of the clock move closer to our target. A piece of my heart leapt to grab hold of the old wives' tale—that, if he made it to midnight, he would make it through the year. The hour, now on twelve, gave rise to sighs of relief: *Welcome to 2017, Dad!* We sang songs, we prayed, and we stayed with him—as a family of four—until it was time to leave. Eventually, when it would be his turn to usher in the new, he made sure to do the same.

Dad *did* make it to 2017, but as my father's history has shown, short-lived relief was never much more than that. This was my last New Year with him. Because of it, I no longer celebrate lavishly inside extravagant, disillusioned palaces. Now, my yearly gatherings are gladly spent in remote spaces, bringing my father's memory forward, and cherishing time with the people who are priceless to me.

**Figure 22**
*Two Peas, One Pod*

# 22

## The Last Birthday

Dad's responsiveness progressively unlatched from his body, but the life-support system locked his breath in place. Even though I was grateful for the confirmed breaths, different parts of the ventilator later formed the images generating my nightmares—the sounds, the sights, the tubes, the preprogrammed rise and fall of my father's chest. The *suctioning*, specifically, was nothing short of terrorizing. Because I held his hand on the hour to help him through the heaving, I had an up-close-and-personal view of the process. His choking and gasping for air that resulted from drawing secretions upward from his airway, winded me. I spent long hours staring at the tube, wondering: *Is it hurting him? Is it helping him? Is it prolonging the inevitable?* My throat dried, sensing the endless brushes against his. Neither of us felt relaxed by the artificial support system now in place. Whenever he regained consciousness, out of fright and confusion, he immediately moved to rip out the mouthpiece. So, before the first day was over, a new element of heartache emerged—my father's hands were tied and restrained to the bed. Now, I became his hands too.

Watching him suffer, the helplessness that transpired from breathing, feeding, and secreting by tubes, shocked my system and contributed to the formation of post-traumatic stress disorder. The equipment visibly showed me that he was dying—that the last stages of his life were here—leaving me powerless to my terror. Hence, every so often, sensing my struggle, Dad managed to do something to lighten the mood. Once, after a bath, the nurse forgot to tie his hands to the bed. Swiftly, my father swooped his palm to his mouth, causing alarm to the staff, but at the last second, he swerved upward and rested his arm on top of his head, scratching his forehead freely. He stayed in this position, carefree, enjoying life. Then, when he was ready, he brought his arm back down and allowed the nurse to tie it again. Those few minutes of freedom brought a smile to our faces, reminding me of the simple pleasures we take for granted, the simplicity of my father.

My best friend and her young daughter joined our family in the ICU daily. Unfortunately, by this point, my attention and patience wore thin, causing me to abruptly tell my niece to stand still while I checked in with a staff member. Noticing my tension spike, the nurse asked if my concern stemmed from something the doctor said or was merely a feeling I carried about his condition. With a faint undertone that acknowledged, *she didn't know what I knew*, I kept my response short: *It's just a feeling I have.* Sympathizing with the situation, she understood and left the room.

Hinting at my earlier premonition received over a month ago, I turned to my best friend and asked, *Do you remember what I told you on the phone that night?*

Without hesitation, she replied, *I think about it every day.*

Blood was spilling from intuition's double-edged sword.

The doctors came by to do their rounds and spoke plainly, informing us that no visible sign of recovery had surfaced, confirming *my feeling* valid. Perhaps it was the *laissez-faire* attitude of the news, but I could not shake the sentiment that Dad was just another patient on the unit. A fire grew within. I needed every person who entered his room to understand his worth was immeasurable. That his family not only loved him, they adored him. I decided the only way to evoke his value was to awaken his character, and I had the perfect picture to do this. In my possession, I had a photo that bore my father's greatest qualities all in one shot: integrity, loyalty, honesty, humility, and most importantly, his unconditional love. It was an image of him with his daughter; it was a photo of us. And because we carry the energy of *twin flames*, I knew it would speak volumes, reaching the center of the hearts of others. I envisioned how this visual would bring life to his room, but I did not know then that the memory would bring life to him also.

# The Last Birthday

***

*On Dad's seventieth birthday, I woke up bright and early and kneeled in prayer. An air of lightness moved me. For the first time since his heart attack, the uneasiness of his death had left. Post-surgery, the cardiologist had informed us that he would only survive a few years at best. However, twelve had gone by smoothly. The fearful grip that tightened my chest with each birthday that passed now loosened, and I gave wishful thinking another shot, "God, Dad made it to seventy! What're twenty more years? Ninety, that's possible, right?" Effortlessly, I prayed with a newfound belief that many more memories would spin.*

*But all the bargaining in the world cannot shift a set date. God set aside my twenty and gave me one year and nine days. And the one well-wish I wrote for him in his last birthday card—Dad, may your 70$^{th}$ year be transformational—came true.*

***

January 5, 2017, my father turned seventy-one, our last mental marker for his safe return home. For his birthday, the nurses curved his bed in an upright position so that he could interact with us. Dad cracked his eyes open but remained unresponsive. I entered the room, canvas in hand, and squeezed my way past the numerous visitors, placing myself directly in my father's line of sight. *Happy birthday, Dad! Look what I made for you.* Though his expression remained dull, curiosity piqued all around me. Slowly, I turned the canvas to reveal a stunning picture of him wrapped in his daughter's arms. What happened next was nothing short of a miracle.

For the first time since he entered the ICU, my father showed clear signs of consciousness. He practically *jumped* out of his chair to get a better view of our photo together. His eyes widened, and he gave a loud chuckle over top of the ventilator—no tube could stop him from sharing his excitement with us today. Everyone was astounded by what was happening. The energy from his heart took a hold of ours as he smiled from the inside out, and not a dry eye survived his momentary return. For a split second, we stretched our limits with this last ray of hope, convincing us, *just maybe*, he would make it after all—myself included. Proudly, I hung the canvas on the wall beside him, fully knowing that only his daughter would garner this type of reaction from him.

By hanging a picture next to him, I not only raised my father's consciousness but the collective consciousness as well. The level of compassion and care that emerged because of one added element to the room was notable, forging a spiritual connection with all who entered. The canvas not only emanated the love we had for each other, but our photo altered the mindset of those who saw it, bringing forward a feeling of love they had for their significant loved one. So, by placing an image on the wall, I opened a door to empathy, granting others the ability to walk a mile in our shoes. Suddenly, all were gentler with my father, softer with us, their approach was more considered, their language kinder, and our interactions became more meaningful. One senior doctor, who said very little to me before this, interrupted his discussion during rounds, turned toward me, and said, *That's a great picture of you two*. I smiled, knowing the energy from the canvas carried too strong a pull not to be acknowledged.

I suppose one picture is worth a thousand words. But more importantly, the doctors and nurses were no longer blinded by the gown; they saw my father for who he was—a remarkable dad. I accomplished my mission, we mesmerized them, and now, I could trust them to take good care of him. This was the greatest gift I could give my father on his *last birthday* with us.

**Figure 23**
*A Perfect Day*

*Note.* Photo courtesy of Jayden Kelli @CustomEyesPhotography

# 23

## The Last Look

The storm awaiting us no longer brewed; now, the murky sky poured. My father passed every test with no diagnosis intact—and with no known illness, no known cure existed. Even the doctor's hope for his survival had visibly decreased as, *I will try to save his life,* slowly changed into, *What level of care would you like us to provide for him?* Mom held the reins over Dad's final directives, humbly requesting the team not to move into level one of resuscitative care, eliminating CPR from the equation. With my brother and I seated in the room, she informed them, *After his open-heart surgery, my husband told me not to let anyone press on his chest. If it is time to go, he wants to go.* Hearing this for the first time, we stayed silent; we did not oppose our parents' wishes. The shock, however, stung sharply enough to break my internal barriers.

The plethora of emotions painting the landscape of a family member's terminal illness provokes either at once or in slow stretches that show no end. The hope, panic, anger, sadness, joy, relief, humility, guilt, self-loathing, compassion, and most prominent—*fear*—gathered on site. And no matter which corner of the building I sought refuge, the chaotic energy surged and rushed through my veins. This outpouring was responsible for the endless adrenaline that woke me each morning and told me to keep going. By now, my meditative drive to the hospital had transitioned into a pre-mourning ritual. I listened to songs my father played for us in our childhood, sobbing out a burdensome amount of pent-up *anticipatory grief.* One Hindi song in particular, which would later be heard during our section of the funeral slideshow, touched the nerve of my sorrow more deeply. The lyrics described the epitome of a friendship bonded by an unbreakable strength. Letting these sentiments sink in, I clung to the phrase that promised the camaraderie would last until *our dying breath*. The sad version of this song repeated to the hospital and back as I cried out the realization that our promise was rightfully kept. To stand tall against the rain—first, I had to immerse myself in the water. This is how I accepted my father's impending death by immersing myself in the downpour first.

Amid all the knowledge and emotional upheavals, small pockets of peace rose to the surface, bringing resolutions of tenderness, ease, and grace. These grief gifts were sparse and selective, appearing only after I hit a dark wall of despondency. Here, the *invisible hand* grabbed hold of my thoughts, the flurry of inevitable regrets that danced through my mind like a whirling dervish and stopped them long enough to attain the beauty of *Sufism*. Involuntarily, I became aware of the only two things in the room that mattered, *God* and *Love*. Slowly, a sensation of gratitude bloomed through my cracked spirit, reminding me to relieve my mind of past and future burdens and stay present using my heart. I was here with my dad now—and in the now, he was still alive, breathing love into the air. God had entered the room to show me that my father was in front of me, resting his eyes on what he loved most, a picture embodying his relationship with his daughter.

Dad's interactions with the canvas always centered me. Since I knew he slept on his left side, I intentionally hung the photo to the left of him. And every morning, even though he started his day lying straight, slowly but surely, inch by inch, his body moved toward the wall as his eyes searched for our picture. He craved to see us, often scanning the room, and easing once he spotted the image. Every so often, the ventilator agitated him, but I watched as he fixated on our photo, using the visual to relax back into a calm, peaceful sleep. A sliver of my human self was always stunned by his actions; it took time to grasp the extent of his love for me. My grief was grand because my father was too.

Gazing upward, I got lost in the picture myself, reflecting on the story of its origin. During a casual conversation with a photographer friend of mine, a seed of desire planted, sprouted, and bloomed to have her photograph my father and me. When I shared the news with Dad, we decided to keep it a secret from our other family members—it was a father–daughter photo shoot, after all. Eventually, my mother and brother came across one of the photos, three years later, hanging in his hospital room. Shocked by the discovery, I bore the brunt end of my mother's envy. Still, it was well worth the emotional tussle. The inkling that formed as a tiny seedling back then was now bearing the fruits of my labor.

Leaning against the backdrop of a Calgary scenic park, I wished to recreate the fondest memories of my childhood, walking alongside Dad as he transferred his wisdom to me. The fall season had just set in, the leaves were painted a freshly colored palette of orange, and my father wore the sweater I bought him to match. Hand-in-hand, we made use of nature's gifts—we played in the leaves, leaned against trees, stood on a bridge, stopped by a chapel, sat on a wooden bench, and shared a strong dose of laughter. Grounded in the earth and surrounded by natural beauty, she captured the essence of our kindred spirit; a forever friendship formed in my early years came alive through her photos. And wrapping up the session, she noted, *It was an honor photographing your profound connection and quiet understanding of each other.*

It was a perfect day. *Does he remember that?* Deflating my doubt, Dad's soft eyes turned to me and communicated, *I remember.* He rested on our image for long periods, carving the nature of our relationship in his heart before he left. Acknowledging this, I whispered, *Sleep peacefully, Dad, and stay with that day.* If he had to leave—I wanted him to leave with the memory of that day.

\*\*\*

*"Well, we're all done, Dad. Ready to go home?"*
*"Let's go and get some ice cream first, my treat."*
*"Oh sure, we can go, but you don't have to pay. I'll buy it for us."*
*"No, you brought me here today and took all of these nice pictures with me. Now, I want to do something nice for you. I want to buy you an ice cream."*

*I watched as my aged father took out his wallet and started counting his change. Ever since I was a small child, Dad would walk me to the nearest ice cream shop and buy me a treat whenever I did something good. And today was no different. Permitting him to follow through with his regular reward system, knowing I had done something good in his eyes, I smiled and conceded to his request. Our perfect day was brought to its rightful conclusion, sitting together, enjoying our ice cream, and feeling satisfied with the life we had made.*

**Figure 24**
*Night and Day*

# 24

## The Last Family Meeting

The three of us took up residence in *that* room, the one located to the right of the critical care facility. We shared the space with another family whose beloved—*father, grandfather, husband*—was also in intensive care. Together, our days and nights brimmed over with extreme medical discoveries and conclusions. If it was not our turn to receive the bad news, it was theirs; and if we were relieved for us, we were equally fearful for them. Through mutual lamentations, our families bonded, swapping stories and sorrows that attempted to comfort one another. Usually, I remained quiet and listened while my mother and brother engaged in conversations with them. Knowing they understood our pain was enough for me. The ICU family room, *I can imagine*, has borne witness to more desperate tears than any other place of gathering. For, the space is an abode that brings the paradoxical element of the opening line of a classic tale to life:

> *It was the best of times, it was the worst of times, it was the age of wisdom, it was the age of foolishness, it was the epoch of belief, it was the epoch of incredulity, it was the season of Light, it was the season of Darkness, it was the spring of hope, it was the winter of despair, we had everything before us, we had nothing before us, we were all going direct to Heaven, we were all going direct the other way…*[7]

Unfortunately, I would not receive the same news as *Lucie*; my shock would not stem from my father being *recalled to life*. Never had I felt so emotionally charged as I did now, pushed and pulled in all directions, navigating the *losing a loved one* spectrum. As my internal navigation

---

[7] *A Tale of Two Cities*. C. Dickens. (2018). Alma Classics.

system collided with the external route my mother and brother took, conflict was created among us. We had already been called into the small, side cubby of the larger room for multiple closed-door meetings and being the guest of honor at that table was nothing short of petrifying, evoking angst, fright, and delusions among all three of us. Every time, I held my breath and turned inward, trying to make sense of the information—while my mother and brother did the opposite, exhaling their opinions in circles, attempting to pinpoint the path of his illness, and trying to convince the doctors of *their* solutions. Quickly, the room became overcrowded with our respective ideologies. But when the day came for the palliative care team to join us, causing us to congregate in the larger space instead of the smaller one, I feared the news had already made itself known. All along, the space and the refutations were not the problems, the pending outcome we all tried to delay was.

*Rapid onset vascular dementia.* Those were the only words I heard leaving the doctor's mouth. Taking a strong, deep breath, I forced my parasympathetic nervous system to slow my body down and conserve energy, allowing my mind to concentrate on what the doctor said. Listening intently, I absorbed and digested the rest of his words:

> *All tests were negative; we can't find the source of his illness; it is either rapid onset vascular dementia or some rare brain disorder that hasn't been discovered yet, you take your pick;* and last, *these people are here to support your family moving forward.*

I zoned in on the diagnosis of dementia. My mind wandered through multiple scenarios that had recently taken place, situations where my father was unable to recall necessary information. Soon, a flurry of questions spun like a funnel cloud:

> *Is that why he didn't recognize those people? Is that why he was confused when I asked him a simple question? Is that why he didn't know where he put his belongings? Is that why he couldn't recite his favorite Bible verse?*

I froze as the last question touched down, *is that why he fell asleep while untying his shoelaces?* Sinking in the quicksand of questions, I placed the wheel of interrogation on hold and returned to the present. The only way to stop my whirlwind of presumptions from spiraling further was to seek clarification. And, as any teacher would do, I asked a very specific question: *What is rapid onset vascular dementia?* As I would soon find out, this was exactly the wrong question to ask.

Purposely preventing the doctors from responding, my mother and brother obstructed my inquiry. Instead, the two of them snowballed through the steps that *each* and *every* medical professional responsible for overseeing my father's care had taken. Exasperated from hearing this story for the *millionth* time, I interrupted their pointless ramblings and staged an intervention to my family's madness. However, as I shifted the dialogue, I suddenly became overwhelmed with my father's presence, communicating a request to me from inside the ICU. Changing my course of action, I looked at the doctors and delivered Dad's message,

> *I know that you have tried everything possible to save him. On behalf of my dad and myself, I want to take a moment and sincerely thank you for everything you have done.*

The doctors' eyes softened. Acknowledging my grounded ability to reason with the circumstances, they tipped their heads in gratitude. As for the other two, I was now on strike two.

Closing the session, the doctors left us in the hands of the palliative care team, who, one by one, introduced themselves and their role to us. Battling the quick turn of events in which the meeting was leaning toward, I turned somewhat bitter. *Why would I need to talk to a social worker?* Beneath the layers, I still held onto a hidden belief that the conclusive result was wrong—that this was a terrible mistake. My silence was my strength and my weapon; now, I used it forcefully, refusing to answer the questions they asked me. Of course, my mother and brother welcomed the inquisition. Their pent-up perceptions were once again released in circular motions, recounting the entire step-by-step sequence of my father's illness from the beginning. I could only hear this story so many times.

Cutting off their repetitive process, I stood up and inquired, *Is this mandatory? Do I have to be here, or can I go?*

Before I could blink, their compassionate concern shifted directly onto me. *No, you don't have to be here, but it might be helpful for you to stay.*

I understood their job was to be proactive and help us, but I had not reached that stage of acceptance yet, and I was done being a sounding board for my other family members. Already on my way out the door, my response echoed behind me, *Great, I'd rather be with my dad.*

My brother and I have always had a complex relationship, and perhaps because of our five-year age gap, a mutual element of respect was missing prior to our loss. Our shade of skin color is different, our blood group is different, our personalities are different, our likes and dislikes are different, and our *handling of grief* is different. Quite frankly, the only evident commonality we do share is our parents. Anyone who walked into the room when we were together knew we were unable to lean on each other. My brother tried to research and reach for solutions; I tried to console and comfort my father. Even though, until now, our interactions were civil, as the end of our father's life drew nearer, so did our inability to stay cordial. I had already had a strong inkling that soon, irretrievable words would be pitched and tossed in my direction. Unfortunately, my asking the *wrong* question was the straw that broke the camel's back.

I waited for the palliative care team to leave and returned to the family area again. And, awaiting me in the small, side room were my mother and brother, guns loaded and ready to pull the trigger. Before I could gather my thoughts to talk to them, I was ambushed.

*Why did you ask the doctor about dementia? Dad does not have dementia!* The mother and son duo pounced, cornering me for reasons I did not even realize were bothering them.

*What's wrong with asking that?* I stammered back.

My brother, already fuming that I had taken the doctors' side and even went as far as thanking them, led the surprise attack. Because of their inability to successfully treat our father, he had grown distrustful of them, and naturally, was the first to explode, *When all of this is over, why don't you sit down and go for a coffee with your new best friend?* I assumed he was referring to the female doctor who, upon seeing the enlarged picture of my father and me, came to console me, letting me know that if she were in my position, she too would be unable to let her dad go. He did not hear our conversation, which from afar may have looked too friendly.

Ignoring his comment, my mother came next, *I'm a nurse, and this is not dementia. I know what dementia is. Why would you even ask that question?*

Having had it up to here with the both of them, I looked my mother square in the eyes and clamored, *When my children ask me how their grandfather died, I need an answer. Do you have one?*

With this, she became silent, but my brother did not. Without thinking his response through, the irretrievable words materialized, *How about when they ask you, you tell them that you're the reason he died!*

The comment I had been dreading, the one remark that days earlier had warned me would make an untimely appearance, was said. And although I knew it was coming, my heart still stopped all the same. All hell broke loose. I gave a long, piercing cry at the top of my lungs, *If you ever say that to me again, I'll kill you.* My anger made infrequent stops, but when it did, my fury had no bounds.

My brother pulled out his phone, flipped it open, and pretended to call 9-1-1, *I'm calling the police. She just threatened me!*

My mother shuffled herself in between us, possibly stopping a physical fight from forming in the very room where the news of our dad's terminal illness was delivered moments earlier. I stepped back and separated myself from them. Storming out of the room, I ran straight to the only person I knew who would protect me. Sobbing uncontrollably, I collapsed on my father's belly—my safe place. And, for the first time since he told me he wanted to go, I wholeheartedly objected. With every fiber of my being, I begged and pleaded and cried out in anguish: *Please, Dad, please don't go. Please don't go and leave me here with them.*

Gaining my composure, I sat upright and looked at my father, sleeping soundly. Dejected, I felt ashamed. The one request Dad made of me was to let him transition peacefully. *He told me he wanted to go. He asked me to let him leave.* Even so, I stood in the way of his final wishes; I asked him to stay for my own selfish reasons. Others may have brushed off my appeal, stating he could not hear me, but I knew better. I knew he was listening and watching our family's drama unfold. *Still*, I never took back those words. Now, more than ever, I needed him here with me.

Moreover, losing him would only be the beginning. This debacle was merely a preview of my life with family members who did not understand me. And I was losing more than them—in the end, they would still have each other. I sat beside him on the bed, scrunching his sleeves, trying to hold him in place, knowing it would not be possible. Gazing down at my father, I wept.

Breaking the spell, my best friend rushed into the room and announced, *I think you should come outside. Your brother is going on a tangent about you.* Instantly, I sprung to my feet. Prepared for battle, I marched out of the ICU and back into the family room, armed and ready for *The Mathew Sibling Showdown.*

I burst into the room and stumbled upon a dozen people from our community, waiting to see my father, welded in place by my brother's volcanic eruption. I looked to find, for lack of a better phrase, that my sibling had lost it. Screaming and shouting at the top of his lungs, his senseless banter boiled over dangerous territory. Then, seeing me approach—his usual target—the magma rose. Marking his prey, the rest of his dormant anger spewed smoldering lava in my direction.

> *You! This is all your fault! You are always putting me down and making fun of me. You insult me and call me an idiot to all of your friends. You think you're better than me and laugh at me in front of them. Some of your friends don't even know you have a brother. They told me that!*

Equipped to defend myself for entirely different reasons altogether, I stood still, surprised by his oxymoronic debate. *What are you talking about? I've never said any of those things about you, and all my friends know I have a brother. They know exactly who you are.*

He retorted by bringing up more specific names of people who I, myself, had introduced him to. Realizing now that his accusations were baseless, I unsuccessfully tried to make him see that he was nonsensical. But no use, the rational aspects of the debate were not getting through to him. A persona creating confabulations—*made-up stories*—arose as a protective measure springing from thick complications of his mourning. To my bewilderment, these actions reoccurred throughout his bereavement. And upon further investigation, I learned that stress and trauma can create confabulated memories that eventually recede. But, in the heat of the moment, they were hard to digest, adding another hurtful layer to our loss.

Feeling vulnerable to the attack, I caught my mute mother out of the corner of my eye and asked, *Why are you just standing there, silent?*

*Why aren't you saying something to him and making him stop? If Dad was here, he would make him stop!*

My mother's usual, helpless response was given, *I love both of my children the same.*

Discovering my pleas fell on deaf ears, I ignored her and turned back to the insults of my brother.

Fishing for reasons to hate me, he continued,

> *It's your fault I didn't take a picture with Dad that day in front of the Christmas tree. It's your fault I didn't come downstairs because you and your friends would have made fun of me.*

My defenses reached their limit, I screamed, *What are you talking about? I came upstairs and asked you to come down!*

He stayed adamant in his position, *No, it's your fault I didn't take the picture.*

My best friend, who was present that night and could corroborate my story, stood to defend me. *No, I was there, and you need to take accountability for your actions. She tried to get you to come down. You chose not to take that picture, and it's no one else's fault but your own.*

The truth in her stance pierced through the layers of sedimentary rock that had solidified months earlier and reached the core of the issue, paralyzing him in place. Frozen by the chill of her words, my brother cooled down.

To my surprise, he softened. Within the blink of an eye, his anger turned into an ocean of tears, and his allegations toward me transformed to reveal a lifetime of regret. *All he wanted was one picture, why didn't I go down and take it with him? It was just one picture.* Registering now that this fiasco had nothing to do with me and everything to do with his grief, I sat down in silence and allowed his emotions to process the news we had just received a few hours earlier.

> *It was the last thing he asked me to do, and I couldn't do it. I haven't done any of the things he asked me to do in the past, and now, it's too late. Look at Linita, she's doing everything Dad asked. If she can do it, why couldn't I?*

Offering to alleviate at least one aspect of his pain, I brought my father's sentiments forward, *It doesn't matter who did what, as long as one of us did it. That's all Dad wanted. I'm fulfilling his wishes for both of us.*

## The Revelations of Eapen

My brother was not soothed by my input. *No, I should have done more. I should have listened and done the things he wanted me to do.* His guilt washed over and submerged him, drowning the voices of others, bringing a quietness to the room.

After the waves receded, those who gathered tried to comfort him, but the root of the matter remained inconsolable. Our father was dying, and he could not change the past, nor the present outcome. The accumulation of his efforts, the Christmas decorations, the daily visits, the nightly Bible readings, the tireless hours of searching the Internet, the consistent questioning of doctors, colleagues, friends, and other family members—had all gone to waste. No one had ever seen my brother this distressed before, not even me.

The disruption of family dynamics that manifests through the mutual loss of a loved one is incomparable to any other family crisis. The interactions, responses, and reactions that stem from anticipatory grief are both unpredictable and unfathomable. While transmuting, the combustible energy tries and tears at you, breaks apart, then unites you. And, *as we walked through the valley of the shadow of death,*[8] we encountered both the separate and the amalgamated emotions of faith, hope, envy, jealousy, anger, sadness, bitterness, frailness, despair, and possibly even sparse flickers of joy. *This is grief*—a locked mansion where only the griever holds the key, and each room explored brings a new color, shade, and awareness of the wisdom of the self. At the pinnacle point of loss, a significant reminder surfaced—that, as I was losing my father, he was also losing his. And, in light of it all, *we can fear no evil*, because at the center of it all, exists love.

\*\*\*

*The evenings were for the three of us. In the afternoon, my mother would leave for her shift at the hospital, and my father would teach us, play with us, feed us, bathe us, and read stories until we fell asleep. Seeing as I had not yet entered my schooling years—I was with Dad all day. And while he usually made us study Monday through Thursday, Fridays were our movie night! On these nights, he walked us to the corner video store and let us choose a feature film. My brother and I alternated selecting the title. Every*

---

8  *Psalm 23.* King James Bible. (1611). King James Bible Online.

*other week, I eagerly awaited my turn to pick out the movie—and this evening, the chance was mine.*

*Waiting for my brother to return home from school, Dad made himself chai on the stove. Turning off the heating element, he specifically turned to me and said, "Don't go near the stove. It is hot." But being the curious girl that I was, the minute he turned his back, intrigued, I touched the ring. Instantly, and for the first time, I felt the burning sensation of pain singe my hand. Because I deliberately disobeyed my father, I could not tell him about my mischief. And as the evening progressed, my seared skin grew more painful.*

*Finally, my brother arrived, and after a quick meal, we were on our way to the movie store. Because it was the middle of winter and an exceptionally cold night, Dad decided to drive us. Sitting in the car, I discovered if I kept my hand on the chilled window, the pain in my palm lessened. I held it glued to the glass the whole way there and back, and once inside the movie store, I stayed close to the large windows, pretending to look out at the falling snow. Noticing my aloof behavior, Dad questioned, "Linita, aren't you going to pick out a movie?" Saddened by my poor choice from earlier in the day, I frowned in response and handed off the honor to my brother. The only person I let down that night was me.*

*Dad set up the Bruce Lee movie, opened the sofa bed, and left to make popcorn. I scrambled around on the bed, covering my hand, trying to rid myself of the excruciating ache, but my efforts were useless, and the scorching sensation would not let up. When the popcorn came around to me, I reached into the hot kernels and screamed. Alas, I could not take it anymore. I turned to my father and confessed. Without telling him what I did, I opened my hand and showed him the sight of raging red.*

*"When did this happen? Why didn't you tell me?" he inquired.*

*"I didn't want to get in trouble on movie night." I whimpered.*

*Dad got up and walked to the kitchen, returning seconds later with a cup in hand. He sat back on the bed and placed my wounded palm in soothing relief. Around midnight, my mother walked in to find the three of us lying on the sofa bed of our tiny apartment. My brother and I were curled up against our dad, fast asleep on either side of him—his hand in a tin of popcorn, and mine in a cup of ice.*

**Figure 25**
*Till Death Do Us Part*

# 25

## The Last Verdict

Like my father's breathing, my movements became mechanical. Every morning, I got out of bed, brushed my teeth, washed my face, got dressed, and drove to the hospital. I cycled through the days without giving much thought to my needs, causing my physical body to feel too depleted to even get out of bed. Each cell of mine dreaded the hardships of loss. But the minute I parked my car, my mind shifted gears, driving out an uncontainable excitement to be at my father's side again. The thought of him lying alone in his bed rocketed my lagging body down the hallway of the ICU.

From the get-go, today felt off; an apprehension grew within. I sat outside the large, flip-flop doors, watching them swing open, waiting for the nurses to draw back my father's curtain. Out of thin air, the kind doctor appeared and sat down beside me, voicing a firm objective, *I wanted to speak with you alone.* In my periphery, the indecisive doors shut closed. Steadying myself using the metal arms of the chair, I straightened and gave him my full attention. Slowly, sympathetically, through regretful eyes, he spoke, *I need you to know that once the ventilator is removed, I don't think your dad will make it. I don't think he will live past forty-eight hours.* Throbbing, my heart beat against the cage of my chest, pacing alongside the high-stakes match of hope and despair. He continued,

> *I'm very sorry. If there is anything we can do to support you, please don't hesitate to ask. I just needed you to know first that this is the reality of the situation before I tell your other family members—before we move forward with extubating him.*

The doctor's empathy allied with the spiritual forces working behind the scenes, unintentionally aligning with my father's last message. Clutching my dad's rings, I tried to catch up to the phrase that bolted past me—*He won't live past forty-eight hours*. Before leaving, the messenger waited to see if I had any questions, but from here on out, no words formed. For the next three years, the trauma solidified by this tipping point created an ongoing inability for me to construct and communicate my words to others.

I imagine this feeling of the doctor handing me *the last verdict*, affirming the death of a loved one, must be similar to the angst created by an officer showing up at the door or being on the receiving end of that one phone call that changes everything. As much as we like to compare and contrast the varying degrees and situations of grief so that we can rank them in some preset order, I assume in the end, the height from which my heart dropped into the very bottom cavity of my chest—must be similar. In one sentence that *pre-pronounced* my father's death, my life fell to pieces. Though I had time, though I knew the outcome for months, the second those soundwaves pierced my ears, I was shell-shocked.

I sat alone in the row of chairs, destroyed. Grasping the truth that my life's greatest fear was materializing, I understood I had come to *Robert Frost*'s fork in the road, and two roads lay in front of me. I could spiral down the never-ending rabbit hole, dictating all the possible scenarios and secondary losses accompanying my tragedy. Or I could listen to the *second self*, asking me to stay calm and present with my father, soaking in every hour of every minute of every second I had left with him—*48 hours, 2880 minutes, 172800 seconds*, to be exact. My head dropped into my hands, and an ocean poured through me. Cleansed and seated in the perfect position to pray, I surrendered to a situation beyond my control. Then, with the *invisible hand* gripping my shoulder, I was lifted to rise to the occasion—I was reminded of what I was entrusted to do. The falling action of my father's life had begun, and now, he needed me most. For his sake, I chose *the road not taken*.[9] And traveling down this path, using the eyes of the second self, slowly, the beauty in our tragedy made itself known. Eventually, my loss would transform into something much grander than fear.

---

9  *The Road Not Taken*. R. Frost. (1916). Poetryfoundation.org.

## The Last Verdict

***

*Since my best friend was staying the night, we pulled out the sofa bed and fell asleep in the living room. By morning, we awoke to the hustle and bustle of my mom and dad getting ready for church. My mother concentrated on the full-length mirror in the room next to us, adjusting her sari and placing her pleats just right, a sensitive task. Soon, my father shuffled down the stairs and squeezed into a spot next to her, straightening his tie.*

*Irate, she blew her fuse, "I came down here to get away from you! You were blocking my view upstairs, and now you've come down here to do the same."*

*"Well, I told the priest when I married you that I would follow you to the ends of the earth," he smugly declared his readily available response.*

*My friend and I started to chuckle, furthering my father's ammunition. My mom, who did not find this funny, took her sari and stormed upstairs.*

*Making small talk, Dad walked to the fridge, cracked an egg on a plate, and made way to the microwave to heat his regular bullseye breakfast.*

*"Mom said you aren't allowed to eat eggs anymore because of the heart attack." I swiftly reminded him.*

*In a matter-of-fact tone, my father retaliated, "If I want to eat an egg, Linita, then I'm going to eat an egg."*

*Spotting Mom on her way back down, mine and my friend's laughter grew. My father, unaware of her looming presence, thought we were laughing with him and continued his amusing dialogue, "Your mom can't stop me, I'm the man of the house, and she is not the boss of me."*

*Patiently, we waited for him to turn and face the wrath of his wife. Slowly, he spun on his feet and, shortly after that, met with her rude awakening, wiping the budding smile off his face. Stunned, my father jumped a foot in the air. Taking a breath to regain his composure, he held out his plate and politely offered her the egg, "Honey, I made you an egg for breakfast." The cut of my mother's eyes stung him straight into silence. Scuttling toward the kitchen table, Dad sat down and quietly ate his meal while we let out an uproar of laughter.*

***

Hearing the news, my mother crumbled. A river ran down her face the instant the words—*he will not live*—grazed her ears. For the first time, I realized her hope was indestructible; she was as in doubt over his loss as my brother. In an attempt to alleviate her startling distress, I offered to take her out of the hospital for a short while to distract her. Uttering words that felt inappropriate, I took a chance and suggested, *We should go and buy clothes to wear for the funeral*. She understood my true intention, and she agreed to step out and *catch her breath in grief*.[10]

The Indian clothing store was on the other side of the city, giving my mother a good forty-five minutes to explore her confirmed loss. Sifting through the natural spousal grief guilt, Mom deconstructed the pivotal points they shared as husband and wife. As if trying to convince me what she was feeling was real, her thoughts wandered through her words, *I know we fought sometimes, but I really loved him. He wasn't just my husband; he was my best buddy*. I had never heard Mom call Dad her *best buddy* before—our eyes brimmed with tears.

Browsing the suits in the store, I tried on a few different selections of black, Indian *salwar kameez*, settling on one I thought my father would like. While in the change room, I overheard my mom whimpering to the woman helping us, *She will wear this for her father's funeral*. The sorrow in those sounds suffocated me, but my mind refused to let the words—*father's funeral*—penetrate my system. I still had a final stretch to go. After purchasing our funeral attire, we ventured into the Indian grocery store. Mom ambled, trying to cope with her sadness as she deciphered what foods to buy. Suddenly, she appeared from around the corner with numerous packs of *papadums* (lentil wafers) piled in her hands—my father's favorite snack.

Distraught, she looked at me, begging for an answer, *Why should I even buy these anymore? He won't be here to eat them.*

Allowing her to process his death one item at a time, I reassured her, *Buy them; I'll eat them.*

Mom's loss was different from ours; she was losing her partner of forty years. The man she created a life with from scratch, in a foreign country, with no other relatives but him, was fading. Their marriage may have been arranged, but their love was planned too, a deep bond divinely guided from start to finish. He was the only person who knew her struggles intimately, whose fibers wove into the depths of her sac-

---

[10] *Catching Your Breath in Grief: And Grace Will Lead You Home*. T. Attig. (2019). Breath of Life Publishing.

rifices, whose spirit intertwined with hers. While grieving, I craved to learn more about their life together before I was born, inquiring into the details I did not stop to ask while he was with us, filling in the gaps in our family's history. Most of the answers were revealed directly through my mother's grief, as fresh layers of stories spilled from her soul. And knowing she considered him as good a husband as we felt a father added a soothing ointment to my wounds.

My mother's challenges following his death were painful to watch, as entering widowhood carries a negative undertone in our culture. When I returned from India, she scolded me for buying her a bright-colored sari, stating, *Linita, I can't wear that now.* Her understanding of becoming a widow in our community stemmed from an instilled mindset at the age she grew in. Consequently, she refused to wear certain items, eat certain foods, or attend celebratory events that *weren't meant for widows*. She stopped attending functions altogether, affirming, *I won't go without your father.* Like many Indian women, she was stripped of her pleasures, shunned society, and felt society shun her. With time, my brother and I persuaded her to live as Dad would want her to live, but life for her had become, in her own words: *Like a wingless bird*; or, *living as though one hand has been cut off and the other remains useless.*

Her grief aged her. Her face was thinner, dulled, and filled with new wrinkles and creases that quickly formed after his demise. She ate very little, smiled less often, and slept even less. To this day, she cannot bring herself to sleep in their bed, being, *Too big and too lonely without him.* When she finally returned to work at the hospital where he died, she locked herself in the bathroom and cried. When my brother's and my grief lashed out, and their lack of parental dynamic stung her, she regretfully burst at the seams. For our sake, her acts of mourning mostly materialized in secret—during their regular nightly routine, in the late hours after her evening shift, sipping the tea *my brother* made for her and dreadfully missing her conversations with him.

Mom's grapple with Dad's foreboding death was the most visible. The day after receiving the tragic result was the only day she could not find the strength to return to the hospital. Later, she disclosed, *Before the doctor told me the news, I still had hope, Linita. I still thought he would come home.* The last ounce of her energy diminished alongside our crushed expectations. She needed to recover, to combat the repercussions that stemmed from the idea of living without him. I took the call, heard her voice, and encouraged her to stay home and rest. She recuperated by allowing herself to succumb to her emotions and sleeping a whole day away. The next day she rejoined us—*rejoined him*—never to leave his side again, not even for a second.

**Figure 26**
*A Girl's First Love*

# 26

## The Last Moment Between Father and Daughter

At last, no one else was in the room, a break from the swarm of people. As the forty-eight hours away from the culmination of my father's life closed in, selfishly, I wanted the time to myself. I left the room out of necessity only, and if someone overstayed their welcome, *as some do in these cases*, I politely asked them to leave. I needed to absorb the last of him without intrusion. Although well-intentioned, I was tired of being pacified with their false sense of security. *Don't worry, he will be fine. He will pull through and recover.* Except, *he won't*. Some timidly cast a rectifying shadow on the visible nature of his death, mistakenly substituting avoidance for hope. Even when the conclusive result stared us straight in the face, many turned a blind eye. Respectfully, I rebutted, *He's dying. I know that he is dying, and I'm trying to accept that. If you want to support me, then let me step into this truth.* Silence believed me.

Witnessing my father's slow but rapid death opened my eyes to a wider prevailing illness—the incessant need to infuse positivity into every situation we encounter, even when we have nothing positive to tell. Life can genuinely take a negative turn with no clear silver lining intact, *let it*. Death can teach us about the function of human suffering, *let it*. When death finally stops and knocks on the door, we have no choice but to open it; we have no choice but to allow the unwelcomed guest inside. In Indian culture, guests are treated and cared for as though we are taking care of God. And the presence of God entered my father's room long before the doctor told me it was time. When I leaned into this knowledge of death, the wisdom of life unfolded. By now, I had learned I could carry hope and acceptance at the same time.

I sat propped with my chin gently resting on the rise of my father's belly, my hand firmly holding his. Absorbed in our stillness, I watched as his automated breaths went in and out and wondered what the odds were of a machine keeping him alive forever. Dad had once again drifted somewhere far away, a place where he felt safe. I asked him once if those dreams revealed anything to him—*Yes, I'm going to get better*. I know now what *better* meant. His life was ending, a stage I had previously feared, dreaded, avoided, and neglected. Now, a gift to be savored—a transition I would not take lightly. A time when love was fully blossoming, peaking, spreading like wildfire between the living and the deceasing; a time of awe and magic and spiritual heightening. As frightening as these final moments were between us, they were equally the most meaningful of my life. If only the end of his days could last until the end of mine. If only we could have stayed in the *just* before.

My gaze shifted from his chest to the soft, elderly features of his face. I spared no effort memorizing every crease, wrinkle, and blemish that had formed on his matured skin. Then, noticing the length of his hair, I reminisced on the times I gave him a haircut, color, and clean shave. Gently examining the locks, I spoke in a convincing tone, *When you come home, we'll get you cleaned up, Dad*. I imagined him nodding. He always bragged to his friends, *My daughter is my barber*. Gladly, I came over and did as he asked, but deep down, I loved the tiny strands of grey hair that budded atop his nose and ears. They symbolized his power; the wisdom he gathered through the ages seeped through his pores. Witnessing my father age was a treasure I never took for granted, and with each year that passed, he became more heavenly. Now, I was in reverence of the man mirroring back to me—silver hairs blanketed his head like a white shawl used in prayer, and a thick matching beard grew around his breathing tube. For the first time, my father sported full facial hair. Mom hated it. But for some reason, my brother and I found comfort in the change. Perhaps for us, growth of *any kind* was a good thing.

Dad had beautiful, deep-set eyes. Sharp, yet soft, they were his defining characteristic. Sometimes, I can still feel their magic—when the full moon shines against a dark sky, I catch a *glimmer* of the luminescent spark that lived in my father's eyes. They were a window to his soul that gave me time-traveling abilities. The pain that lived in them, the struggles that accumulated over his lifetime, transferred to my body within seconds, leaving me capable of feeling his suffering directly. Because of this, I knew how to assuage his fears, particularly as his illness worsened. Often, I entered the room to find my father visibly agitated, his body shaking from head to toe. He had gotten into the pattern of suddenly waking from short, heavy sleep, severely distressed, and these abrupt sleep-wake cycles occurred in dozens, leaving others unsure of what was causing his angst. However, placing myself in his line of sight, reading the alarm in his eyes, *I could feel* the source of his anxiety. Gathering that his affliction stemmed from the uncertainty of where he was, I stationed myself at his bedside, knowing my touch would quell his fears. When panic emerged, I located his heart with the palm of my hand and gently patted his chest reassuringly. Post heart attack, the doctor informed me that by massaging his chest when he first complained of the pain, I might have kept my father alive—perhaps I thought I was doing the same now. Caressing his brow with the tips of my fingers, I subdued the storm that had stirred: *It's okay, Dad, you're okay. I'm here, you're in the hospital, but you're okay. I'm right here with you, and we are in the hospital.* Dad's desperate eyes found sanctuary in mine. He relaxed his body, communicating he understood. Within minutes, the cycle repeated.

Noticing his agitation had vanished, the nurse questioned, *How did you do that? We have been trying to calm him for the past hour.*

Without breaking eye contact with my father, my natural response flowed, *We've always been like this.*

My response was normal, natural, and necessary. My father relied on me for self-regulation; we were each a haven. Others became aware of this while he lay in the ICU, as they observed our interactions and took note of them. They mentioned that if I stepped out of his line of sight, my frightened father would scan the room until he found me. Then, catching a glimpse of me, he would breathe a sigh of relief and calm down.

Or when he could no longer engage verbally, they discovered we had a language of our own, suggesting in disbelief, *It's as though you two are communicating with your eyes.*

The uncommonness of this ability never struck me, *We've always been like that.*

Onlookers referred to my actions as inspiring, openly commenting on my persistence to tirelessly tend to my father's needs: *What's the secret to your strength? No matter how many times he wakes up scared and afraid, you are there to comfort and console him.*

The question mortified me. *Can't you feel the fear in his eyes? Doesn't it hurt you? Wouldn't you do the same for your dad?*

The short answer was no—not everyone had a dad like mine. But after watching us, two of my friends went home and mended their relationship with their fathers. And when they told me this, the rainbow of our story appeared. My heart swelled with gratitude for him, *for us*. Only after he died did the rarity of our connection fully register, as my soul ceaselessly went in search of him. Through this endless searching, I discovered a tie knotted beyond blood. I was not simply a good daughter performing my daughterly duties—I was one side of a flame who felt the light dimming. My body was not moving by sheer will alone; it moved to soothe the matching aches within my own bones. After watching both his children and his wife dote on him day and night, my father's friend revealed, *I learned more about your dad in these past few weeks than I have in our decade of friendship.* My father came into the world with nothing and left in the same manner, but still, he was the richest man I knew.

Awakening from the introspective meditation that had formed from watching my father, my issue surfaced, *How do I live without you, Dad?* I surveyed his movement, searching for his reply, but he lay motionless. My question had come too late; he could no longer give me an answer. Soon, I would have to navigate this world alone, companionless, without my one solid connection. A movie reel of our legendary storyline as father and daughter projected against the back of my mind, each scenario playing out smoothly. I gleaned the qualities and characteristics that made him a wonderful father, his actions consistently showing me unconditional love. And I recognized this man, lying on his deathbed, was my definition of the *perfect man*. All I had ever asked for was his brilliance, softness, humor, compassion, and profound ability to care for me with his whole heart. The man I had been searching for *everywhere* and *elsewhere* was with me all along. A sea of water emerged, carrying me toward my own revelation—a girl's definition of love is shaped by her first love, and my first love was my father.

With sincerity and softness, clutching his hand even tighter, the revelatory words came out: *I could have married you, Dad.* Reverting to my childhood insistence that I would never leave my father for another man, I stared at him in awe. Now, the second revelation followed suit. That, with his death, I would indeed fulfill my childhood promise.

***

*At twenty-seven, I decided to move out, a decision I knew would upset my parents greatly. It was not common for women in our culture to take this step and leave home, but the invisible hand had opened, revealing it was time. On the drive back from work, I repeated the mantra, "strengthen the bond, loosen the grip" as I did not want to hurt my parents. But the minute I delivered the news, their grave disappointment was evident. My mother immediately listed off her reasons why this was a bad idea. She spoke of abandoning them, abandoning culture and tradition, and abandoning the comfort and safety found at home. But still, I would not budge. My father's reaction was worse—he did not say anything at all.*

*I walked upstairs and sat on the bed beside him while he pretended to nap.*
  *"What do you think, Dad?"*
  *"It's not a good idea. You just started your Master's, and you won't be able to afford both your tuition and your living expenses."*
  *"You don't think I can manage both?"*
  *"No. If you leave, you will fail."*

*Those words "you will fail" had never left my father's mouth before. I was disheartened, but I would manage. I knew I had hurt him deeply.*

*A month went by, and out of respect for them, I stayed mute on the subject, causing my parents to brush off the possibility of me leaving. Instead, I formulated a plan on my own. And on the first day of June, I showed them the listings I had found online. When the day came to look at the apartments, I made sure to bring my father along. He stayed steel silent at each showing, but still, he performed a thorough inspection of the building. Even though he sulked about me leaving, he selected the final apartment.*

*A few days later, I picked him up to go furniture shopping. Our salesman was an older Pakistani uncle who took us to each showroom. Before choosing an item, I stopped, turned to my father, and asked, "What do you think of this one, Dad?" He refused to respond in words; he shook his head for 'no' or nodded 'yes' instead. For each purchase made, I sought his blessing first, involving him in the decision-making process. I wanted him to feel okay, to feel like he had control over the situation. He was hurting, but still, he selected all of the items with me.*

*The next day, I returned to the store to make a payment. Again, the same uncle from the previous day helped me.*

*As he waited for my transaction to go through, he enlightened me, "You know, I went home and told my wife about you."*

*Caught off guard, I questioned, "Really? What did you say?"*

*"I told her how a father and daughter came into my store and how I appreciated watching you interact with him. I described how much you loved him, how clearly I could see it, and how you wouldn't make any purchases without his input and approval. You know, I've lived in this country for twenty-five years, and yesterday was the first time I saw a daughter give her father that much love, devotion, and respect. It really touched me, and I felt like thanking you."*

*Struck by his compliment, I thanked him. I did not realize our bond had this effect on others or that they were even paying attention at all.*

*I went home and shared the heartwarming message with my dad, but his silent demeanor did not change. He was still overwhelmed with emotion at the thought of me leaving. But, over the next year, as he watched me bloom into an independent woman and excel, my father, himself, spoke of my accomplishments the loudest. As for the uncle, his astute observation reminded me that my love for my father would get us through the obstacle of separation—both back then and now.*

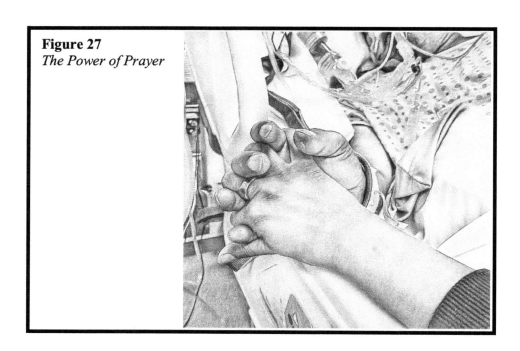

**Figure 27**
*The Power of Prayer*

# 27

## The Last Day

My father's fate was no longer in limbo; he was ready to cross over. His body moved into preparation mode before the ventilator was removed. As he sweated profusely, I tried regularly wiping his face, neck, and chest, but the drenched towels could not keep up. Then, in what felt like a nanosecond, the three of us had to finalize *when* to remove our loved one from life support. Keeping the doctor's forewarning at the front of our minds, we probably stretched the date of the extubation longer than we should have. But it is tormenting, convincing your mind to consent to the action that permits your loved one to die—a traumatizing decision. The pressure of the weight God must carry, tipping the scale of life toward death, is not meant for human hands.

Ironically, our readiness coincided with receiving the last inconclusive test result, which arrived on *Friday the 13th*. The fables, myths, and superstitions of an unlucky day would now depress under the weight of my father's death. As we gathered to listen to the next step of care, the double-edged words—*we will keep him as comfortable as possible*—eliminated all comfort from us. And when the time came to remove the tube, my mother and brother could not bear to watch. We had all heard the excruciating sounds of another patient's procedure from the day before. But I refused to let him go through the removal alone.

The walls of his room were whiter and brighter than I remembered, granting me a clear view of what was about to happen. I moved into my father's line of sight without creating interference for the nurses.

Securing his hand firmly, I steadied his anxieties. Caressing his forehead, restrained, I repeated, *You're okay, Dad, you're okay.* Glancing at the clock, I memorized the time—*1:40 P.M.*—marking the beginning of the end. My father squeezed my hand tight for the entire length of the tube—coughing, hacking, wheezing, rasping, *struggling*. Within minutes, he was liberated. But for the next twelve months, those sights and sounds would imprison me. My body's retaliation for my intentional choices formed the visuals of my trauma. For him, gladly, I would endure again.

The machine was unplugged and turned off, and Dad would have to breathe on his own, a *free will* he had already surrendered. The doctor's eyes met mine to remind me of his conditional term. I nodded but knew otherwise. My father was clear. He was ready to leave two weeks ago; he would not stay past *twenty-four* now. And a mere twelve hours later, barely brushing past the credulity of this bad omen of a day, I would prove our extrasensory perception to be accurate one last time.

What seemed like seconds after the ventilator came off, Mom barged in to shave the beard that my brother and I had grown fond of. The nurse, overhearing her comment daily that, *He was a clean-shaven man*, gave her the honors. Our family friends soon followed and gathered around him, making my brother uncomfortable. He vocalized his desire to limit the visitors, perhaps a humble request he sensed from our father, a private man. But his ask was a moot point. For the remainder of our father's *last day*, a bombardment of people stopped by. Family, close friends, community members, colleagues, and old students flooded in to say their final goodbye. Observing the continuous herd of people circulating through his room, the nurse commented, *Your dad must be a very special man to be loved by so many.*

An understatement.

\*\*\*

*Every night, at eight o'clock on the dot, my father religiously called out,*
*"Linita, come down. It's time to pray."*
*Dragging my feet, I joined him on the floor.*
*"Again? Why do we have to pray every day?"*

"*Because, Linita, a family that prays together, stays together.*"[11]
"*But it's just you and me.*"
"*We are enough. You won't understand the importance now; you are young and carefree. But as you get older, in times that matter, and when you reach the end of your life, having a strong relationship with God will make all the difference. Now, let's pray.*"

***

The time had come to perform my father's last rites. He partook in three separate ceremonies—two in his native tongue, Malayalam, and one in mine, English. The repetition of this ritual brought solace, a sense that he was leaving in the right way, a promise delivered through sacred words. I rose to my feet, watching the *anointing of the sick*, and listened intently to the sounds and sacraments responsible for cleansing my father's soul, not knowing, but *feeling*, them cleansing mine simultaneously. Unconscious, he wore a peaceful expression, absorbing the prayers wholeheartedly. I bowed my head but kept my head held high, strong in the knowledge that his faith was leading him safely to his next destination, a place more deserving of him. An odd sense of relief emerged through the understanding that no one would be able to hurt my father again. That, the goodness of his soul remained unconquerable. Witnessing these final blessings bring his life its rightful conclusion confirmed this truth for me, strengthening me at the same time they were relieving him. Knowing what these prayers meant for him, I tried to be courageous. I tried to emanate *Gandhi*'s definition of having an *indomitable will*, as taught to me by my father. Many commented on the quality of my strength, wishing they, too, could be strong like me. Yet, *strength* also comes disguised in robes, worn to mask our fear and, ultimately, our denial; flickers in the heart still attempt to spark the possible, even when the impossible is known. Truthfully, I was last to accept death's knock at my father's door.

---

11   *Al Scalpone*. (n.d.). Oxford Reference.

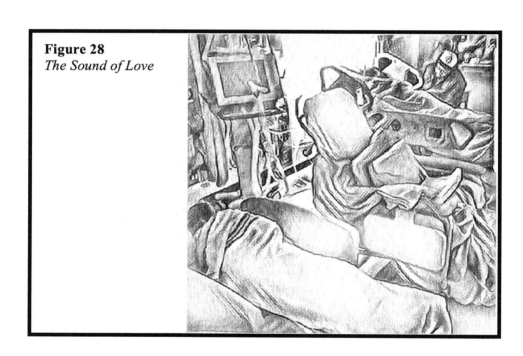

**Figure 28**
*The Sound of Love*

# 28

## The Last Night

An unrelenting hope rose from my chest, *Do you think there's still a chance? No, I don't think so. I'm sorry.* She looked away, responding earnestly. Intertwining my hands, I lowered my head. Her words blew past me.

The last visitor left us at midnight. Dad was right—*everything is planned accordingly.* This morning, my father's roommate transferred, leaving the room on this night solely for us. My brother, who had already gone home, returned an hour later, choosing this night to be the only evening he stayed over at the hospital. The *invisible hand* had intervened through a friend who convinced him to come back. Even in his death, Dad was intentional, and deferred his departure for *the four of us.*

I waited to enter the room to not disrupt the space gifted to a father and his son. My brother and I had not interacted since the big eruption in the family room. Thus, I crept in, avoiding his line of sight—not because I was upset with him, but because I did not want to *upset him.* I decided to initiate a service no one could find fault in; I massaged diabetic lotion onto my father's legs for the last time. My brother sat at the head of the bed, playing old, familiar songs for him, while Mom slept on the cot beside us, giving her children time with their dad. As the three of us quieted, each attending to my father's needs in our own way, the mood in the room shifted. A holy atmosphere crossed the threshold, permeating the space around us, exuding a feeling of serenity that granted us the ability to *accept the things we cannot change.*[12]

Obediently, I sat at the foot of the bed and applied lotion to his arms and legs. This task was a part of my higher calling, infusing humility, servitude, and love into my palms. Moving the lotion up and down, the thought of my hands no longer having purpose brought forward a rushing cascade. Bringing an ancient truth to life, *I wept on his feet as my hair brushed past, soaking the tears.* The holy atmosphere now transcended to pure transparency.

The songs my brother played were nostalgic, the same Malayalam melodies our dad used to play for us in our tiny apartment. The essence of our childhood danced through these tunes as snapshots of our life with him twirled alongside them. Thinking back on the simple pleasures our parents could afford to give us back then filled our hearts with gratitude for them. And now, when luxuries were more readily on hand, the only possession we needed all along was slipping through our fingers. In a cruel twist of fate, the scales were balancing.

My brother broke his silence, *Do you think he will die tonight?* He did not know I had asked the same question to my best friend an hour earlier, but mine spun on the chance of survival.

Surprisingly, a daft response came through, an uncontrollable reflex, *No, I think he will be okay.* Quickly changing the topic, I compared Dad's legs to *Beyoncé*'s, patting myself on the back for keeping them in such pristine condition. Humour, a reliable defense mechanism.

However, here, I opened the door for my brother to engage in this aspect of his health, *That's just it. Physically, he looks fine.*

Denial brewed between the both of us.

*\*\*\**

*A typical Saturday in my teenage years consisted of watching Indian movie marathons with my father. Storytelling is a prominent feature of our culture, and these stories overflowed with unrealistic plots, dramatic dialogue, extreme comedic relief, and colorful song and dance. The purpose of Indian cinema is to escape from one's own life for a short while. Dad and I—we broke free together.*

*Yawning, I tried to keep my eyes open for the second feature film, but it*

---

12 *The Serenity Prayer*. R. Niebuhr. (n.d.). Beliefnet.com.

## The Last Night

*was late, and the three-hour storyline made it hard to stay alert. Lazily, I slipped further and further down the couch. Until finally, I was fast asleep. Noticing I had dozed off, Dad walked over and shook me awake, "Molae, ezhnelkku—Daughter, wake up." Groggily, I murmured nonsense in my sleep. My father repeated himself, "Daughter, wake up and go sleep in your bed." The second warning gave rise to a few tosses and turns but stopped short of that. Firmly now, he stated, "Linita, I know you think if you stay down here, I will carry you, but I can't. I'm too old for that now. Soon, you will have to carry me." Grumpily, I got up, put one foot in front of the other, and made my way upstairs, burdened by the fact that my father had awoken me.*

***

A solid hour passed. I pushed my cot next to my father, and my brother set out to play one last song before retiring to bed. Listening to his playlist, it registered that *he, too,* knew Dad well. That, *they* had spent five years together, without me. Staying with this awareness would later soothe the tension between us. Tucking myself in, I fastened onto my father's arm and rested my heavy head on his shoulder. Satisfied, I shut my eyes.

*Molae, ezhnelkku—Daughter, wake up.* The words were lucid; my father called out to me in Malayalam. I jolted awake, surprised by what I had heard, and questioned the extraordinary experience. *Why did I hear Dad say that?* I looked to my left, but he lay on the bed unmoved, eyes closed and unconscious. I smiled at him, remembering the countless times he woke me from the couch after one of our movie marathons. Wishing to go back to those blissful days, I clung to his shoulder tighter than before and closed my eyes once more. Then, his resounding voice echoed again, *Molae, ezhnelkku—Daughter, wake up*. I opened my eyes but did not move. His sound was solidly faint—far but close, quick but slow, spoken but not uttered. *My mind must be playing tricks on me*, I settled. Determined to blame the illogical occurrence on my severe lack of sleep, I forced my eyes shut a third. Yet, just as I touched my head to his shoulder one last time, the nurse burst in. And in two words, our world shattered—*it's time.*

# Figure 29
*The Arrival of Dawn*

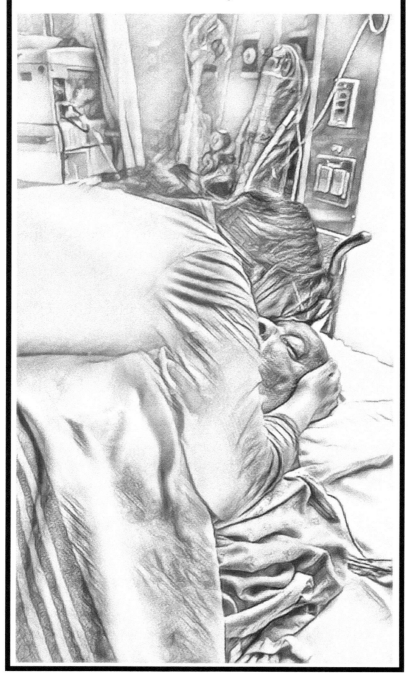

# 29

## The Last Breath

*A few months shy of eighteen, I traveled to Mexico with my church to build homes for less fortunate families. It was the first trip I took alone, independent of my parents, and I was beyond thrilled to go, raising the expenses on my own. When the day arrived, my father, mother, and close friend came to see me off. And after packing my belongings on the bus, I moved to part ways with them. Effortlessly, I said farewell to both my mom and my friend. But when the time came for me to say goodbye to my dad, suddenly, panic and alarm washed over me. Right then, it occurred to me that we were separating. That, for the first time in my life, I was choosing to be away from him. As a full-grown adult, I cried like a baby on his shoulder, and I continued sobbing all the way to Tijuana. People were astounded by the pain I felt leaving my father for only ten days. Imagine the toll it took on me when I had to say goodbye to him forever.*

***

"And Joseph's own hand shall close your eyes."

—Genesis 46:4

Understanding the finality that follows the words—*it's time*—the three of us sprang to our feet. My mother lost all color as she held her beloved's hand for the last time. My brother lost all hope as he looked down helplessly at our dying father. And—I—lost all control as the forceful feeling of terror swept over the rest of my senses. The woman who stood courageously tall for the last fifty-four days came crashing down, stripped to her core of *Daddy's little girl*. And this girl, who remained poised, calm, and quiet throughout his final days, generated the loudest uproar on his last one. In a split second, the soul-destroying mark of his death made itself known and punctured an infinite hole in my heart.

A painful explosion in the center of my chest caused me to scream in anguish, cycling one phrase *over* and *over* at the top of my lungs: *Oh my God! Dad, don't go! Please don't go!* Never had I begged someone to stay with me before, but on this night, relentlessly, wholeheartedly, I did. Cognizant in all respects of his desire to leave—*still*—I expended every last morsel of energy and pleaded with him. And as my grip on that whom I loved most was pried open, I clasped on as tight as humanly possible. Grabbing hold of both my father's arms, I shook him uncontrollably, determined to wake him back to life. But he was not responding to my touch—*for the first time*—my sway had no effect on him.

A sealed valve hidden in the abyss of my heart burst open, showering down on his body. Heavy tears flowed like freshly spun silk, wrapping him in a shroud. Quivering, shrieking, unraveling—I continued to shake him. *Please, Dad! Please don't leave me, please don't go!* My madness was unstoppable. Knowing this, my mother did not move me; she stayed silent, allowing me to come to terms with the source of my affliction. *Mom, I can't breathe! What's happening to me? I can't breathe!* The suffocation was unlike anything I had felt before, as though my spirit forcefully decided to leave with his. My brother stood behind me like a solid, sturdy statue; when the pinnacle part played out, we had switched places. Softly, striving to calm me, he spoke, *We have to let him go, Linita*. But I would not stand down. I screamed louder, attempting to latch onto my father's soul and hold his essence in place before he left entirely.

Yet, no use, no matter how powerful I am with words, I could not rewrite an ending already written.

A prolonged, hollowing breath released. *Five seconds, ten seconds, fifteen seconds*. Then, a second, shorter, sunken wheeze rattled. *Five seconds, ten seconds, fifteen seconds, twenty*. I collapsed onto my father's body, trembling, as only the word *no* came out. With ease, one final, liberating breath exhaled onto my right shoulder, causing me to lurch upright and exclaim, *He's still alive!*

But *he wasn't*. My father had merely saved his last breath for me, blessing me with all he had before he left. And, with this final act of love—He was gone.

***

*"One day, Linita, you will have to learn how to live without me."*

## ~A Year of Firsts~

*And, when he shall die,*

*Take him and cut him out in little stars,*

*And he will make the face of heaven so fine*

*That all the world will be in love with night*

*And pay no worship to the garish sun.*

—William Shakespeare, *Romeo and Juliet: Act III, sc. ii, 21–25*

**Figure 30**
*Empty Spaces*

# 30

## The First Night

The room went *dead* silent. Staring at my father's lifeless body, mine went terrifyingly numb. My eyes staggered back and forth—from mouth to belly, from belly to mouth—searching for breath. But for the first time, my routine check had failed. His belly no longer rose, and not another ounce of air came out. The desperation of my eyes—the seeking, the searching, the tremoring—stayed for a year. As my jaw dropped in disbelief, I caught the taste of something brand new to me. On this night, *the first night*, I tasted the sting of defeat.

Delicately, the nurse approached, offering my brother and me duplicates of our father's hospital bracelet, a warm gesture.

Distressed, I clung to the keepsake and naïvely posed a senseless question, *How did you know he was going to die?*

Recognizing my disorientation, she supported me, *His heart stopped on the monitor.* The equipment had been removed from our room, and it had not occurred to me that they were tracking his progress outside. I never regretted asking the question, but my remorse grew from hearing the answer. Those words—*his heart stopped*—haunted me long after. Softly, she continued, knowing one of us needed to borrow her lens, *It was one of the most beautiful deaths I have seen.*

Grasping at the speck of light that managed to squeeze into the entryway of our dark tunnel, my eyes widened as my heart, leaking hope, innocently inquired—*Really?*

She turned her eyes and met mine. *It isn't often that you see a patient in the ICU surrounded by his loved ones, dying while his daughter's head rests on his shoulder.*

Lowering my gaze to his body, I buried my face in my palms and wept.

*What was his time of death?* My mother's first words traveled in the nurse's direction.

Keen to keep track of each milestone, I, too quickly, responded, *1:40*, exactly twelve hours after the extubation.

However, this was the time I noted before collapsing on his chest. The nurse corrected me, shifting the clock to precisely 1:41 A.M., making his last breath—expired on me—his official time of death. The *invisible hand* tapped my shoulder, telling me to take notice. Spiritually, numbers have always been symbolic; I studied patterns as they appeared in my life and knew their meanings. Noting my father passed away on 14/1 at 1:41 felt like my first message from him. I understood that he had undergone a positive transformation, a new beginning, surrounded by angels. My father's voice echoed around me: *Linita, spiritually, I am always with you.* These numbers became the code I used to cut the key, which opened the door to communicating with him still, enabling me to continue a bond with my father.

We were given as much time as we needed with his body. As a family, we decided to stay until three o'clock, allotting space to gather our hearts off the floor and capture our last intimate moments with him. When my turn was over, I stepped into the side room, a home no longer ours, and took it upon myself to inform our family in India and close friends that he had died, sparing my mom the burden. The conversations were brief, as every time the words *he died* rolled off my tongue, my heart jumped upward and blocked my airway, preventing me from saying anything further. The suffocating notion traveled both ways, as the news delivered to those on the other end of the line left them stunned too.

The brewing anticipation of his loss and the stone-cold experience of death were two different pages of the same book, the latter lines causing a profound piece of me to slip away when he did. I had been anticipating his death for so long, for half my life, that when it finally happened, I was left speechless. And as I was transported to that liminal space, *the state of in-between*, utter shock overwhelmed me. I pulled out my cell phone, searched for the names of visitors who came to see my dad, and texted as many people as possible, informing them

## The First Night

*he died*. Almost uncontrollably, I hoped the more those two words flashed in front of me, the more my mind would believe he was gone. That I had just lost my father.

Packing our belongings, we were about to leave at the promised time when, to our surprise, our closest family friends, all of them, showed up. We were not expecting them to join us at three in the morning, but they did, ready and willing to bear our initial shock, mourn with us, and say goodbye to their beloved friend. This instinctual and instantaneous act of compassion directed at all four of us made a positive and impactful difference at the onset of our bereavement. When our world went dark, they brought their light, and this shining presence offered in the hour of our despair reinforced the life lost—*his life*—mattered. Gathered around my father as a larger group, his casing was sheltered, protected from harm's way. I felt his value emerge from head to toe.

After another hour, we prepared to leave him a second time. The spark of my soul, I touched my father's feet and held them firmly, taking his final blessings with me before leaving. But as I moved toward the door, a *holy spirit* came over me, preventing me from crossing over the threshold—an unfinished task was at hand.

Stopped in my tracks, I pivoted and returned to where my father lay peacefully. Raising my arms over him, I spread my palms and prayed, *Into Your hands, we commit his spirit.*

A force of finality ran through my veins as those witnessing concluded, *Amen.*

Now, he had closure—now, I could leave.

***

*After I graduated from high school and entered university, I was given more freedom to spread my wings. A young adult in my early twenties, I became a social butterfly, reaching the peak of my extroversion. I loved hanging out with my friends and getting lost in conversation. Yet, though Dad eased the ground rules, I still had to report to him on the hour—if he did not hear from me, surely, I heard from him. And for the twenty-six years I lived under my parents' roof, a curfew was enforced.*

*I crept up to the porch and looked through the window. The light was on, which meant my father stood guard. Slowly, I turned the knob on the handle and hid in the shadows of the entryway. As usual, Dad was sitting in his reading chair under a dimly lit lamp, waiting for me. Carefully, I removed my jacket and shoes and tiptoed to the edge of the staircase.*

*Gaining momentum, I made swift movements up the stairs and let out a rushed, "Goodnight, Dad."*

*Bringing his book down to his lap, he peered over his glasses and sternly inquired, "Do you know what time it is, Linita?"*

*I let out a sigh. I was way past my curfew and patiently awaited my earful. The lecture never changed—his words and warnings were standard. Sometimes, I made excuses; most of the time, I blamed someone else; rarely did I argue but never was I angry. I knew his actions were a measure of love and that our family only had each other. Until I returned home safe and sound, Dad would not be able to sleep.*

*Every single night, my father waited for me, stationed in his spot in the corner. And, as much as it scared me to walk in the door and face my consequences for being late, when the first night came that I entered our home and found his space devastatingly empty—I was terrified.*

*\*\*\**

The three of us drove separately, either accompanied or followed by our friends. We arrived back home, without my father, and entered the house of a *newly deceased person*. His vacant spaces stung me. I looked to my father's rocking chair for comfort, but it remained motionless like him. I looked to his empty reading chair in the corner, but the light was off, and he was not at his post, waiting for me. I walked over and placed the canvas of us, taken down from his hospital room, here. All of his books, belongings, and trinkets had lost their owner. Suddenly, the value of these meaningless items increased immeasurably. Replacing my father's warmth, a biting cold took over our home, chilling me to my bones. His bedroom, in particular, carried a crisp, arctic air for the first year of his passing; even after the rest of the house had stabilized, his room remained the same. Hints of metaphysical happenings were evident: in our family of electric candles, *one burnt out*; the clock in the living room beside my father's chair *stopped ticking*;

## The First Night

and the battery in his watch *died* the same night he did, leaving the date stuck on *14*.

Out of all the mysterious occurrences that ensued his death, the rarest sight we saw was the personification of sadness found among my father's plants. They were equally his children, he tended to them meticulously, and our house was filled from top to bottom with his greenery. But on the evening of his demise, their leaves drooped to the floor. My brother maintained their care while Dad was in the hospital, so a logical reason was lacking. The only rational explanation I could come up with was that they knew what had transpired—they knew their caregiver had died. Until this night, they stood sturdy and upright. But then, like the rest of his family, they wilted. And they, too, would take a long time to revive and look alive again.

The level of care infused through our social interactions immediately after my father's death made a difference. Whether it was the careful medical attention given by the ICU staff, the special permission we were granted to stay with him on his last night, the understanding of the nurse who took care of our aftershock, or the friends that woke in the middle of the night and drove across the city to share in our grief—every action mattered. At the pinnacle point of death, our tragedy was witnessed and our pain was held, teaching me to pass my presence onto the next person. The aspect of coming together to infuse a deeper level of empathy and compassion into a newly bereaved family secured that we would keep breathing, even after my father had stopped.

When the house went hauntingly silent, my mother walked to the closet and reached for a folded white bedsheet, seemingly awaiting her. Tearfully, she wafted the fabric, delicately spreading the linen across hers and my father's bed—a solemn reminder that his spiritual presence was tied to the earth still. She wore white cloth to start their fairy tale and initiate a life with him, and now, she used white cloth to close their chapter and enter widowhood.

This symbolic gesture spoke to the holiness of death, proclaiming the colors of our life had been covered. To remind us that the light of Christ illuminates our darkness, she kept an electronic candle burning beside the bed. These rituals signaled the commencement of our ceremonial fasting. For the next forty days, we could not sleep in this bed, consume alcohol, eat meat, initiate new projects, indulge, or celebrate.

Though the lives of others would keep turning, ours would not. Though the world kept spinning, ours was not.

**Figure 31**
*Grieving Together*

# 31

## The First Day

I startled awake on the couch at nine in the morning, not knowing when I had drifted. Moving forward, I would regularly wake in this fashion, as if trying to snap myself out of a terrible nightmare, one that would never end. The truth of my father's death remained incomprehensible to me, cross-wiring my nerve impulses and short-circuiting my brain's electrical activity. I sat up disorientated, feeling my body and surroundings were now unreal.

My sleepless mother was on the phone all morning, taking calls from those offering condolences, inquiring into the nature of his death. At times, she cried, other times she spoke softly, and every so often, she vented her frustration loudly, *Why are you calling now? He already died!* Her towering sorrow caused her to lash out, a warranted reaction. The underlying issue was that when some heard the news of my father's hospitalization, they did not take his condition seriously—a common problem for illnesses with no visible sign of distress or diagnosable symptoms. Even though I told her not to answer the phone begrudgingly, I did not reinforce my efforts to stop her. He was sick for fifty-four days. If they could not bother to visit or muster a phone call in that amount of time, *then why bother now?* The only plausible reason was to relieve their burrowing guilt.

The wrath of grief was sharp, stemming from losing our loved one unfairly. A molten fury rose in all three of us, twisting and tormenting our minds. Even now, when my father's loss stings me, it comes out in a disorderly and ill-tempered manner—an unstoppable force, moving without my consent, matching our choiceless matter. Still, I wish his death had not happened to us. I envy families intact, and I feel resentment toward those who abandoned me in my time of need. However, I rarely put this emotion on display; the anger merely festers inside and amplifies my perception of them. My heart does not allow grief's venom to snake-bite and poison another.

The most prominent, consistent, and noticeable rage exhaled from my brother. And though I have seen his anger plenty, this shade was different. This hue was deeper, but *softer*; clearer, but *masked*; explosive but *contained*, and inexplicable but *understandable*. Only grief has this capability to reveal an impassioned new layer of different emotions. Grief is not sadness, it is *intense* sorrow; grief is not longing, it is *intense* yearning; grief is not despair, it is *intense* desperation; and, grief is not hatred, it is *intense* anger. And my brother was intensely angry. As he clamored, any mention of funeral arrangements or burial plans had come too soon for him: *My father just died! It hasn't even been twenty-four hours yet! I need some time!* He was right, but time was also of the essence; like death, funerals do not wait for our acceptance. We pushed him to the edge of his comfort and forced him to make decisions he was not ready to take. Later, when reading about *male grief*, I learned his reactions were not out of the ordinary—they were pretty close to the textbook definition.

My phone exploded with condolences before my feet even touched the ground. Sifting through the messages, I responded, *thank you*, to as many of them as I could. Part of me was trying to reinforce positive grief mannerisms, while the rest had yet to believe my father had died. Grievers do that—they take care of others attending to them. My pain was so potent, *a raging fire*, I assumed those who came near me were burning too. I wanted to save them, so I desperately tried to douse the rising flames. Yet, soon, I would learn they were fireproof.

Unexpectedly, a call from my best friend popped on the screen. She worked at the hospital where my father lay admitted, and she took her break every day and visited with him. Today, she unknowingly fell into the same routine. However, upon reaching halfway to the ICU, the matter of his demise snuck up and struck her. Unable to control her grief, her manager let her go for the day, and now, she was on her way over.

## The First Day

Weary to the bone, my mother forced me to rise and eat my breakfast. Despairingly, I fixated on the empty seat at the head of the table, a painful hollowness filling my chest. Without taking my eyes off my father's chair, I sat in the vacant seat across from my best friend. My body was numb, drained of vitality, leaving me with no desire to eat. Avoiding the food in front of me, I used a fork to move the items back and forth on the plate. I darkened. An otherworldly sensation overpowered me; a feeling of being *here* but *not here* caused me to wonder, *am I still alive?* My physical body remained, but my spirit had left to search for him—and, recently, I learned a corpse with no soul barely breathes. I was fading. Exactly then, out of the corner of my eye, *someone* appeared. For a fleeting moment, sitting at the table, my spirit succeeded. And a visage I would recognize anywhere materialized.

Following the image intensely, I became increasingly invested in what I saw. A solid form, dressed in ash gray sweatpants and a half-zip blue pullover, sauntered the bend. My eyes widened to such an extent that my best friend took notice. Gradually, inch by inch, I rose from my chair and pointed in the direction of the kitchen island. Shockingly, I screamed, *Dad!* For one swift, split second, an enormous wave of relief washed over me as the notion that he died sincerely reversed in my mind. But just as fast as the mirage of his likeness came to life, the ephemeral vision vanished in equal measure. *Dad, he was just here. I saw him! He walked around the corner, right there, I saw him!* The eyes in the room stared at me in disbelief, saying nothing.

Detecting the truth of the fantasy, that it was all a figment of my imagination, I sank in my chair, distraught. Sobbing profusely, I shoveled food into my mouth, attempting to distract my tears from falling. Every so often, I mumbled, *Dad was here, I saw him.* Eventually, I would read multiple reports from grief researchers, confirming these hallucinations are associated with acute mourning. Seeing a loved one shortly after their demise is common and can be attributed to shock, desperation, or the griever's high attachment to the deceased.[13] A person's perceptions take time to match the knowledge of the death.

Whether the figure of my father was real or not remains a mystery to me. But catching a glimpse of my friend's steady expression as she sat watching me from across the table, one thing was evident—*she*

---

[13] *Bereavement: Studies of Grief in Adult Life, fourth ed.* C. Parkes & H. Prigerson. (2010). Penguin Books.

believed me.

***

*I sat in the passenger seat as my father drove to our destination.*
 *"Where are we going, Dad?"*
 *"A member of our community has died. We are going to their house for a prayer."*
 *"Will lots of people be there?"*
 *"Yes, I think so."*
 *"Why is the prayer different than the funeral?"*
 *"A prayer is immediate; it occurs on the same night of the death. The funeral remembers the life of the person and lays their body to rest, while the prayer gathers the community to guide their spirit, supporting their final journey. And right when a person dies is when their family needs their community the most. Nothing matters more than the support we give one another during a time of death—everything else is secondary."*

*We arrived at the house, and my father was right. The home was packed with people who came to pray for the deceased's soul. Christian hymns sounded, prayers recited, and my dad delivered a spiritual message to those who attended. I stood and watched as empathy spilled from him, his compassionate words comforting the crowd around him. Dad always used his knowledge and actions to support the common good, especially when it mattered most.*

***

By evening, our home was blessed with an abundance of condolences. The dining table overflowed with pictures, cards, flowers, and food, brought to us in our time of need. Any gesture, small or large, played a role in comforting us.

As the sun set on *the first day* of my father's death, our house filled with members of the Malayalee community and close family friends, ready and willing to carry my father's soul on their voices. Dad often brought me to these cultural prayers of mourning for others, and now, the unfathomable had occurred, and I was attending his. People gathered, wall-to-wall supporting us, expressing their love for my father, preventing our walls from collapsing. I tried to give them my full attention, but my mind was spinning and swirling around the same simple question. *Did he die?* Every second without him was surreal. But when the prayers began, I shoved the intrusive thoughts down, focusing solely on the words that would initiate the closing ceremonies of my father's physical life and the opening ceremonies of reaching his spiritual destination. The ritualistic chanting offered through select songs and prayer entered my core, acting as a spiritual grounding, *guiding his spirit upward*, bringing mine back into my body. I listened intently to the sounds and syllables responsible for transporting him, effecting a ceremonious closure. The smoke of burnt frankincense swayed through our home and wafted toward the ceiling, supplying a sensory experience to envision his journey. I closed my eyes, pictured my father, and allowed the community's prayers to wash over me, cleansing me for what came next.

The first prayer held the night after his death lived up to its expectations, providing immediate support and relief, a feeling that we were not alone, and a knowing that this is how he would have wanted the evening to be. The next day, after the prayer concluded and the funeral arrangements became clearer, I decided the time had come to announce *my father's death*. Using Facebook as the outlet, reaching family and friends worldwide, I sat down and allowed the pen to flow freely. I inhaled, I exhaled, and I poured the most intimate contents of my heart onto the page:

> *My father's last breath was taken at 1:41 A.M. January 14th, 2017. At that exact moment, the essence of my heart left my body. An unbearable emptiness replaced it instead. And, for the first time, I do not have the ability to put that pain into words. I have no doubt this essence will not return, as he took it with him—that's okay, Dad, it belonged to you anyway.*
>
> *Not for one moment did I doubt the power of your prayers. The hundreds of messages of love and compassion received were so cherished. Unfortunately, there is an indomitable strength that resides in my own prayer—and I prayed for his suffering to end. God has the habit of granting me whatever I ask for; in this way, I am blessed.*
>
> *I can have no regrets of how his last days were spent. Being a woman of service, I was granted the gift of caring for my father over the course of 54 days. I went beyond my own understanding of service and felt a strong presence as though I was*

*caring for God himself. As the scripture says, in the book of Matthew no less: "For I was hungry and you gave me something to eat, I was thirsty and you gave me something to drink, I was a stranger and you invited me in, I needed clothes and you clothed me, I was sick and you looked after me, I was in prison and you came to visit with me... Truly I tell you, whatever you did for one of the least of these brothers and sisters of mine, you did for me."*[14] *I did for my father what any daughter can only aspire to do for theirs. The memories acquired over these 54 days will take me through till the end of mine.*

*My beautiful journey with my father was a true honor placed upon me by God. We walked hand-in-hand, but I always lagged a little behind, learning to be his shadow. Because of this, in the end, I had the perfect view as my eyes witnessed a genuine transition from man to angel—no resistance, no struggle, without suffering. Now, he will no longer walk in front of me leading the way. Now, he will walk alongside me, revealing it.*

*Rest in peace, my sweet, sweet father. My eyes refuse to stop searching for you. I feel their hope and suffering wishing to see you again. And they will once more—when my work here is done.*

---

[14] *Matthew 25:35–40*. New International Version Bible. (1973). New International Version Bible Online.

**Figure 32**
*Picture Perfect*

# 32

## The First Confrontation of Changing Family Dynamics

The week leading up to the funeral was nothing short of frantic. If we lived in India, the funeral arrangements would have been in the hands of the community. But since we were burying my father here, we were thrown into a bombardment of decisions that needed to be made and needed to be made *now*. Unfortunately, we were the family with no prearranged plans for death, and an array of decisions weighed heavy as we stood on the quicksand of loss. We needed to inform the church; purchase a burial plot; pick out a headstone; pick out a casket; pick out a vault for the casket; meet with the funeral director and choose the necessary prearrangements; meet with our priest to discuss the format of the service, and receive spiritual guidance; arrange pictures for a slideshow; arrange food to be catered after the service; arrange money to cover the costs of the outrageous expenses; write the obituary; write our eulogies; and, somewhere in between all of this—we needed to come to terms with the fact that he died.

***

*Dad and I did not spend much time apart. Even after I moved ten minutes down the road, I called him twice a day, every day, visiting multiple times throughout the week. And when I spent ten days in a nearby city marking government exams, I taught him how to FaceTime to manage our separation. But because of my work hours, the conversations were usually cut short. So, naturally, we made plans for my return.*

*Driving back into the city, I picked up my father and took him for lunch at our usual spot. Dad, who was typically quiet and reserved, talked nonstop for hours. I let him divulge to his heart's content, and when a reasonable break formed, I inquired into the reason.*

*Jokingly, I fished, "You're talkative today, Dad. Did you not talk to anyone else while I was gone?"*

*Subtly, he replied, "No. When you aren't here, I don't feel much like talking. I can't have these kinds of meaningful and intellectual conversations with others. So, I stay silent."*

*I knew he was trying to make me laugh, but I also knew he spoke his truth. And his truth and mine are the same.*

\*\*\*

Thankfully, members of our community surrounded us, offering their support in organizing the material aspects of the funeral. Driving us from one place to the next, they accompanied us to our appointments and helped finalize the financial expenses. Because my father turned seventy-one for *nine* days, most of his insurance policies became null and void. Fortunately, one safety measure survived the age cap, assisting with costs that would have otherwise buried us in debt alongside him.

Moving from one establishment to the next, my brother was the most uneasy on these unfamiliar grounds; for him, the funeral parlor was *too cold* and *too eerie*, exacerbating his anger. To help *him* feel more comfortable, my mother consistently and specifically, directed the choices, such as selecting the design of the casket and vault, toward his opinions—and his only. Culturally, the eldest son usually makes these decisions, but I was used to a father who made no such distinctions. *If Dad were here, he would ask me*, I thought. But he was not. And now, I had to live with this new system shunting me.

A more prominent understanding of our invisible, changing family dynamic surfaced, pushing me under in the process. I was much *unlike* and *separate* from the other two; my attributes intertwined solely with my father's. I was also quiet and not as vocal as them, both *pre-* and *post-*loss, unconsciously melding me into the background. My quietness was then mistakenly labeled as strength, and because I was viewed as *the strong one*, most people coddled my brother and left me to fend for myself. But now, my counterpart had died, and the feeling of aloneness and separateness expanded by the second. And contrary to popular belief, this was when I needed their support the most. Yet, what started as two fingers of a hand, eventually shaped into two full fists that strangled and suffocated me as this sense of isolation moved beyond my mother and brother and dispersed into the larger world.

At times, I wondered if I had made more of a fuss, or if my mourning was more visible, *would the intensity of my grief had gone so unnoticed?* Other times, I wondered, *if it was me who died, and this was my hell*, a life without my father and a story of no recognition. Sensing I was the shorter side of a freshly formed isosceles triangle, I became visibly upset. And as these irritations continued to fester, the mounting pressure between my mother and me only worsened. In the middle of one of our heated arguments, she accused me of purposely distancing myself from them, deepening a wedge she claimed she knew I would drive. She could not see that the void always existed, that my father bridged the gap. And now, I would have to move my feet on my own—without him holding my hand, lovingly walking me toward them. Even though I had committed to sleep at the house for that first week of loss, her spousal sorrow, and my overprotectiveness of my father, brought me back to my apartment in less than three days.

The shape of one's grief molds long before a loved one dies—my father, the potter, coiled the clay. The twists and turns in the entanglement of loss stemmed from each of our experiences with him, continuously pulling from the family dynamic as we once were. Thus, our unique relationship with him manifested paths of mourning that were trilaterally different. My brother's bruises left him angry at *everyone*; my mother's heartache left her angry at *my father*, and my stifling despair left me angry at *them*. The sorrow for all three of us was moving in different directions, and so, for the time being, it was best for us to do the same.

Because of the distressing change in our family system, I funneled all of my energy into planning the intimate details of the service, ensuring they aligned with my father's unsaid wishes. Sitting at my desk, I cried out words that formed an obituary. And although his death notice was one of the most challenging pieces I have had to write, summarizing my father's life *just right* brought immense healing. Ritual, through writing, permitted my body to shed the first layer of pain, and writing it out was therapeutic.

*Eapen Mathew, born January 5$^{th}$, 1946, peacefully passed away on January 14$^{th}$, 2017, at the tender age of 71. Born in Kerala, India, as the son of Dr. M.J. Mathew & Mariamma Mathew. He is the third oldest of nine living siblings. Eapen continues to be loved dearly by his wife, Mary Mathew, and his two children, Lincy and Linita.*

*Eapen was a gentle soul who enjoyed the simple pleasures in life—gardening, reading, writing, and going for walks. He spoke very little, but when he spoke, everybody stopped to listen. He was an educator at heart and spread his knowledge wherever he went. While in India, he received a double Master's degree in Economics and English, and was teaching at a college in Bhopal. In 1978, Eapen traveled across the seas to Newfoundland to marry his soulmate with whom he would share 38 wonderful years. Upon moving to Calgary, together, they would build a small, tight-knit community of friends who then turned into family.*

*Eapen Mathew was a parishioner at St. Peter's Anglican Church for 35 years. He devoted many years to the Bible Study Fellowship Men's Program as both student and leader. Eapen thoroughly enjoyed his involvement with Calgary Toastmasters in which he earned several awards, including the highest achievement of DTM in 2006. He volunteered much of his time in schools and around the community, always lending a helping hand to those in need. Eapen, a proud Calgarian, was awarded for his volunteer efforts through the office of Immigration Services. Eapen's inspirational soul, pure heart, and humble nature will be missed and cherished among all those who were blessed to have loved him.*

*Relatives and friends are invited to pay their respects at St. Peter's Anglican Church in Calgary on Saturday, January 21$^{st}$, 2017, at 11:30 A.M. Funeral services will be held at St. Peter's Anglican Church on Saturday, January 21$^{st}$, 2017, at 1:00 P.M. Eapen will be laid to rest at Mountain View Memorial Gardens. Photos, memories, and condolences may be shared with Eapen's family through the funeral services' website. By donating to The Canadian Diabetes Association, together, we can continue on Eapen's legacy of generous acts of service. A special thank you to the ICU medical staff for their loving care and support during Eapen's stay.*

The obituary, coupled with my eulogy, was a turning point, allowing me to absorb the positive correlation between writing and grieving.

And, as a bonus, when my mother and brother read my words, the sharp edges of our three-person triangle softened. Gradually, I understood that when grief is the trigger, a family turns on each other, and then, with time, they turn to each other.

Continuing the creative process, in consultation with the priest, I chose from memory the readings, poems, and songs for the service I knew my father loved. With each selection I made, his voice reassured me, *You always know what I'm thinking.* Then, with help from the funeral director, I finalized the design of the memorial pamphlet, verifying Dad's images aligned perfectly with the prose. Choosing these pictures was difficult as my favorite photos were now also a symbol of his death. And, saving the most arduous task for last, I worked through the night until four in the morning, putting the finishing touches on the slideshow, memorializing him. I had gathered and organized these photos on my computer shortly before his extubation, amid the doctor's forewarning. Now, with my brother's input for the serenades, I created a visual story responsible for narrating our father's life in the span of seven minutes. As daunting as the task was, the emotional eyes of the congregation told me I had succeeded. And the tears in my own affirmed his story was visible.

In the ongoing debate of whether a funeral is needed, my advice is this—truthfully, the funeral is not for the person who *left us*—the funeral is for those *left behind*. With each decision made, each choice that takes priority over the other, and each creation that tells a story, our lost loved one springs forward, takes our hand in theirs, and heals us. During the chaos of tragedy, organizing my father's funeral service brought a structure that settled me. And while replacing a funeral with a *celebration of life* can be a beautiful tribute to death, we must walk the fine line carefully. Choosing one over the other, hoping to remove the element of sadness from loss, hinders us from fully experiencing a crucial emotion associated with death. And the more we surrender to our suffering, the more joy awaits us on the other side of healing.

In due course, with hard work, dedication, and ongoing persistence, I learned to open a door to my mother and brother, discovering that a different layer of love exists with them. I grasped that my immediate family held a key and, depending on how it turned, either alleviated or aggravated my grief. And as we moved past our initial conflicts, I tried my best to turn toward alleviation.

Our love for each other grew through our combined experiences with loss and grief. My mother was given a rare opportunity to take back the countless hours lost with her children, the time she sacrificed to support us financially; my brother was able to empathize with us more easily, connecting through stories of our father; and I discovered that by bringing my walls down and letting others see the true rippling effect of grief, writing became a therapeutic tool that provided healing for all three of us.

**Figure 33**
*My Father's Funeral*

*Note.* Photos courtesy of Riana Lisbeth Studios @rianalisbeth

# 33

## The First Funeral and the First Burial

January 21, 2017—Today is my father's funeral. Awake, the words washed over me as I planted my feet firmly on the floor, initiating the steps I needed to take to get through my first milestone without him. My brother selected the date of the twenty-first because it fell on the same number as his birthday, and he felt this was promising. He was right, making it so that my father was *born* on a Saturday, *died* on a Saturday, and *buried* on a Saturday.

Sunday, the day of rest, was nearing.

Staying in the shower longer than I should have, I permitted the warm water to embrace me, to comfort and calm me. Within this timeframe existed my only moment of solitude—to be still and silent as needed—before facing the agonizing trial of today. I was not opposed to crying at *my father's funeral*, but I knew if I drew tears from his well, they would not run dry. And today, I needed to fulfill my obligations as his daughter without wailing like I was his daughter. The fifty-four days of turmoil we endured boiled down to this. I paused, I prayed, and I asked God to allow me to embody my father's spirit, the epitome of unbreakable strength. He listened, and without hesitation—He granted my request.

Shutting off the water, I got out of the shower and dressed for *my father's funeral*. My bereavement consisted of repeating phrases, ideas, and concepts, emphasizing truths my mind could not grasp. Certain parts of his death would not penetrate the deeper level of my consciousness and lay unreachable from me. And so, I repeated them *over* and *over* and *over* again—to my grieving family, to my fading friends, to attentive strangers—until they moved closer and clicked. The trauma of my grief was beginning to show, but only to those who were brave enough to talk to me directly, and their courage earned my respect early in my mourning period.

Glancing at my phone, two types of messages appeared. Some offered spiritual sustenance, preparing me for the day ahead—and they did. Others offered weak excuses, not meaning to hurt me—but *they did*. Scrolling through the texts, I was subjected to menial reasons and unconvincing rationalizations that prevented a person from attending *my father's funeral*. At the time, I was numb to the messages and tossed my phone aside. But later, when I revisited their ignorance, I resented them. What better time to salt a person's wounds than the morning of the funeral? The Earth *did* rotate seven times in between. *Sorry, I can't make it; I already had plans today*—I am sorry my father's death was an inconvenience to you. Grief's intense resentment cut through staggering friendships that perhaps lingered too long anyway. Brené Brown's research is accurate—*funerals do matter*—and not attending one creates mistrust of the absent person.[15] For me, this was instantaneous.

Dressed in the black and gold salwar kameez purchased the day I found out my father was not going to make it, I garnered protection wearing his jewelry, wore my hair down straight the way he liked it, slipped on a black pair of heels, and headed in the direction of our family's home. Pulling onto the driveway, suddenly, our loss felt real. And, crossing the threshold, everything felt like a movie, *literally*. A videographer was present to film the funeral so that our family back home could witness the day. Living abroad, this was common to record the service and burial; I partook in my grandparents' final ceremonies through the television. Later, I realized that viewing the recording was as crucial for me as it was for them. The day itself flew by, leaving me no time to process fine details. But on his death anniversary, I rewatch the service and absorb those things that swerved past me back then. I can witness the love and affection received from others, the interactions between the people who gathered, the facial expressions of those listening to our eulogies, and my courageous reactions and responses to losing my father. By paying attention and being present in a dif-

---

15 *Braving the Wilderness: The Quest for True Belonging and the Courage to Stand Alone*. B. Brown. (2017). Random House.

ferent way, I feel grateful for the beauty that did bloom that day. That said, my brother still cannot bring himself to watch the recording, and that is fine too.

Dad's final *yatra*, or journey, was inaugurated from our home. My mother set the wheels of his chariot in motion, singing songs and reciting prayers in our native tongue. I listened to her requests of the Lord to *guide His son* and reinforced them through my thoughts, hoping to manifest a seamless transition. Her cousin and his family bound to us, offering strength and support. So, thankfully, we traveled to the church as eight and not three.

Outside, a black limousine waited to take us to *my father's funeral*. And staring from afar, an old memory pushed its way to the front of my mind, carrying his voice forward: *I always wanted to be chauffeured in a limousine.* My eyes welled at the thought that my father's wish came true, yet, tragically, only while transporting his deceased body to his funeral.

My father's final moments would have been different in India. We would have washed his body and dressed him in pure, white clothing. He would have been carried in a glass carriage from our home directly to the church, crossing significant spiritual landmarks along the way as we walked alongside him, guarding both sides. Instead, he reunited with us in the chapel, missing the cultural significance of the final procession. I sat in the car, fixated on his body. An uncomfortable feeling of separateness emerged; he was alone and unprotected, leaving me vulnerable. But, *what could I do?* He had forfeited his security long ago in exchange for mine, and here, I had to return the sentiment.

Throughout the trip to the church, the same question—*what will he look like?*—ran through my mind. It was not the service, the people, or the speech that made me nervous—it was seeing my father's dead body. From a young age, I insisted the first corpse I saw would be that of a family member, so approaching the venue, I lacked the skill set to cope with this brutal blow. I knew the appearance of his face alone would cause my soul to split and my heart to rupture. That, I would lose all control over my faculties. Walking in, I reminisced on my bond with the building—I was baptized, confirmed, and grew up here. I had lifelong memories steeped in these walls. But now, viewing Dad lying lifeless in an open casket would trump them all.

Respectfully, we gave our mother, *Dad's beloved*, precedency in line. Gently, her hands went to his face and cupped his cheeks as though trying to keep him in place. She touched her forehead to his chest and begged him to stay, spilling her grief in tears. Then, she held him firmly, squeezing the last bit of love she could give him in this lifetime and stepped aside.

Fearfully, I moved forward, and as expected, I fell apart. At first, I was startled; a body lay there, but not my father's. Examining the corpse closely, I could see how others were mistaken. But I was not fooled by the imitation, and for a few seconds, a bearable scenario of irrational thoughts ensued: *That's not my dad. I can get through this because that is not him; this looks nothing like him.* My heart cast my mind aside like a jilted lover.

Gradually, the wrinkles, creases, and blemishes I had earlier memorized shone through. I squinted my eyes to adjust to his light—and slowly, I saw it was him. Caressing the top of his head and wiping his brow like I did all those days in the hospital, I felt his ice-cold skin and cracked. Immediately, I rubbed my palms against his arms and chest, trying to spark warmth. Yet, once again, I had failed; his daughter's touch was unable to render him heat. I put my cheek down to his forehead, but our heart-to-heart signal was no longer active. Still, I released one last wave from my end, *I love you, Dad*, and then, I, too, shaken, stepped aside.

My brother went last, shuffling toward him in small steps. Surprised by who he found lying inside the casket, he, too, was struck by the changed appearance of the father who had loved him unconditionally for the past thirty-six years. The look on his face matched that of a person who unsuccessfully attempted to revive someone. The frozen edge of Dad's skin shocked my brother's senses, so he put his head down, released his tears, and joined my mother and me on the bench. The three of us sat on the right side of the man we loved deeply, unsure of our ability to let him go.

Before opening the doors to the public, we held a small service for close family and friends in the chapel. My brother read my father's favorite passage, *Psalm 23*, while I read one of his favorite poems, *Daffodils*.[16] The selection was a secondary choice, as Robert Frost's—*Stop-*

---

16 *I Wandered Lonely as a Cloud*. W. Wordsworth. (1807). Poetryfoundation.org.

*ping by Woods on a Snowy Evening*—was being read in the service. And though I knew Frost's brilliance well, it had been a long while since I had heard my father recite the lines of Wordsworth. As I read the verses, the uncanny resemblance of the character's mannerisms to those of my father's unexpectedly tugged at my heartstrings.

Dad's wisdom was unparalleled. His life taught him to walk with but little material wealth; instead, he treasured the simple joys that an ordinary life offered. He was the one *wandering lonely as a cloud* among those who could not find value in his role as a househusband, a man who did not earn a living. Yet, rather than complaining, desiring more, backlashing, turning bitter, or numbing himself—he turned inward, to nature, and God. When he pondered more deeply upon his fate, *his heart with pleasures filled* in the beauty made visible around him. Stumbling on the real reason why the metaphor resonated with my father, seconds into the reading, I wept. My brother offered to finish the poem for me, but I persisted, knowing I had to get to the end of the character's fate myself. With each line that brought Dad's likeness to life, I paused and allowed the depth of his sweet soul to sink in, weeping some more. When I finished, I folded the paper in four and tucked the lyric into the left chest pocket of his suit coat alongside our family picture, burying a few of his favorite things with him.

My brother and I stood at the entryway of the chapel, receiving condolences from others, witnessing a continuous stream of farewells brush past us. Mom did not budge from Dad's side. People from all faiths entered and made the sign of the cross in front of my father's body—in death, we are equal. Before closing the casket, his rings were removed and placed in a small, suede pouch handed to my mother. Next, the priest held out her palms and blessed my father. Last, my brother, the eldest son, stepped forward and performed a final Indian Christian ritual. Covering Dad's face with a white cloth ensured his dignity was preserved, emphasized the purity of his transitioning soul, and marked him with an emblem for the second coming of Christ. The lid lowered, the casket sealed, and the last glimpse of our beloved was gone.

Exiting the chapel, I was overwhelmed with emotion at the sight of the attendees. The church pews were filled to the brim, overflowing into the lobby and spilling over into the upper hall. The day progressed rapidly, a blur. But I remember the faces of those who took the time to attend. I remember the solid efforts made to pay their respects to my father. Their attendance had little to do with supporting me and everything to do with honoring their love and loyalty to him. Every person was a measure of my father's love, like rays of sun stretching to usher in the dawn.

Eapen Mathew was a man of principles. His life followed stringent moral conduct that suited his spiritually sensitive nature. Before beginning any task, he made sure to read the instructions and followed them carefully, firmly believing one must do things the right way. He taught me, *Ellathinum oru reethiyundu—There is a correct way to approach everything*. Heeding his advice, I planned the funeral using the same format, meticulously scanning each detail that went into his final ceremony. I structured my eulogy the way he would have wanted, acknowledging God, his parents, his family, and his life because of them—in that order. Truthfully, I wrote my tribute while he was still alive, during the silent moments we shared in his hospital room, over those last forty-eight hours together.

Dad was a teacher, a natural-born speaker who delivered spiritual messages at religious events in Canada and India. Because of the abrupt onset of his illness, I wanted to channel his words of wisdom, not bury his essence with him. I waited for opportune, tranquil pauses when only the two of us were present. And wedged into the corner, I grabbed my laptop, listened closely, and wrote. The words formed were his; they were too beautiful to be mine. Hence, I knew I could not deliver his last lecture without breaking down. Accordingly, my best friend and I found an isolated area where I could read my eulogy to her first. My tears overtook me, the sounds stuck in my throat, and I barely managed to squeeze out the end. But, by surrendering to his life lessons that first time, I was prepared to uplift them a second. I was ready to deliver his final message without fail. And the person who needed to hear my father's words the most was my brother.

Our cortège consisted of family members and close friends; a long line of loyal people who loved my father dearly walked behind him. Together, we entered the narthex to one of my father's favorite hymns, "Nearer, My God, to Thee", whose lyrics broke through a barrier I had brought up in my system. We followed him the length of the narrow nave, gliding behind his casket, covered by a white, holy sheet, symbolizing the purity of his departure. Dad stopped front and center of the golden protruding cross while we took our place on the left-hand side of the church, near his usual seat. Sometimes, *still*, his casket rests there, unmoved.

His children, we summed our affection for our father through our eulogies, a last attempt to embody, share, and process the love he had for us—and that we had for him. Being firstborn, my brother went first. I sat back and listened to his speech, recited from memory. He summarized our father's greatness using anecdotes that conveyed how lucky we were to have had him as a devoted father and husband. His eulogy was vibrant, encapsulating Dad's humor, wit, and lighthearted spirit. The congregation was left in an uproar of laughter, leaving me squirmy and nervous, pondering, *my eulogy isn't funny at all*. Yet, ending on an emotional note, he set me up perfectly:

> *In the end, my dad took every ounce of his strength and held onto my hand. When people tell me that my dad is lucky to meet all those famous people in heaven, I say they are lucky to meet you, Dad.*

Silent, I searched for my father's face in the crowd, but he was no longer in front of me. He was to the left of me and behind me. Breathing in, steadying myself, I began. To set the tone, I quoted Shakespeare's metaphor of undying love—*of dying and stargazing*—advising how our paths will converge with his now. Next, I touched on my father's background and spoke of his family, upbringing, and education. Then, my protective nature kicked in, laying my father's struggles bare, opening the minds of the congregation to his sacrifices. With restrained firmness, I brought his trials and tribulations to the table, explaining how he survived the judgment of others by putting his children first. Last, I touched the center of their hearts using my father's own wisdom, a solution to conquer loss. To conclude, I affirmed that through it all, and in the end, today was a celebration of his victory, returning among the angels where he belongs. The laughter vanished, the congregation quieted, and not a dry eye survived my tribute to my father.

Even in our speeches, my brother and I differed. But our dynamic together, as siblings, provided the whole picture of who our father was. Moving to close the service, we sang a traditional Malayalam farewell song, *Samayam Radhathil Njan*, alluding to his beautiful journey home. And when the service concluded, Dad led the procession once more, exiting his church for the last time.

Although the act of love may seem small, those who attended Dad's funeral played a significant role in our family's ability to reconcile our loss. During the reception that followed, many approached us and shared stories of him, some of which were brand new to me:

> Your dad helped me find a job; your dad gave me a connection within the community; your dad prayed for me when I needed it; your dad visited me when I was sick; your dad helped me when I first came to this country; your dad saved my life when I was on a dangerous path, I'm indebted to him.

The last testimonial came from a person who sat beside my father's bedside and cried, a man I had never even met before. Dad was too humble, too quiet, and too private—a lot of these examples heralding his good deeds only came forward in the last few days of his life. And when bordering bereavement, an insatiable ache appears, accompanying the griever everywhere, a wish to have asked more, and a desire to uncover the hidden aspects of a loved one's life. Yet, no matter how hard I searched for these answers on my own, it was only through socially interacting with others that I could piece and weave narratives, filling my void. Those who attended not only shared their presence and personal stories but confirmed *his* presence also. And that recognition of Dad's spirit appearing as the guest of honor was the ethereal element that got me through *my father's funeral*.

Before rushing to the cemetery, we thanked as many people as possible, grateful for their witnesses.

Transitioning quickly, we made it to the burial site on time and performed the last tradition of the day. Despite being mid-January, the weather was ideal, and the extreme cold held off to avoid interfering with our customs. The sun was shining, and the ground was soft enough for us to permanently lay my father to rest, permitting our journey of the bereaved to continue in an orderly fashion. The divine effort that materialized did not surprise me.

The gathering at the graveside was intimate, and we welcomed this. The three of us spoke our final goodbyes before Dad descended.

Peering out at the sun, placing my palm on his wooden casket, I mustered a few words on the spot:

> *I'm the woman I am today because of you, Dad. Thank you for loving us more than you loved yourself and giving us everything you had to give. We will see you again—one day.*

The priest recited the Book of Common Prayer, pouring sand on my father's coffin, bringing the earth to earth, ashes to ashes, dust to dust imagery to life. As the casket inched further underground, long-stemmed white roses adorned him. His grave left a visible mound of dirt for all to see—communicating that, *yes, he is lying under the earth.* Before we left his resting place, the three of us each received one of four metal crosses; the fourth one, attached to his casket, remains with him.

Although losing my father was agonizingly painful, his closing ceremony was spiritually sound. In hindsight, my father's funeral was a perfect day, embodying the truth, beauty, and goodness of a life well lived.

***

*My Father's Last Lecture (My Eulogy)*

*And, when he shall die,*

*Take him and cut him out in little stars,*

*And he will make the face of heaven so fine*

*That all the world will be in love with night*

*And pay no worship to the garish sun.*

—William Shakespeare

*It was at this very lectern that I first began speaking in public. I was around the age of seven. My brother came to practice as a new lector for our church services. While he was reading, I turned to my father and asked him if I could read too. My father walked over to our instructor and said, "My daughter would also like to read the scriptures." She asked him if he thought I was ready to start at such a young age. Fearlessly confident, my father responded, "Anything my son can do, my daughter can do too." And just like that, I became St. Peter's youngest lector. This would be the first of many fearlessly confident moments my father would have in my abilities.*

*Today, I have the obligation as a daughter to deliver a powerful and transformational message. I must epitomize a man for whom no words can truly depict in his entirety. My vision is not only to tell you who he was but also to vividly paint a picture of his essence. And so, may God guide my words and deliver his final message, from my father's heart to yours.*

*Eapen Patchamkulam Mathew, the son of Dr. M.J. and Mariamma Mathew, was born and raised in Kerala, India. He was the third-oldest of nine children—favorite below and now favorite above, the first one they called up. He obtained a double Master's degree in Education and Economics and taught pre-degree studies at a college in Bhopal. Not only was he a brilliant man, but he was also genuinely a kind human being with a fiercely good heart.*

*My father was my mentor and guide. He was more than a father—he was also a mother, a brother, a sister, my best friend, and confidant. His life was filled with silent struggles and, at times, criticized by others for his choices. During a time when work could not be found, he decided that it was God's will for him to stay home and take care of his children. This decision was not always socially or culturally accepted.*

*I became very overprotective of my father. They did not see the gentle care and concentrated attention my father gave us. They did not see my father wake up every morning to make our lunches and get us ready for school. They did not see him waiting with us at the bus stop in freezing temperatures and waiting once more when we arrived back home. They did not see him sit at the table with us and help us complete our homework, and then assign us his own set of questions. I learned of Chaucer and Shakespeare and Whitman and Frost—I could recite poems and verses as a small child. They did not know how he brought culture into our lives. They did not see him feed us, bathe us, and tell us stories until we fell asleep, night after night, day after day, year after year. And when they made comments that would hurt my father's feelings, I would sit on his lap, and he would say,*

## The First Funeral and the First Burial

*"I am blessed to spend all of my time, hours, and days with you."* It became my most comforting habit to sit with him in silence, ignoring the rest of the world, simply enjoying each other's company. This therapeutic act of healing would benefit us both until his final breath. This would be how we made it through his final days, energized in our own silent company.

My father was not a showy man or needing merit—his life taught him how to survive on very little credit if any at all. He raised me to be humble, to be grateful, to be God-fearing, and to always do what I can to help those around me. It prides me to say that his very last act was an act of service.

On December 28$^{th}$, 2016, at 5:30 A.M. my father spoke his final words to me:

> Linita, are you awake? Come here. What is today's date? Write it down. What time is it? Carefully watch the time. Do not neglect the words I am telling you today—because today, I am going to die. I have met God. He told me my time has come, and I will not live. God told me to go back and prepare the girl—she is having a hard time. If you do not prepare her, she will suffer greatly. Linita, I am going to die. Why are you crying? Look at me, I am not worried. I am sorry I cannot cry with you; I no longer feel emotion. Where I am going, it is not needed. I want to be with God. It is your choice to keep me here. Never worry for me, daughter; I am happy to be with God. Everything is planned accordingly. Look how beautiful God is—look how He gave my last moments to you. That is how I wanted it to be. The beauty of a daughter belongs to her father. Linita, even if I die physically—spiritually, I am always with you. Stay by my side today. Today, do not go anywhere.

I stayed. Within twenty-four hours, my father would be rushed to the ICU. And this would end up being our last intimate conversation as father and daughter.

Millions of beautiful stories are shared between a father and his daughter, and our story is no different. Ours is a story meant to give hope, inspiration, and promise that God's pure and unconditional love does exist—and we were merely a living example through which it was told.

In our lifetime, we will cross paths with many different types of relationships—acquaintances, friendships, and close bonds. Beyond the physical knowing, there will be spiritual knowing as well. We will feel a deep con-

*nection with another, and we will refer to that person as our soul mate, whether it be a mother, father, sibling, friend, or spouse.*

*Yet, even still, if we reach beyond the realm of soul mates, there exists a bond so inexplicable and rare that words cannot contain it, a relationship known as a twin flame. My father and I reside here—one flame, separated by two bodies. Twin flames appear identical in nature and, when brought together, fan flames so vibrant that their energy is felt by all. Some search their entire lives and never experience this kind of relationship. I was so blessed that I was born and placed directly into his hands.*

*I considered my father God's best-kept secret, a fountain of wealth and knowledge accessible to me at any time, my problem solver. He would not only listen but listen deeply. He would not only respond but engage from soul to soul. My father would walk me through multiple paths to a solution: the scientific, the logical, and the always last, spiritual. "You have to find the root cause of your suffering to eliminate it, Linita." Ironically enough, toward the end of his journey, the root cause of his suffering remained undisclosed. I like to imagine that this was the way the universe balanced itself.*

*And so today, because he is no longer here, I would like to share my problem with all of you instead. The root cause of my suffering, of our suffering today, is that I have lost my father; collectively, we have lost a wise counsel and best friend. I have no ear to turn to, no lap to sit on, and no belly to lay my head upon. I, myself, must bring forth my father's comfort for all of us as though he, himself, were giving us an answer.*

*Here's what my father would have said:*

> *If we approach the situation from a scientific perspective, Linita, I have surpassed a pinnacle age and reached seventy-one. It is not old, but it is not young either. I have multiple health issues that are counteracting my recovery. When one issue is resolved, another issue begins, and these complications keep my chances slim. Listen to what the doctors are saying—they are educated, have experience, and are trying their best, even though we know they are puzzled by my illness. Unfortunately, the scope of science is limited, and you may not receive a definite answer. That is okay because I have raised you to understand life beyond the limitations of science. There*

*are two dates already written for us that science can monitor but not control: the day we are born, and the day that we die.*

*So then, Linita, let's approach the situation from a logical perspective. You were well aware of my signs and symptoms long ago. You noted the times I failed to recognize familiar faces. You saw my weariness and extreme tiredness when I fell asleep mid-conversation with you. You silently observed my decline at the hospital—first, I stopped walking, then I stopped eating, then my consciousness began to fluctuate. You saw a steady deterioration through a rational sequence of events that led to my death. But, still, I know you, this answer will not ease your suffering. You will search deeper to find a more meaningful answer.*

*And when you search deeper, you will exhaust yourself with the possibilities. Then, you will finally look at death through a spiritual lens. Here, you will see that death, in fact, does not exist at all; it is merely an illusion. When we live life through the human perspective, we suffer because death becomes something definite. Our need for instant gratification, now, will no longer be met. You will not be able to pick up the phone and hear my voice on the other end; you will not be able to run into the house and see me sitting in my chair, and you will not be able to place your hand in mine and feel comfort. This is how you perceive the meaning of death—the loss of instant gratification. Instantly, I will no longer be there.*

*Linita, a spiritually aware person, does not need instant gratification. They know that, just like the body, it will only be temporary. Search beneath the layers of the body, and you will find me still, alive, and well. If you take the time to quiet the noise around you, you will hear me guiding you. If you take the time to block out all other distractions, I will appear before you. If you bring your hand to the center of your heart and wait, you will feel me comforting you. Because Linita, even if I die physically—spiritually, I am always with you. And, when you forget, I will leave gentle reminders along the way.*

**My father's advice is always straight and simple because it is in the simple pleasures where we find our loved ones again. In the simple joys, we find the presence of God.**

*This is the magic of a twin flame. I feel the pain on the side of my light that has dimmed, but by mastering patience, he will burn brightly through me. I carry my father as a torch inside of me. And, when the time comes when you, too, feel his light is missing, I invite you to sit with me, and once again, you will feel his presence in mine. He fought with my mother to name me—Linita Eapen Mathew—and now, in between my name is where he remains.*

*When my father realized medical hope was lost, he said, "And so you see Linita, my illness will remain unknown. In the ongoing battle between God and science—God always wins."*

*My father celebrated God's victory, and so should we. His son, Eapen Mathew, has returned home—among the angels—where he belongs. And today, I celebrate my father's victory over his suffering, Hallelujah!*

**Figure 34**
*A Spiritual Sanctuary*

# 34

## The First Trip to India

During the early hours of a winter morning in January, I sat upright at a ninety-degree angle on the couch of the ICU family room, contemplating the *right* steps forward. My father's death was pending; the profound loss had not happened yet, but I knew it was upon us. And, auspiciously, I wanted to make sure I performed my spiritual and religious duties, as emphasized in Indian culture. The sacred rites and rituals undertaken during the designated mourning period are some of the most ancient eastern traditions that exist, where rituals are the wooden planks laid down for the deceased to walk on, bridging their peaceful passage into the afterlife. Thus, the night before he died, I turned to my mother and announced, *I'll go to India after the funeral*. Nineteen years had passed since my last trip with my father, and this would be my first time traveling to the country alone. And despite being in my thirties and living on my own, my mother's overprotectiveness continued to hover over me. But I was adamant, knowing one of us had to go. Understanding the importance of the longstanding traditions and family awaiting us back home, she agreed. Besides, I would still be accompanied by my father, albeit in different form.

From the second I decided to go until the minute I arrived back in Canada, every step sailed smoothly. I booked my ticket within a day, and my rushed travel visa landed on my doorstep a few days before takeoff. The *invisible hand* was as in control of the journey as I was. Mom struggled with leaving me at the airport, and her call rang through at each Indian home I visited as soon as I entered. I could not blame her; the anxiety and dread that had spiked from losing her husband would take time to settle. Yet, I was not anxious at all, fearless energy circulated through me. My greatest fear grew around my father's death, so I had nothing left to lose. Wearing his shawl, I moved forward confidently, knowing his protection cloaked me.

Before boarding, I sat in an isolated row of chairs close to the gate. For the first time since his death, I was alone. I was freed from the people, the shackles of caregiving that forced me to witness his slow demise, the endless responsibilities tied to his funeral, and from the intentional distractions created through my work. For a few fleeting minutes, a psychological break from the relentless effort to save him materialized. Then, all at once, the rising thought—*he died*—sunk in. At last, the turbulent waters of grief smashed through the walls of a cracked dam, barely holding me together.

Bursting open, waves of water washed over me, baptizing bereavement, releasing the toxins of loss. These heavy rains fell for the entire length of the journey—two days of travel, two layovers, and twenty-three hours of flight time. I cried sitting down; I cried standing up; I cried on the plane; I cried watching Indian movies on the plane; I cried pointing to the endless reminders of him, passing my view; I cried helping an *ammachi* (elderly grandmother) buckle her seatbelt, sparking memories of the infinite times I buckled his; and I cried when I landed and India's warm air brushed his spirit over me. Giving in to grief's wanderlust, I succumbed to my sadness and surrendered to processing my father's death in his birthplace.

As I stepped onto the soil, Dad's embrace welcomed me to his homeland. Though the spirit is transparent, it reveals itself on the ground where it sprouted. I sensed him, and I detected him instantly. I was so accustomed to removing his boots and tending his feet that now I received the honor of watching my father step into my guardian angel's shoes directly. And from the onset of this spiritual pilgrimage, his warmth accompanied me. *He's here*, I thought. *If I can feel him this strongly, then maybe, death isn't as final as I thought.*

Navigating the motherland, I learned of the multiple truths of this phenomenon—of sensing a loved one's presence. However, upon returning home, I grasped my one misconception. Even though my father's essence remains with me, his spark was the strongest, as per our custom, during those first forty days. After the ascension of spirit took place, profoundly feeling him only came in waves. Nevertheless, throughout the initial stages of my grief, being surrounded by his soul soothed me.

Dad's youngest brother retrieved me from the airport. Two decades had passed since we last saw each other, but we communicated regularly. On the car ride home, I caught us searching for my father in the other. Our ancestral home was three hours away, so I sat back and absorbed the sights and sounds of India. I was born in Canada, but my heart is divided by this country. Perhaps it was because my ancestors originated from this land; or because my parents were traditionally sound in our upbringing. Regardless, I was adamant about keeping our cultural practices intact, which was easy to do as a Canadian. I read Indian literature, cooked Indian food, watched Indian cinema, learned Indian classical dance, listened to Indian music, and strongly understood the various cultures, languages, religions, and traditional practices in both the northern and southern regions. It was not an instilled love; it was a rooted love.

Visiting as a child, I remember feeling a deep sense of belonging as though my spirit had finally returned home. An aunty of mine hit the hammer on the head when, after seeing a westerner adjust too easily to their way of life, suggested: *Mol vere oru janmam ivide janichathu arrikum—You must have been born here in some other lifetime, daughter.* Her statement resounded to the bone. It was not an external attachment but an intimate knowing, as each time I deplane, a spiritual extraction occurs, rising to the surface. *How could anyone not feel a sense of spirituality in India?* The practice is settled in her soil, nourished through her roots, grown into her stems, and released into the very air we breathe. When my father's death destroyed me, I chose the proper place to mend my spirit.

*Keralam, land of coconut trees*—gave birth to my ancestors. My mother and father were born here, raised here, and bound to each other's spirit *here*. Gazing outward, the natural beauty of the state enchanted me. The palm-lined beaches, lush hill stations, and stretches of still, emerald backwaters exuded healing. Gazing inward, I ascertained, *I will be okay, I'm safe in the hands of God's Own Country.* My eyes and ears moved with the Malayalee peoples, speaking the Dravidian language, Malayalam; interacting amicably with one another; and practicing their respective traditions with religious freedom. I often awoke to the prayers of Christians, Hindus, and Muslims, blaring through the traveling loudspeakers or stationed in the streets. The strength of the spiritual sounds and vivid vibrations of multiple prayers from multiple faiths traveling to heaven provided a vehicle for me to meet with my father once more. Spiritual healing, which I found essential for my grief, protruded from every nook and cranny of Kerala. Hence, not only did I engage in the rituals laid out for my arrival, I actively created and executed my own as well.

*Appachan*'s (grandfather's) house was already a sacred sanctuary for me, a home that carried generations worth of my family's love. My grandfather, Dr. M.J. Mathew, was respected and disciplined in nature; everyone rose to their feet when he walked into the room. He was a well-known family physician who dually specialized in Ayurveda, healing many under his roof. Often, I gathered around relatives, eager to hear old stories of people lined down the street, waiting to see him. Legend has it he could diagnose a person *just* by looking at them. Due to his stroke, before my last visit, we could not communicate at length. But I was a perfect companion for my grandfather—I was good at being *still* and *silent*. Appachan and I sat on the front porch for hours, immersed in silence, watching the downpour of the monsoon rains, absorbing the meditative qualities that accompanied them.

Gaining his trust in this way, soon, he let me follow him everywhere, asking me to assist him with various tasks, leaving others surprised by his quick taking to me. I was not shocked at all. Like my father, I won him over with my ability to enjoy quietude; essentially, the three of us were the same, calm and quiet, and he recognized that. We only spent a few short months together, but we had a special bond. He was my father's *father*, and I doted on him for this reason alone. I observed him eating by himself, and I befriended him. I grew fond of him and became overly attached to him. His loss was my first painful experience with grief, and on *his* death anniversary, my father fell ill. Reminiscing on the cross my father bore after Appachan died, I understood now why he grieved his dad so deeply—I am the one carrying the weight of that torch now. And for the first time since their deaths, I returned to the place that solidified our transgenerational tie. That front porch, for me, symbolized the settling of the storm.

Every morning, before the break of dawn, I awoke and made use of the space that already carried a restorative element of healing for me. Swaddled in my father's shawl, I grabbed his picture from the mantle and kept him beside me as I took my seat on my grandfather's throne. The love and spiritual energy of two fathers surrounded me. And, with one on either side, before anyone else could interrupt the flow, I leaned into their shoulders and cried. Using this self-made ritual, I stretched to the spirits of my ancestors to console me. Their warmth derived from the rising sun slowed the tsunami within. And when the ceremony closed and I had extracted as much solace as I could, I looked in time to see a white butterfly dance across my path and land on the wall to the right of me. A good omen, I practiced this act of intentional crying in a structured and repetitive way every morning for all three trips to India over the next two years. I freed my pain by bringing attention to my concentrated sorrow, embedding it into a solid routine, and then allowing for release.

Soon after my arrival, we held the seventh-day *Aradhana* (communal worship) in the *Kudumbum* (ancestral home). I walked outside into a constructed space and saw rows of red chairs that would soon fill in memory of my father. Due to the vital weight placed on communal grieving, my understanding of community solidified from the sureness that these seats would not stay empty. I watched as priests, relatives, church members, and nearby neighbors flocked to bring my father's soul peace.

Traditionally, women sit on the floor, but since I was the guest of honor, my uncles guided me to take a seat among the men—synonymous with how my father raised me. As it would turn out, my placement aligned with Dad's picture, resting on the mantle above. And when the prayer started, I felt a strong pull coming from the direction of his visage. A warm gush of energy descended from the top of my head to the bottom of my toes, carrying his voice forward: *I chose you to be here. That is how I wanted it to be.* Acknowledging a message that mirrored our last conversation, a well of water poured forth. My father's uncle, who sat next to me, noticed the tempestuous storm and held my hand firmly, *Karayenda, molae, njangal ninte kude illae? Don't cry, daughter, are we not with you?* Not having had a lot of physical contact with my relatives, I did not realize how deeply their touch would console me. A profound sense of comfort arose from mourning the loss of my father among his own flesh and blood.

Embedded within the religious structure of the ceremony were moments to pause and reflect on Dad's life. His eldest brother recounted stories of who he was in childhood while I supplemented the knowledge of who he became into adulthood. Our synergy painted a life more visibly whole, embellishing a story of loss *I could* reconcile. As I spoke of my father in Malayalam, the nostalgia of hearing him speak, and the depression of never hearing him again, struck me. Choking back the whirlwind, I managed to deliver a summary of his life, ending on the note of my one firm truth—*Pappa ente etovum adutha suhurthu aayirunnu. Dad was the closest friend I had.* Now, the funnel fell. Deconstructing our relationship in his mother tongue reached deep into the cellar of my stomach, uprooting sheltered sentiments. And when the tornado of tears dispersed, we fulfilled our ritual. Afterward, those who attended sat down and shared a vegetarian meal. Then, when the seventh-day prayer concluded, something lifted.

That night, I fell ill. But it was not the common cold or flu I was used to—for three days, my body drenched in sweat, leaving me weak and bedridden. Lying still, trying to sleep off my sickness, scenes of my father's body preparing for death, and my inability to soak the sweat from his system, resurfaced. Notably, I was going through a similar transition, mimicking his process. However, I was not preparing for death; I transformed to live anew. I was purging and purifying toxins produced by grief, perspiring a girl I no longer knew. And when the third day passed, I felt born again, reset, and ready to relearn my identity.[17]

In honor of my *late* father, I was responsible for enhancing the lives of those less fortunate than us. Accordingly, our charitable acts must embody the humility of loss, infusing a relentless reminder that we are all equal in the eyes of God. In Canada, we made traditional monetary donations in my father's name. While in India, these acts of giving continued, but the emphasis differed as a reciprocal relationship between the griever and receiver was necessary.

First, I gifted a golden chalice and paten for Eucharist to my father's church, and by handing these items from my hands to the priest, Dad's devoutness persists. A sense of him living through me arose. The

---

17 *How We Grieve: Relearning the World.* T. Attig. (2011). Oxford University Press.

priest received liturgical vessels to feed the congregation, and I received blessings to sustain my mourning. Next, I visited an old age orphanage and treated the residents to an afternoon lunch, sitting down to share the meal with them. The abandonment of these *appachans* (grandfathers) and *ammachis* (grandmothers) hurt me, and a looming sadness lingered. Images of me tending to my father spun as I wondered, *who would leave their parents like this?* A flicker in the dark, bolded Malayalam lettering caught my eye. Turning to my uncle, I asked him what the message on the board read—his response, *In Memory of Eapen Mathew*. The residents received my father's love, and I received onus. Last, I purchased a month's worth of groceries for a low-income family in our neighborhood, hand-delivering the items to their door. As I entered the small living space of a single mother and her two children, our tiny, two-bedroom apartment flashed through my mind, seemingly not so small anymore. They received nourishment, and I received perspective as to why my father brought me here. I awakened.

Most of the rituals were communal, but some were private also. A few weeks into my trip, my uncle brought me to a famous church in Kerala known for its healing power. He informed me that people journeyed long and far to ask for forgiveness in this sanctuary. That, anything I asked for here, *would be forgiven*. My mind zoned in, pinpointing a specific situation eating away at me for some time, a rare occasion when I had gotten upset with my father. Some years back, I had picked up Dad from home, intending to take him for his daily walk. While sitting in the car, he made a small request to stop at the store that sold diabetic socks, footwear I had previously purchased for him. My patience wore thin; I became short with him, irritated by my earlier warning that we would not have time to make this specific stop. In the end, I *did* take him to the store, but once his sock shopping was over, I drove him back home without going on our walk.

Kneeling in the scorching sand, I bowed my head to the ground at the foot of a flaming cross and begged my father for forgiveness. *Dad, I'm sorry about the diabetic socks! Please forgive me!* Instantaneously, an emotional upheaval surged to the surface, blocking all common sense from me. My uncle had no idea that *this* is what caused *that*. The matter was trivial and mundane, but my selfish actions tortured me. I did not realize a small situation would leave such large, gaping holes in my soul. Yet, grief alters the mind; even when the relationship I had with my father amounted to sheer perfection, my sorrow-filled spirit clung to the tiniest action and amplified my self-image into that of a monster. Grief's intense guilt found a way to punish me. But now I stood on sacred ground, a holy place where many had sought forgiveness before, and many will come in search of it after, offering me redemption. A crucial element to the power of rituals, aged for centuries, the structured repetition reinforces and elicits a mystical, reparative vibration.[18] And as I lit the candle that burned my guilt away, the incessant and intrusive murmurs spotlighting my selfishness around the diabetic sock incident reduced to ashes. I am not sure how my remorse eased—I only know *it did*. A candle, *a symbol of light*, provided a means to bring distressing aspects of my grief out from the shadows, lessening my pain. The materials required to sew ourselves back together post-loss reside within. Rituals merely task us with committing to reach inward and pull the thread through the eye of the needle, so we can suture our wounds and recover.

The social interactions that emerged from my trek through India were mostly beneficial for reconciling my grief. Escaping the hometown that held memories of my father's death was not only welcomed but helpful for my healing, as specific spaces stung me deeply. Eventually, I would have to find my way through those parts of the city I avoided—the long stretch of road, the hospitals, the coffee shop, our restaurant. But for now, certain freedom existed in being far away, limiting my ability to relive the trauma encountered with spatial triggers. Instead, I spent quality time with my relatives on my mother and father's side. I recounted the story of his death and watched the funeral numerous times, strengthening my mind's ability to process the events. I visited my grandparents' resting places, auspiciously asking for their blessings before birthing a new life. And, at times, I shared my struggles with our morphing family openly and honestly, without worrying about the backlash or judgment that came from disclosing kin conflicts. I had found myself in a home away from home.

Yet not all cultural exchanges were seamless. Because my father was not of ripe old age to die, often, family members needed a clear and concrete reason behind his death, a solid diagnosis I could not give

---

18 *The Wild Edge of Sorrow: Rituals of Renewal and the Sacred Work of Grief.* F. Weller. (2015). North Atlantic Books.

them. Every so often, the blame fell on our family for not attending carefully to his needs. Alternatively, it was determined that our lack of a true relationship with God brought calamity to our household. Respectful, though crushed, I tolerated the noise for my father as visuals of the three of us working tirelessly to keep him alive played through my mind. Setting our story of loss aside, a full account of where his life should have taken him was detailed, without empathizing with the challenges of migrating to a foreign country. The knowledge that he was the most educated in the family, but remained unemployed in Canada, *still* managed to slide its way into conversations. Conflicting ideologies of how one should regard death and the deceased made it hard for me to hear situations I had long ago surrendered, circumstances I did not feel I needed to control. For me, this was the epitome of having a confident relationship with God.

Last, and perhaps the most frustrating, I was faced with relatives who took it upon themselves to question my past and settle my future—specifically, in the area of marriage. With my father's death came an ongoing, somewhat shaming, cultural invasion of privacy. *He died before seeing your wedding. Don't let your mother suffer the same fate.* My stomach churned, my chest deflated as though I had been convicted of a criminal offense—which being thirty-one and single was equivalent to in their eyes. Being an independent Canadian woman, I was not used to being called a *spinster* or forced into making hasty decisions about choosing a partner.

A month before Dad's health declined, we broached the subject ourselves after the *invisible hand* nudged me to return to school. I left my fate in my father's hands, allowing him to choose which direction I traveled, education or marriage. Straightaway, he responded,

> *Linita, you have time to get married, complete your doctorate first. Now is the right time to finish your education and fulfill what you set out to do. If you start your family, it will be harder for you. Once you have children, you won't leave them.*

His wisdom grew from his experiences. Consequently, whenever painful exchanges regarding my life choices were brought to the table, my father's firm guidance trumped their criticisms. My chest inflated, knowing God deliberately chose this man as my father. A man who placed my higher calling at the forefront of our decisions. Without a doubt, I trusted him. And thankfully, I listened. *Thankfully*, he left knowing I had initiated the steps to achieving his dream. In terms of my grief—*the girl would have suffered greatly*, had he left without knowing that much.

\*\*\*

*The year was 1997. My father and I were boarding a train in Mumbai, making our way back to his brother's house after a day of sightseeing and shopping. Since I was born and brought up in Canada, I was sheltered from the experience about to unfold.*

*Patiently awaiting our train on the platform, the vehicle arrived in a flash. My father hoisted me onto the cart within seconds and hurriedly got on himself. Then, out of nowhere and at lightning speed, thousands of bodies ravaged their way onto the railcar. Mumbaikars crammed, trying to fit in every crevice, even climbing and sitting on top of the train. My dad, ready to rumble, instantly pushed his way to the back wall and domed over me. The men standing around pushed back, shoving him, visibly jabbing his arms, back, and sides. I stood still, closing my eyes, waiting for the moment to pass. And, in the forty-five minutes it took to reach our destination, not a scratch befell my body.*

*My father, my human shield, protected me from suffering at the hands of the herds.*

\*\*\*

I entered my father's home, *right foot first* like he taught me. I reunited with his brothers and broke bread with them. We held a memorial prayer together, and I spoke of his goodness and immeasurable worth in his native tongue. I gifted his church, sanctifying his memory, and partook in their holy communion. I traveled to Bangalore and spent time with his sister so that she could feel closure after his death. I sat with the hungry and fed them in his honor. And before leaving, I filled the room with his strong presence, quiet composure, and subtle sense of humor. When Dad humbled me in the hospital—*as long as you are in the room, I feel at peace*—I prayed these deeds, overflowing with love, were examples of me still staying in the room with him.

## The First Trip to India

The truth of my father's statement was always visible; he calmed at the sight of me. But the extent of that verity, the requited dynamic, was only disclosed to me later. As I navigated through a world without him, it was I who no longer sensed peace. Aimless, I searched for my father, craving to hear him call for me, *Linita, molae—Linita, daughter*, again. I yearned for the sound of his voice, his comforting touch, to engage in our meaningful conversations, and to see his glorious smile once more. His physical absence was profound, drying my eyes like drought. And secondary losses of the simple, everyday, taken-for-granted things were killing me slowly.

Then, when I was in Kerala, the land that comforted me when no one else could, my father was found. Astonishing, ephemeral moments materialized. When one brother called me *molae* (daughter), my father's voice echoed through the house. When another conversed with me endlessly, my father's wisdom carried through their words. When one smiled or laughed at their *dad jokes*, my father's mannerisms fleeted by. When one reached out and held my hand, my father's palms replicated. When one reminded me that my dad is with me *even now*, my father's final message rang loud and clear. The countless catchphrases and witty comments that all nine siblings share made my heart leap to join in with my father's clever sarcasm again. And when I watched as they wept and fought the outcome of his death—*Oru urambine polum novikathilla. He wouldn't even hurt an ant*—they gave voice to my feelings of injustice. The stories they shared and the visible sadness that spread over their faces while thinking of his loss penetrated and uplifted my heart, resounding loudly, *he mattered*. They felt his loss as I did. Quickly, I realized as each of his siblings aged and entered various stages of life, the sting of his death would resurface; my father would resurrect and die once more. Nonetheless, I reveled in the beautiful ability to experience someone's physical presence after they died. Adapting to this, my father's promise beyond doubt revived: *Physically, I will no longer be here, but spiritually, I am always with you.*

To perform our death rituals, I visited India twice that year. Culturally, the first year of mourning is prescribed in a way that lessens the load on the soul. With every tradition I partook in, my cosmic understanding grew. Ritualistic ceremonies allowed my spiritual ache to transform into something tangible, and by translating my grief into human action, I found a way to let my suffering go. Moreover, the practice of communal grieving fortified me; I found a community that would accompany my prolonged grief long-term. My extended family lit a lamp, then, encircling me, they prevented the light from leaving.

Before I left, I placed my aunty's arm on my lap, stretching, examining, and memorizing her features as I did with my father. My tears streamed with the same painful consistency as they did then. The fragility of life and the quickness of loss were no longer a secret to me. I no longer knew who would live to see another day—I only knew my time with my loved ones was precious. And moving forward, the impermanence of life would no longer elude me.

Grieving in the home where my father grew, I felt his child-like spirit running wildly through those halls; he was free from the body that caused him affliction. Returning to Canada, after the evening prayer on the *nalpathu divasam* (fortieth day), marking the ascension of spirit, we folded the white sheet on my father's bed and placed it under his pillow. In the physical act of *folding the sheet* and *putting it away*, I felt catharsis, a liberation through bodily knowing. I knew my father's soul no longer tethered to me—the time had come to let *his spirit soar*.

**Figure 35**
*Like Father, Like Daughter*

# 35

## The First Time Back in the Classroom

*Dropping the pen onto the paper, I tilted my head back in exhaustion. Two months had gone by in my new position at a new school, teaching two new grades. And no matter how hard I worked, I could not seem to get caught up, leaving me at my wits' end. So, for the first time since the summer, I took the afternoon off and headed home to spend some time with my dad.*

*Walking into the house, I found my father sitting in his rocking chair, one of his staple spaces. I was a grown woman, but I felt no shame collapsing onto his lap. Jokingly, he complained how the weight of my body was crushing his legs, but still, he let me rest. My mother was at work, and my brother went out, so the afternoon was ours just like the old days. Deciding a movie marathon was long overdue, I put on the latest Hindi film and joined my father on the couch. Dad sat upright while I sprawled out with my head resting on his lap. Every so often, I looked to find him sleeping in his seated position, but I did not think much of it then. He slept through most of the movie, jolting awake in time to catch the funny parts, letting out his contagious chortle.*

*When the movie was over, I insisted on watching another, this time in Malayalam. Dad was surprised by my actions. Lately, I was always in a hurry—to eat, to visit, to talk. I got in the habit of cutting our time short and hurrying out the door to rush back to the piles of marking and planning. Leading the life of a teacher, I was constantly sacrificing memories made with my family, thinking I had more time with them later. But today, I took a stand and put my work life on hold, soaking in each second spent with him. When I finally got up to leave, he turned to me and thanked me. Driving home, I felt rejuvenated, like a missing part of my life had returned.*

> *Later that night, Mom called me on her break,*
> *"Dad was happy today."*
> *"Really? What did he say?"*
> *"He told me that, after a long time, his daughter spent so much time with him."*
> *"Yes, I spent most of the afternoon and evening there."*
> *"Good, you should do that more often. He misses you."*

*Her words cut through the illusion that placed my work on a pedestal. I vowed to spend less time working and more time enjoying quality visits with my parents. And I stayed true to my vow until his last breath, taken two months later.*

***

The tidal wave of my father's death crashed into me, and gradually ripples of secondary losses multiplied. One was the loss of reverence I held for my profession. I am a teacher because my father was a teacher, and this profession runs in my blood beyond that. Yet, as much as I love the teaching aspects of teaching, the amount of other work that continuously piles onto an educator's shoulders caused me to reexamine my career post-loss.

With each passing year, the responsibilities of a teacher change and compound, moving further away from mastering the art of pedagogy. And though the spectrum of my workload was, for the most part, manageable, in my family's time of need, my attention was seriously divided. It was not that I frequently checked my emails or held meetings with my substitute teacher in the ICU lounge, nor was it my constant worry about deserting the individual needs of my students. The lingering wake-up call sounded when I caught myself sitting in a hospital room, watching my father die *and* writing one hundred fifty report card comments in the corner. A compelling realization kicked in that my job as a teacher overtook my role as a daughter. Still, I continued to write them. Not because I was forced to—but because

I had to. Most teachers exude this *have to* quality, ensuring the best interests of students trumps our well-being. In this way, school staff members carry out some of the direst forms of self-sacrifice I have ever seen. But in times of crisis, this mentality shifts from mastery to illness, and no one will point this out or assertively try to stop it. I insisted on writing the comments. I wrote them through the end of his life, the funeral arrangements, the onset of my bereavement, and the early hours of the morning right before boarding a flight to India. Repeatedly, I told myself, *it's okay, I can rest on the plane*. However, when I finally sat with the consequences of my actions, I awoke to the knowledge that I would not maintain both my health and this profession for much longer.

Touching down from India on a Saturday, I rejoined my students that Monday. It is safe to assume that I was not in the right frame of mind to return. But my *four days* of bereavement leave, aiming to cover the loss of my father of thirty-one years, had been used to plan and attend his funeral. Moreover, my spiritual trip to India to perform our obligatory prayers and death rituals, though granted, cut my paycheque in less than half. Truthfully, I had not given much thought to this system beforehand. But through my loss and lengthy conversations with others, I discovered the death of a loved one almost always incurs punitive repercussions in the workplace—financially, socially, emotionally, or status-wise. Our society is not structured to soften the blow; its framework ensures the opposite. I suppose I could have taken a leave of absence based on my generalized anxiety disorder, and not specifically my complicated mourning, but a third of me felt as though I had abandoned my students, a third of me was conscious our society would view me as weak, and a third of me welcomed the distraction.

Right foot forward, I entered my classroom, touched my hand to the ground, and then to my heart. My grief had taken on a life of its own, severely affecting my day-to-day functioning, and I needed all the blessings I could get. I had prepared for the emotional tide of loss, but the physical, neurological, and social disturbances blindsided me. My neurons fired around my father—thus, pulling the plug on his life support, concurrently pulled out my wires, leaving me damaged and in disarray.

Fumbling around my desk, I tried to organize my affairs, but my *fight-or-flight* response stayed activated since the scene where I shook my father; watching him die slowly had traumatized my brain. This unrelenting surge of adrenaline, combined with a significant drop in my weight, drained me. I was lighter, but my limbs grew heavier, and dragging dead weight made it impossible for me to maneuver from point A to point B without sustained mental effort. For the rest of the school year, I generally stayed put.

A profound helplessness coiled through my spine, hunching me over and forcing my shoulders to sink, leading to fluctuated breathing and spasm pain. I either took short, clamped breaths that tightened my chest, causing my heart to race as I huffed and puffed through lessons. Or, I released all my air at once through automatic, uncontrollable deep, deep sighing. Oxygen was circulating inside me, but my suicidal cells refused to take the nutrient in, so the accumulating air blasted forcefully. Whether I was aware of my soughing, I exhaled like this throughout the day, and others took notice. While in India, hearing my raging sighs, my aunty explained that those who carry heavy sadness stuck in their heart have no option but to suspire it out—grief literature suggests that one is physically *choking* on grief.[19]

Drifting through the days, I was unaware of my surroundings—people and places became unreal, and sounds were swallowed by the unwarranted physical disturbances connected to my deep psychological pain. First, extreme nausea rode alongside my breathing issues, bringing continuous vomiting sensations throughout the day while eating, driving, sitting, reading, and talking. Frequently, these feelings turned to action, causing me to run rapidly to the nearest bathroom. Then, the personification of fear forced my eyes to shudder, leaving them stuck in *searching* mode, disallowing my brain to read or retain information. Insidiously, my pupils staggered back and forth, making it so that when I picked up reading material, the words shook. And though my external vision was weak, my internal sight was overactive, pushing scenes of my father taking his last breath to the front of my mind, sporadically, while teaching and in the middle of my lessons. This trait, materializing images out of thin air, tipped me off. These symptoms had collided with me before; I knew my grief had coupled

---

[19] *Bereavement: Studies of Grief in Adult Life, fourth ed.* C. Parkes & H. Prigerson. (2010). Penguin Books.

with post-traumatic stress disorder.

Next, my speech became slurred and impaired, preventing me from sustaining long-term conversations with others. When people assumed I was silent out of pain, I was also speechless because I literally had no words that would form—or I forgot how to say them. A surprising manifestation of traumatic grief was memory impairment. I struggled to connect thought to action as a block prevented the two from meeting. I forgot basic instructions like *watering a plant* or *cutting carrots*, and completing these small tasks became great victories for me, even if others did not see it that way. They did not know that I had little recollection of short-term events; I could not match names to faces, leaving both parties feeling awkward; I could not recall student names, forcing me to use common pronouns; and that all of my belongings went into hiding. In short, I could not bring forward information that was deemed unnecessary, and anything outside of my father's death was unnecessary. Before I learned that this was a symptom of complicated grief, I wondered if his demise left me with early-onset dementia. My body mimicked all sorts of conditions from my father—*why not this too?*

Finally, the most crippling aspect of my grief was enduring violent pangs of pain, lightning bolts striking the center of my chest—repeatedly, relentlessly. Unconscious of my actions, I walked around tapping or palming my breastbone, trying to soothe the untameable ache. At home, I sat like this for hours, *tapping*. I could feel the muscle squeezing, aching, yearning, missing him. Searching the web, I diagnosed myself with takotsubo cardiomyopathy, *broken heart syndrome*, a plausible explanation. But when the symptoms increased and heightened, the doctor eventually labeled the invasion as *psychosomatic pain*. My mind, undergoing severe emotional and chronic stress, was manifesting real, excruciating, and unbearable physical pain. Now I suffered from two stigmatized syndromes, prolonged grief and what some considered *made-up* pain. These symptoms progressed for six months. After that, a few fell away, several lingered, and most worsened. My body, unable to recalibrate and adjust to his death, steadily shut down. And no one could empathize with me. The best they could do was offer senseless counsel: *get over it, move on, let it go*. Grief was suffocating me, not the other way around. And because of their ignorance, I stayed mum on both, sharing my health concerns with doctors, psychologists, and grief counselors only.

With all of these issues operating in the background, I attempted to reintegrate back into my workplace. But since my grief had created monstrous confusion, leaving me mute, I mostly kept to myself. I resided in a separate, faraway world, transported by daydreams that persistently sought to meet with my father once more. My mind, a trickster, stung me into new routines, and a wild craving in my chest created glimpses of him standing at my classroom door. Stationed at my desk, I would straighten in a sigh of relief—only to hunch back down seconds later in despair when the mirage disappeared. To be sure, I lunged into the hallway, attempting to cross the threshold between us, but his silhouette shattered and dispersed in the air as jasmine and incense, cultural indications that a loved one is near. Alone in the evenings, more desperate searches ensued, and our roles would reverse, whereas I imagined fatal ways of reuniting with him. My destroyed heart had decided nothing was more painful than living, lacking him.

Stepping back into the classroom, I resumed teaching a subject that amplified my grief. I sharpened my father's expertise for a living; his voice lingered on every letter of literature that left me, solidifying my sorrow. On more occasions than I would like to admit, I closed my door during my prep period and cried. But, despite the endless, abounding heartache, I went to work daily, thinking my private demeanor hid my inner chaos—that nobody could *see* my suffering. Later, I learned my grief was transparent; the complications were crystal clear.

Within the walls of the school, I felt supported. The teacher who took over my class carefully looked after my students and workload, ensuring my seamless return. My administrative team was compassionate and caring; my students were understanding; and my colleagues kept a watchful eye on me. Thankfully, these elements aligned, as I have seen the detriments caused by an unsupportive workplace. Even though I was brand new to the school, many of my colleagues attended my father's funeral or arranged food delivered to the house, communicating they stood with me in ways they could. Those who were already members of the grieving community took me under their wing, carrying me along. They checked in on me regularly, dropped by my class at scheduled times, and helped me behind the scenes. Their subtle solace made a visible difference. Perhaps the *invisible hand* assigned me to this school on purpose, knowing the blustering storm headed my way.

That said, not all social exchanges post-loss were perfect. The first week back, spotting me ambling around aimlessly, a colleague pulled me aside and asked, *How are you handling things since your dad died?* Gratitude spilled, and my eyes wet with relief as I burst at the seams. At last, someone directly addressed my grief. Uncontrollably, I sighed out nonsensical ramblings, voicing my internal chaos outward. But sadly, my explosion detonated our discussion.

One split second later, shockingly, the person retracted their compassion. *I'm not really good with the emotional stuff. I'm probably not the best person to talk to.* Taken aback, the interaction rendered me speechless as I thought, *but you—asked me.* My father was my first primary loss. I did not know how to adjust to his death, nor did I know how to interact with others and seem normal. I had not been exposed to their grief-illiterate lingo, those raw questions that are asked but do not want an answer. An unsolicited interplay that teases the mourner's pain and transforms their sorrow into a comfortability issue with the other. Stunned, in the middle of the hallway, I was forced to unravel a code that clarifies to the griever that they should never make the non-griever uncomfortable with the *actual* experience of death. Instead, a silent, one-sided compromise unfolds, deeming bereavement as best handled alone, away from the support of others, even if community is needed most to reconcile and heal.

After this crass exchange of words, I learned my first lesson in *grief illiteracy* instantly, a horrible moral of the story moment that led me to believe my visible expression of mourning was burdensome. That, those who are not good with the *emotional stuff* will continue asking the vulnerable questions, even when they cannot handle the fragile answers, as though the inevitability of death will blow past them. From this insensitive interaction onward, the complexity of my feedback flattened, delivering the response they wanted to hear, a simple reply reassuring them, *I'm fine.* This obtuseness was the first of many social interactions that caused me to question our culture's ability to companion grief. And as similar stories compounded one on top of the other, I awoke to the alarming rate of grief illiteracy that exists in our society. Stirring these sentiments through my doctoral dissertation, I was pushed to lead what I like to call—*A Grief Revolution.*

After completing my Master's degree, relationship building became the cornerstone of my pedagogical practice. The lessons and activities in my classroom derive from the foundation of social pedagogy, which aims to develop solid bonds with each student in my care—mutual respect that continued to grow while I was away. Thus, when death stripped me to my core, the unfiltered compassion I received from my students was a restorative aspect of returning to work. The innocence of children, who had not yet been tainted by the unrelenting expectation that I suppress my suffering, welcomed me and my grief with open arms.

Transforming back into their teacher, the first conversation I initiated with my students was to share my pain. Grief was seeping from me—even if I tried to restrain and contain my suffering, visibly, I could not. They would spend the most time with me and be on the receiving end of my inability to adapt, so I needed them to understand my reactions and responses to his death more deeply than others. Thus, I leaned into my grief, revealing my wounds and bringing my walls down long enough to show them what his death was doing to me. Standing at the front of the class, barely breathing, I explained:

> *My father was the closest person I had in my life. We all have that one person, and he was mine. He is the most painful loss I will experience in this lifetime. I cannot explain my reasoning beyond that, but I can show you a glimpse into our life together.*

I projected the funeral's slideshow onto the board for every class, five periods in a row. Attentively, they watched, noticing things like my father's favorite poem hung on the walls of my classroom, that even here, I had infused my love for him. They were silent, respectful, and still—and this was how they approached me for the rest of the year. Later, when parent–teacher interviews rolled around, a handful of parents thanked me for inviting their child into my sorrow, showing vulnerability around the topic of death, and teaching them a lifelong lesson that will remain with them during their time of loss. When I exposed my tragedy, I had no idea how my actions would be perceived. But what emerged, vital discussions highlighting the need for grief education, went far beyond my expectations. I simply wanted them to meet my dad at least once, and by introducing him to others, as expected, he brought a more signficant lesson on life to my attention.

## The First Time Back in the Classroom

The 2017 school year was the year my students saved me. Being surrounded by them during my grief was a blessing—with them, empathy always presided over sympathy. They connected with and acknowledged my pain more easily than most of my adult friends; they were kind and caring when their handmade cards were delivered to the unit; they asked questions about my dad, wanting to know how he lived, instead of tiptoeing around the event of his death; they decoded my repetitive, jumbled jargon, filling in the blanks I could not construct; they reminded me of things I had trouble recalling; and they were sensitively sound. When my birthday came around—forgotten by most of my friends—my students surprised me with uplifting messages, addressing the day as *the first birthday without your dad*. When my anxiety spiraled, they were patient with me and they waited for me to catch my breath and return to reality. During my distressing juncture, they were my lifeline, genuinely lifting me back to my feet. For all of the endless expectations we place on our students to successfully learn from us, I think we, as adults, have as much to learn from them.

\*\*\*

*Sitting in my room, marking, I overheard a conversation brewing between my parents downstairs.*

"One day, I want to sit in her class," *my father remarked.*
"Why?"
"I'm curious to see how she teaches. I want to observe her approach to teaching the English language and watch how her students respond to her. You know, to see if her techniques are the same as mine."
"You want to see if she's another version of Eapen Sir," *Mom laid out bluntly.*
"Well, I already know she is. Now, I want to see it."

\*\*\*

Crawling back into a world that kept spinning while I stood stock-still was no easy task. All I needed to do was communicate my over-exertion to others, clarifying what they could expect from me, but my words refused to release. And as a teacher with a strong *have-to* mentality, my inner frustration grew. I realized the pressure I placed on myself to normalize my grief was as severe as an outsider's. So, taking a step back, I examined my work ethic and formulated a different approach to handling bereavement in the workplace. Caring for myself, as I would a struggling student, I chunked tasks into levels that correlated with the intensity of my grief. Using a one to five scale, I created a *Grief Check-in Chart* that monitored my well-being and delegated tasks accordingly. If my grief was at a low 1, *I completed as many tasks as I could that day*, but if my grief was at a severely crippling 5, *my goal was simply to get to the end of the day*.

The physical aggressions of prolonged mourning prevented me from teaching at full capacity. Since I typically ranged in the four–five zone, I spent most of my time sitting with students and learning the layers of their struggles. A clear connection between mental wellness and academic achievement formed, shaping my future role as a mental health support teacher. Because my eyes would not adjust to their assignments, a day of marking took me a month; thus, minimizing the strain on my eyes, I delivered verbal feedback and on-the-spot assessments. I pushed the boundaries of my teaching techniques and found value in these new methods, diversifying my criteria for evaluation. Inch by inch, I managed to get through the last half of the year using an evolving system. Yet, despite my resourcefulness, papers would need to be marked; the second set of report cards would need to be written. And when my reserve hit dangerously low, when I felt like I could not go on further, a memory shone through. I remembered, finally, my father had taken his seat in my classroom, comparing our teaching techniques from afar. Then, *somehow*, I got to the end of June.

Floating on air, handing out assignment sheets, all at once, the fire drill unexpectedly sounded. The loud noise latched onto my obliviousness, shunting me back to the hospital and stunning me into a fight-flight-freeze frenzy. Because I actively participated in my father's death, a state of hypervigilance had emerged, triggered by environmental stressors. And although I was ever-present elsewhere, the senses surrounding me processed through my system in acute form, leaving me thinking I was constantly in danger.

Mimicking the students, I made my way outside. But trapped in ravaging torment, my mind exploded with images of my father's eyes pleading for my help while lying attached to a similar, flittering beeping machine. The forewarning—*it's time*—rang through my ears louder than the alarm, transporting me farther away from the school. Luckily, a student noticed my distress, grabbed the attendance sheet, and took over. *Don't worry, Ms. Mathew, I'll take attendance. You just relax and breathe.* As appreciative as I was, I was still the adult in charge, and traumatized or not, I needed to operate more effectively. Hence, my active pursual of grief work was not optional.

Since my days brimmed with excessive stimulation and intentional suppression of my grief, my evenings had to revive me through the opposite. I had to work hard to bring my body back to homeostasis. I engaged in a deeper level of self-care—what I deemed *grief care*, defined as nourishing my grief from the inside out, replenishing my physical, emotional, psychological, and spiritual health.

When I was alone, my grief could breathe. Winter wound the sun down early, mirroring my inner landscape, and my body desired to dull. Turning off the lights and technology in my home was a meditation that calmed me, as sitting still and silent in the pitch-black darkness settled my nerves, soothing my system. Moving through the shadows, I forced myself to eat small meals, and slowly, my diminished appetite grew. I took salt baths, softening my stiff muscles, ridding myself of the plentiful grief toxins overcrowding my health. I floundered in the water for long hours, unsure if the tub overflowed from the tap or my tears, both of which cleansed me. My physical grief care regime aligned with shielding my nerves, nourishing my body, and releasing my aches—strengthening my shattered structure.

My best friend supplied me with emotional support; she was one of the two left in my intimate social circle. Every night—for 365 days—her call came through. And every night, *for 365 days*, she gave me an outlet to process my story of loss through retelling, repeating, and relearning. My thoughts and words wrestled one another, barely forming comprehensible explanations, but still, she listened. Because I could not connect my mind to my thoughts or my words to emotions, mostly, I sobbed through statements—so she stayed on the phone and wept with me. She knew I needed to talk through the tortured tale tangled inside me. And through this persistent twisting and turning, grief's thick knots unraveled.

Storytelling was a thread of my grief care used to sew my psychological patches, stitching the scattered dots of Dad's death to a sensible plotline. First, I wrote to him: *Letters of a Broken-hearted Daughter*. Once the ink flowed, my hand would not stop, mulling over our tragedy, reaching out to my father daily. Eventually, I succeeded as these letters writ a bridge to him still, filling him in on the ongoing pages, leading the way to these 41 stories. Next, to stop my eyes from shaking, I held pictures of my father in front of them. The act of seeing him still—stilled me. And the more I surrounded myself with visuals of him, the less concrete his loss felt. In time, this led me to organize an album of photos that captured his final moments, restoring a chronological timeline of his last days on earth. All three of these outlets—my friend, my letters, my photo album—emphasized the importance of narratively engaging with my story of loss to reconcile his demise. Before I had chosen my research topic for my doctorate, it had chosen me.

The spiritual aspects of grief care, the essential healing, emerged through consciously engaging in the powerful act of mourning—of *expressing my sorrow*. Craving my father's physical presence heightened my grief to unbearable extremes, conjuring dark, invisible storms. I had never felt the ruggedness of calamity until my mind started unevenly comprehending that I was now permanently cut off from him. And no matter what I did, the torrential tears spilled. I clung to my father's belongings to calm the storm, keeping his physicality close to me. Most people wanted me to move forward and rid myself of these things, but I knew spiritual healing resided in them, that they would help regulate my nervous system.[20] So, my wardrobe transformed, fretting less about fashion and more about feeling the threads of Dad's clothing on my skin.

Merging with the dark, sitting in his chair, playing his favorite songs, wearing his oversized sweaters and jewelry, clutching his valuables to my chest, and gripping his cane firmly—I encouraged myself to hold on to my father still. Absorbing the sensory imprints that lingered on his possessions, I leaned into these objects and permitted the rain to pour. They were not small sobs or trickling tears—I cried heavy monsoons, matching the ones I used to watch with my grandfather in India. My sorrow was too heavy; frankly, I had no other choice.

---

20 *A General Theory of Love*. T. Lewis, et al. (2011). Oxford University Press.

Setting aside two to three hours each night to cry was the only way to find refuge, liberating my pain. And as my grief squeezed out in tears, my brain processed the events of his loss. This act of encouraging myself to cry—without judgment, inhibition, or constraint—was the smartest discipline I put in motion. Because I allowed myself to weep, wail, and sob then, I was able to feel the opposite later on.

I kept my grief care in place until I no longer needed it. Now, I no longer need to cling to my father's possessions to feel his presence; his spirit flows through me freely. I no longer need to sit and sob for hours; gratitude and joy have reemerged. My nightly mourning rituals may have faded, but the traditions that stem from my eastern heritage remain intact. Gladly, I light a candle, *a symbol of my father's spirit*, and leave fresh flowers, *an expression of my love and reverence*, in front of his picture—acknowledging his ongoing role in my past, present, and future. When I must make a vital decision or seek his spiritual connection, or my writing needs to flow, these traditions allow me to secure his blessings. By implementing grief care, heavy acts of mourning have subsided, and smaller tributes of remembering have replaced them. These auspicious markers are an indication that I have relearned my place in a world without him, while keeping him with me still. Light symbolized my way out of the darkness of his loss, signaling our bond persevered past the shadows of his death.

As a consequence of my *first time back in the classroom*, I realized to a greater extent the toll grief took on me. When my strength returned, I worked hard to uncover the layers of my grief and learn how to move through them. I ventured into the grieving community and gathered resources from different avenues: I attended grief counseling and joined grief support groups; I volunteered at the local hospice and worked with children and teens who suffered parent loss, discovering a boon of resiliency in their eyes; and I researched and read a vast amount of grief literature to supplement my grief literacy. Steadily, a complete picture of my role in education bloomed—to address grief and trauma in schools, healing loss using the art of storytelling. The silent leader who observed, aided, created, and supported from behind the scenes, joined forces with the companion leader who empathizes, listens, sustains, and walks alongside the suffering of others.

My new understanding of educational leadership and grieving

solidified a topic suited for my doctoral dissertation: *Can written first-person narrative storytelling be used as a tool to actively process and effectively move through grief?* By synthesizing the wisdom I gained from listening to a wide range of losses, my rigorous research, and my own grief story, I organized a grief toolkit designed to address bereavement in schools. In due course, I led Working With Grief and Writing Through Grief workshops for colleagues and community members. Last, I designed a unit plan for educators—*Storytelling Through Your Sadness*—as surfaced from my doctoral study findings to support bereaved students in schools, the data for which are these stories.

When I decided to lead the necessary task of bringing death education and grief work into Canadian classrooms, a purpose higher than my pain emerged and transformed into a mission to serve, the joy for my profession returned, and reconciling my father's loss became inevitable.

**Figure 36**
*Crossing the Bridge*

# 36

## The First Time on Social Media

Grieving in the digital age brings its own added complexities; the proper etiquette for social media grief norms has not been adequately laid out. Thus, the raw, throbbing wounds that accompany loss can be shredded open as fast as the click of an *updated status*. Public networking sites fill a void because they provide an outlet to announce life's greatest feats—and greatest feats only. An underlying thread draws us in through an insidious assumption that our value is determined by how happy we appear to be or how much egoic wealth we have. Our culture's need to feel as special and privileged as possible is then normalized onto a platform where nothing is normal. And when tragedy strikes, it does not fit into the standards of social media postings, at least not for an extended period or without a clear silver lining intact. Being *too sad* or *too negative* quickly leads to a mass unfollowing. Hence, as a new member of the grieving community, I was restricted by a lack of socially constructed web spaces that could help me process, cope, and work through my grief.

During the first year of my bereavement, I interacted minimally online. Losing my dad thrust my life onto the opposite end of the desired social networking spectrum. I had nothing to brag about and preferred not to compare my lack of happiness to the abundance of others. Mid-February, the last post I made was on January 14, announcing the biggest *defeat* of my life. This one admission ended up being my most liked status throughout my social media lifespan; a post that traveled to the other side of the world and, without my knowledge, was read at vigils held for my father in India. And though it was one for the books—beautiful, heart-wrenching, and a full-fledged reveal of my talent as a writer, silver lining included—it is the only status I cannot bring myself to go back and read, even now. After that, as a consequence of the heaviness of my grief, my desire to post ceased. The instant gratification delivered through net culture had vanished; I never posted a *selfie* again. I found it hard to take pictures, as my inner workings no longer allowed me to produce a meaningful smile. Melancholia, coupled with my steadfast commitment to honor our sacred forty-day ritual of devout fasting for the deceased, I declined to engage online until the designated time of cleansing was over. I stopped going on social media altogether, as the digital detox was relieving—except for this specific time, on this specific day.

Stirring from a deep, exhaustive sleep, I spooked myself awake, reaching into thin air, grasping at a father no longer there. A solid routine, recurring for the past thirty-five days. Mornings were the roughest part of the day—and so were the afternoons, and so were the evenings. But mornings carried a different challenge altogether because as I woke, I had to shake off the dreams that kept him alive and re-remember that he did, *in fact*, die, that he was, *in fact*, gone. And every time I awoke to this dawning realization, again, my heart descended back into the bottom of my chest, my lips quivered with fear, and a wave of tears, reaching high tide, surged forward. The aftermath of embodying disbelief lasted until I got back into bed, and the whole scenario would repeat again in the morning.

Yet, in the wake of my suffering, my grieving was divinely guided to an extraordinary extent, a knowing I received in the anticipatory stages of loss. An *invisible hand* shepherded me through its thick, preventing me from experiencing more pain than I had to. On this morning, the hand was heavy, prodding me to see things for what they were. Without warning—a warning came over me. A feeling seeped into my bones that someone *out there* had broken tradition. So, I gave in, and I checked my social media. Scrolling through my Instagram feed, my inkling was unfortunately confirmed before even hitting the third frame. Debaucheries that should have stayed hidden sprawled out in front of me. Photos that should have spared my grief-stricken line of sight were determined to do no such thing. At once, the cells in my body collapsed. Situated in sorrowful sadness, I sunk further into a deeper state of shock, draining the last tinge of color from my face. She was present for his illness, witnessed his suffering directly, and fed him with her own hand. But the actions we put forward when the world is watching, and the desires we maintain when we are not as visible is *two-faced* behavior.

The ongoing partying, lingering in the background of my father's death, had finally caught up to me. My soul knew the solution, but my mind refused to concede. I paused and reflected, grasping at straws to save a friendship submerging. But there was nothing left to hold onto; the last straw had previously been drawn when my father lay ill with delusions. At my most critical crossroad, when I needed strong allies to push past their limits and reach into the fragile mind of a woman who had lost everything, she could not empathize with me. Instead, these images wildly proclaimed that nothing was lost at all—life, for her, remained utterly unchanged. With one outrageous post, ripples of poor and insensitive choices made throughout my father's illness formed a tsunami, staring me straight in the face in the form of distasteful pictures. The irrevocable had become the inexcusable. Realizing the farce enacted in front of me, a retching sensation drew from my stomach, swerved past my respiratory system, and landed full force in the middle of my throat. My inability to breathe, amplified by my complicated grief, mimicked the spirit of *Caesar* in his final moments. A person who was supposed to be my lifeboat on the sea of sorrow created unexpected waves, pushing me further under the water. In that one reckless decision, that one inability to control the craving to gain *likes* by the fifty-some people viewing these shameless selfies, my father's mourning period was tainted.

\*\*\*

*The turnout for the party was a success; more than one hundred guests made time to join us and celebrate Dad's birthday. After the surprise was over and the shock faded, I noticed my father searching for a face in the crowd, looking somewhat perplexed.*

*I interrupted him, "Dad, were you surprised? Look at all the people who came!"*

*"Yes, I was." He smiled. "But someone is missing."*

*Taken aback by his astute observation, I briefly paused and then pro-*

*ceeded to make excuses, "Oh, she couldn't make it tonight. She already had other plans, but that's okay."*

*"No, it's not, Linita, she is like a daughter to me, and she should have been here."*

*Solidifying his argument, Dad turned to greet the other guests. My father was right, bringing a hard truth to light—one I have trouble fully coming to terms with. Even though we consider some our own, viewing them as extended members of our family, their actions, when it matters most, readily reveal they do not reciprocate the feeling.*

***

While grieving, some stood at the shoreline, ensuring my safety from afar; some dove in and swam alongside me; and some refused to acknowledge the ocean's depth, fearing they would drown. And *who* landed *where* shocked me. However, once they solidified their stance, I left them as is, knowing eventually, the tide would turn—with time, they would face and feel their grave insensitivity. If ever there exists a time to evolve into our higher selves, it is in the time of great grief. And if I did not allow this natural evolution to occur, this organic process of elimination to unfold, then, later, I would continue to suffer. I thought long and hard before making a final decision, a sentencing that would cause self-imprisoning emotional repercussions for the next few years. Maybe if my heart knew remorse or regret would surface, that a sincere apology would be made, things could have ended differently. Yet, I already knew the *hard truth*, and before the hour was up, I *unfriended* and dismantled my longest friendship.

Dad's death left my heart frail and my spirit soaked in sensitivity. An ultra-vigilance emerged in the form of my deceased father's protector, and actions that usually would not have fazed me became a loud source of betrayal. I admit my standards are high, and my expectations of those close to me are higher, but what I value most is empathy—a gift that breathes freely from me. Consistently, I have shaped my actions to support the situations of others. But, at the height of my sorrow, I was devastated to learn the same rules would not apply. When the *light of my life* extinguished, approaching my darkness delicately was inconceivable to many and met only by a few. And though I had adjusted to the apathy of others in the past, now, as sheer ignorance interfered with the rituals put in place to bridge a peaceful path for my father's spirit, room for leniency was not tolerated—not even on social media.

Second-generation children grow in cultural hybridity, so I often faced an ongoing dilemma within my social circles, an implied battle of understanding age-old traditions beyond the fads of pop culture, immersing oneself in the meaning behind our rituals. The sacred ceremonies and communal grieving observed by my ancestors were quintessential components of healing, known to *make* or *break* a person's grief. And fasting from toxic or celebratory behavior at a time of death conveys that a pivotal person—someone fundamental to our being—has died. That, our grief is so damaging we must work to restore our body to its natural state. In a moral and spiritual act of service, we bond closer to God to uplift our well-being, and by purifying ourselves, we preserve the purity of our beloved's transitioning soul. Thus, when the time came for me to strip away my luxuries for forty days, I gladly held on to a full year for my father—my principal comfort died with him anyway. But witnessing a lack of reverence for his life splattered on a social media platform shattered my perception of community—a perceived level of pain I thought others felt for his loss was marred. When I believed *they, too* were reeling from his death, I learned I was wrong.

This is not to say that I expected my closest friends to maintain strict adherence to our mourning customs; I simply did not predict his grave would be walked on through the social media limelight. I did not pretend the parties would stop on the occasion of his demise, as I did not imagine there would be parties at all, at least not flashed out so soon in front of me. And I did not presume that those around me would solemnly mourn my life's greatest loss; I just assumed they understood that I was. It was, after all, *only* forty days.

As a teacher, I have seen the effects of digital platforms up close and personal, the detrimental and irreversible indent they can leave on one's spirit. Even though social media garnered fame by boasting of strengthening community ties worldwide, we feel more isolated, anxious, and depressed than ever. The dangers associated with digital actions that make us feel good in the moment equally come with the risk of hurting ourselves or someone else. Slowly, we have come to understand that social networking sites are not the reality they portray themselves to be, nor do they induce the long-lasting connections we all hope to have. And still, we often choose these outlets over real, living, or *once-lived* people because, in the digital age, time is of the essence. We post what we want to post, and we post it now, giving little consideration to the full consequence of our actions.

Although instances arose when a person did not have time to visit my father in the hospital, or have time to attend his funeral, or have time to postpone their celebrations a little while longer after he died—time was always readily available to update one's social media standing. In the end, the quality of one post during a close friend's mourning period can measure the friendship. And the inability to empathize with the greatest loss of a friend can sum up one's character as a whole.

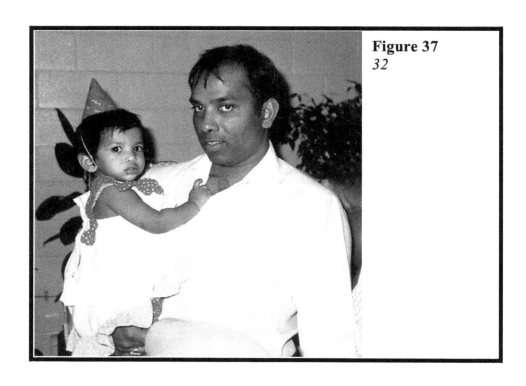

**Figure 37**
*32*

# 37

## The First Birthday

Of course, my birthday had to come first. Contemplating the *why* behind this synchronicity, I pulled at a string that revealed my father's logic. Mine had to initiate the year of firsts to supply strength to our other two family members, whose birthdays would soon follow in three-month intervals.

April 10 was always a source of excitement; I loved celebrating my birthday. But now, the joy of the day, and my child-like nature, had vanished, leaving me no desire to continue acknowledging special days. With each birthday that passed, I stayed encased in the shell of who I was when he died. For three years after his death—*and sometimes still*—my age remained 31. Frozen in time, I often unconsciously wrote the date as *January 14, 2017*, or repeated the year, rendering shouts from the room: *Ms. Mathew, it's 2019!*

Snapping out of my trance was difficult; my mind stopped operating when he died, and I could not grip onto the turning years. Thus, when my thirty-second birthday arrived, all fifty-two weeks blurred, holding little to no significance for me—except that it was the *first birthday* without my dad.

A month before the day, I was driving home from work when, all at once, the damage unexpectedly hit. A greater understanding of what a birthday without Dad was, dawned on me. A *fatherless* birthday meant I would receive no big bear hug, no sweet little trinket for a gift, and no handpicked birthday card. Dad always patiently searched through the rows of greetings, reading multiple inserts and selecting one he felt summed our relationship *just right*. Now, the abrupt realization that I would never get a card from him again sent me over an emotional edge, landing headfirst in troubled waters. My thoughts spun out of control, thinking back to every card and gift he gave me. This *griefburst*[21] happened so quickly that I shocked myself, and I needed to get a hold of my emotions.

Avoiding my lonely apartment, I drove straight home. I parked on the driveway, exploded through the front door, and ran straight up the stairs to our usual spot. Only this time, my father was not waiting for me; instead, the room was cold and empty. I threw myself down on the bed and wept.

My brother entered our parents' bedroom. Confused, he questioned, *What are you doing home?*

*I just missed him*, I murmured, keeping my face pushed into the pillows.

Without asking anything further, he let me be.

A typhoon moved through me, but I lay still, unmoved. Suddenly, standing in the doorway, a familiar form emerged. A resuscitating whisper arose, *Molae, nee vanno? Daughter, have you come?* I sat up. I stared blankly at the space, searching for a solid form to reappear. But the vision had vanished.

Stuck in my seated position, as if magnetized in the direction of my father's filing cabinet, *the invisible hand* pulled me toward a treasure. Slowly, I rose to my feet and shuffled toward Dad's meditation chair. Sitting down, I opened the top drawer and ruffled his belongings, sifting through the items. I did not know what I was hoping to find; I only knew something wanted to be found. Then, this year's gift appeared in the blink of an eye. Underneath my father's files and folders lay two blank birthday cards—one addressed *Dear Son*, and one addressed *Dear Daughter*.

\*\*\*

*As a small child, I unknowingly started a tradition with my father on our*

---

[21] *Understanding Your Grief: Ten Essential Touchstones for Finding Hope and Healing Your Heart*. A. Wolfelt. (2003). Companion Press.

*birthdays.*

*Whenever the day came around, either his or mine, I awoke bright and early, ran to him, and screamed, "Dad, it's our birthday! Happy birthday, Dad!" Even back then, I thought we were the same. I continued this celebratory ritual every year without fail even as I aged. And, though I was always excited out of my wits, Dad stayed cool, calm, and collected.*

*Nodding gently and replying, "Yes, it is."*

\*\*\*

The week of my birthday, my anxiety steepened. Anticipatory grief does not only materialize before the primary loss, but it accompanies every secondary loss too. And even though the year of firsts constantly triggered me, the anticipation of each milestone always created more angst than the actual day itself. The more I thought about the day, the more frequent my chest pains, breathing difficulties, and jumbled words became.

Fearing the attention of others, I turned the birthday notification on Facebook off, and without it, not many remembered. At midnight, calls from my relatives in India flooded in, attempting to shelter my ache: *Remember, Linita, he is always with you.* Then, the three of us prayed, and I shifted upstairs and slept in Dad's bed, knowing a dream visitation[22] was likely. Laying my head on his pillow, with him clear on my mind, surely his image would conjure.

Waking, my mother and brother greeted me a little extra, attempting to bring forward some form of happiness today. Grateful for their efforts, I gathered my thoughts, and when I felt ready, I got out of bed to face the dreaded occasion. Deliberately, I walked into the attached bathroom and headed straight for the walk-in closet. My father's garments hung untouched as he left them.

Staring at the vacant stitched threads, a fearful feeling swept over me. Impulsive, I grabbed hold of as many articles of clothing as I could and held on to them tightly. Trying to resemble the shape of him, I hugged the bunched wardrobe with all my might, squeezing, whimpering, *Dad, it's our birthday. Happy birthday, Dad.* The tears fell

---

22  *Gifts from the Unknown: Using Extraordinary Experiences to Cope with Loss & Change.* L. LaGrand. (2001). Authors Choice Press.

fast, so I cried into his clothes, preventing my mother and brother from hearing me. They tried so hard to make this a good day. Leaning back, I straightened my father's suits and disguised my sadness behind a brave mask before heading downstairs.

A fine balance, masking one's grief to protect others.

Together, we visited the cemetery and adorned his grave with his favorite flowers. *Dad was right*—I had to go first. From my birthday onward, we established new routines, adapting our way around his loss and ensuring that all significant days still included him. In my thirty-second year, our family's strength aged upward.

**Figure 38**
*A Family of Four*

# 38

## The First Wedding

Per our eastern traditions, our family was excused from attending celebratory functions during the first year of bereavement, a restriction to which we gladly adhered. Birthdays, holidays, religious ceremonies, and weddings were all *off-limits*. We evaded most social events, except for a wedding that sprang up in my father's best friend's family. Since they were close to us, unanimously, we decided to see it through for Dad's sake. Although only four short months had passed since he died, we had hoped we would be ready to reintegrate within our community. Yet, in the end, we were wrong—the cultural restrictions were rightfully in place.

    Indian culture is patriarchal, making the father the head of the household, the figure we revere and respect, leveraging the final input into our decisions. Dad was integral to us, our tribune and strongest pillar, raising our family structure and supporting us equally. Therefore, attending a family function without him left long-veined cracks in the remaining three columns. This wedding was the first social event we attended after his death. And, oddly enough, the same couple's engagement was the last gathering I went to before he died, with the same group of people but with my father at my side—a deadly combination alone, setting me back before my foot passed through the door. I could not foresee the size of the storm headed my way. How other people held in their hands a button, igniting my grief in seconds. Disillusioned, I believed my suffering would sit on the shoulders of our community. But social gatherings tend to do the opposite, as large crowds are known for watching the ball drop. Hence, my father's death not only broke my heart; his demise created friction that tore our social web. Suffice to say—*the first wedding* was my first and last social event of 2017.

Grief is the unwelcome guest at most get-togethers, but especially at weddings. In hindsight, with my functioning eyes restored, I am astonished by how bereavement blinded me. *Really, Linita? A wedding?* Out of all the social situations I could have put myself in, I chose to attend the most festive, flashy, and exuberant option—*an Indian matrimony*. My reactions and responses to my father's death set off an alarm for anyone within a fifty-foot mile radius of me, let alone those crammed under the roof of a banquet hall. Thus, mixing this extravagant affair with a scoop of my complicated mourning was a recipe for disaster, and I would not leave the occasion unscathed. I would not be able to fool others into thinking my sorrow was under control, that I remained coolly unaffected. Then again, *why did I feel I had to?*

At the onset of our decision, a chemical combustion occurred, causing me to sweat the various shades of our loss I was not yet equipped to handle. And as the wedding inched closer, so did the vividness of my night terrors. It was not the union, the festivities, or the forced interactions with guests that haunted me; my nightmares stemmed from a pinnacle point more significant than these. Stirring at night, I mulled over the notable father–daughter promenade I would soon be subjected to see. For most girls, the beauty of their wedding day revolves around the person waiting for them at the end of the aisle. For me, it centered around the man walking me down it. *The beauty of a daughter truly does belong to her father*. My wedding was as much for him as it would have been for me. I, *more than anyone*, wanted that moment so badly. And I, *out of everyone*, was forced to leave it behind. Now, as I witnessed two hearts joyfully unite, mine would split straight down the middle.

***

*I strolled into the living room to find my father watching the televised nuptials. Catering to his poor vision, he stood close to the screen, with his back turned to me. He was unmoved by my entrance. That's cute, I mused, noticing how he fixated on the bride and groom.*

*"Dad, you're watching the wedding! Nice, how was it?"*

## The First Wedding

*My father stayed silent. Taking a second to settle, he turned and revealed an emotional dad I was not expecting to see. The tinge in his eyes, his glistening cheeks, and his short sniffles communicated he had been crying.*

*Instantly, I moved to comfort him, "Dad! What's wrong? Are you okay? Did something happen?"*

*Dejected, he explained, "I watched her father put her hand in his, and I thought, how will I ever be able to do this? How will I give you to someone else? I will never be able to put your hand in another man's hand. I will never be able to give you away."*

Stunned, I stood still. Without waiting for my words to form, Dad walked upstairs, closed his bedroom door, and remained in his room for the rest of the evening. I have only seen my father cry a handful of times—the Royal Wedding was one of them.

*\*\*\**

Jolting from a bad dream, I lay in bed, reflecting on a time in the hospital when I had to dissect these feelings before. Alone in the room, I contemplated the question that reverberated one evening, early in his illness: *Are you okay if your father is not here when you get married?* The time had come for me to answer.

Silently, watching my father sleep from an arm's length away, I asked him, *How will I ever get married without you, Dad?* Moving to hide my tears, I balanced my head between my thumb and forefinger, resting my elbow against the arm of the chair. Perhaps, because I had relaxed into his thinking position, somehow, I entered the depth of his mindset, permitting the *invisible hand* to retrieve his response. Without conscious effort, flashes of instances arose, showing me numerous occasions where he had already given me his answer: *I will never be able to put your hand in another man's hand.* Blinking rapidly, I returned to the present moment and looked at my dad in disbelief. His intentional choices struck me. Comprehending him loud and clear, I smiled, certain my father knew what he was doing. Reassuringly, I spoke, *It's okay, Dad. I didn't want to let go of your hand anyway.*

Although I eventually let Dad off the hook, my spirit was not strong enough to watch other fathers and daughters take our place. I tried to navigate this exhausting predicament alone, but my mind was foggy, and my heart grew weak. My body began rejecting my decision to attend, flaring into full-blown anxiety attacks. Rotating through extreme agitation, hot flashes, cold sweats, and insomnia—my mental preparation became a *Sisyphean* task. My stomach tied into small bundles of knots, twisting with nausea, begging me to embody my grieving rights and stay home. As an empath, I felt all the signs and symptoms point to a hard no—but as an empath, I put myself in their shoes first. Emphatic grievers are more concerned about the feelings of others when the compassion should be the reverse. Because of my foolishness, I blocked my ability to think rationally, act logically, and listen intuitively. Deep down, I was convinced, *I had to go through with this, no matter what.*

The morning of the wedding arrived, and my body was bedridden. My limbs, solidly frozen in place, had no intention of moving. I managed to get out of bed, vomited, and fell to the floor. Every fiber of my being knew the repercussions that would follow, so my bones collapsed, preventing me from experiencing the griever's pain associated with socializing with others. My legs refused to walk out the door of my apartment, let alone get me to the church on time. I was powerless; I had no choice but to give in to my grief. Debilitated by my losses, at the eleventh hour, I conceded and stayed home. I missed the service, I missed the ceremony, and most importantly, I missed the *father walking his daughter* down the aisle. In all its glorious beauty, I would not have gotten through this defining detail without shattering the last fragments of my heart that managed to linger past his death. Leaning into this truth, I evaded the guilt surrounding my actions. But the question—*what will they think?*—remained strong.

Picking myself off the floor, I used the next five hours to prepare for the evening ahead. Taking unprecedented action, I settled on wearing western attire to an Indian wedding for the sole purpose of conserving my energy. I needed every ounce of my life force for the upcoming interactions, not wasted on tying a sari. Somehow, I made it out the door, and then, again, I made it to the hall's parking lot. Sitting still and silent in my car, I drew the *shakti* needed from my backbone to embody the spirit of a warrior. Leaning into the understanding of whose daughter I was, I held my head high and crossed over the threshold, reminding myself, *it's just one evening, Linita.*

Except that *it wasn't*. It was an evening, the *first* evening, without my father walking in on my arm. It was an evening, the *first* evening, that we would be seated for three and not four. It was an evening, the *first* evening, that our loss would be ignored. It was an evening, the *first* evening, that I—*the strong one*—would be unable to keep my grief contained in a socially acceptable box. It was not *just* one evening. This night was so excruciatingly painful that I can only relive it in moments. Moment by moment, the crown I placed on my head in the car gradually transformed into thorns. And as my head lowered further into the night, those who gathered to witness my decline pierced my side to check and see if I was still alive.

**Moment One—*The Mingling*.** Walking in quietly, I made a loud entrance. Multiple eyes pinned to me as I was still the girl whose father had died. Moving through the crowd, one or two people offered me solace. I was not there to receive sympathy, but it is important to note that out of a room filled with three hundred people, only *one* or *two* expressed their sincere condolences. Naturally, death has no place at a wedding, even if it was my first time out in the open. Besides, four months had passed, and knowing our modern culture's death-denying attitude, I am sure most assumed I was *over it*.

Ignoring the egoic chatter spewing from my mind, I shifted my focus. Quickly, I learned that saying nothing was the better choice of the two: *Linita, long time no see! How are your parents doing?* The rhythm in my chest flatlined. *My parents?* I thought. *My mom is fine, my dad is dead.* Holding back grief's intense bitterness from expelling from my mouth, I muted myself. With one question, my father's death reduced to ashes, my grief was disregarded, and I realized I no longer had a set of parents. *Do people really not know he died?* Before the throes of loss could embroil me, I nudged my way through the masses and located a bathroom. Within ten minutes, multiple layers of the protective skin I grew in the car had punctured, and I needed to lock myself in a stall and hold myself together.

Lowering my head, I avoided the stares of others, but I was spotted on my way into the washroom. Two older uncles, my father's friends, pointed me out. *Athu Moncyde mol annu—That's Moncy's daughter.* Only at an Indian event do I get to hear my dad's Indian nickname. A double-edged sword drew, one side carrying the pain of hearing his affectionate name and the other side offering bittersweet relief, acknowledging me as his.

**Moment Two—*The Reunion*.** Exiting the bathroom, I walked right into the next trap, eyeing a hurdle I had been dreading to jump through. Straightaway, I faced off with those friendships I had earlier disbanded—the ones who had established indifference to my suffering. Not only did I have to see them, but technically, I was a guest at their family wedding, and this was our first interaction since the social media blunder. Although grievers often feel pressured to justify their stance to non-grievers, I chose to stay silent. I had learned to restrict my social support system based on the *Rule of Thirds*: one-third will harm or hinder my grief, a third will remain neutral to healing, and a fortunate few will help.[23] Leaning into this theory, I tightened my relationships accordingly. And consciously, I eliminated dangerous mines hidden on the heath of grief. But now, I found myself among those who had previously detonated a blast and were consequently squeezed out.

Perhaps, deep down, I hoped for an apology, a small acknowledgment of my insufferable pain, or even a warm smile—any three of these would have been considered a win. I was already the black sheep of the party, resembling a saddened shipwreck, gliding across each room as my grief continued to topple me. Yet, once again, the hard truth came to light. Culturally, guests are supposed to be treated with the highest reverence, but this made no difference to them. My heavy heart was met with cold shoulders and colder cut eyes, clearly communicating I was not welcome. Now, the question—*why are you even here?*—echoed from both parties. Before the sadness could swallow me whole, I snapped back to reality, reminding myself that even now, continuing the party was more important than acknowledging my father's untimely death. *Still*, the ego outweighed the scales of Lady Justice.

Realistically, I should have paid no heed to them, I was the one who ended the friendship, and this was merely a ripple riding the repercussion wave. But I was not prepared to see the unshakeable sadness on my mother's face, who stood afar witnessing their dismissiveness. Mom's heart was too pure; she was sure our broken friendship would

---

23 *Understanding Your Grief: Ten Essential Touchstones for Finding Hope and Healing Your Heart*. A. Wolfelt. (2003). Companion Press.

be sewn back together after seeing the severity of my sorrow. However, the harmful hindrance laid bare for all to see. The treatment was no longer a false impression cast through the lenses of my grief goggles. Before this moment, my mother consistently tried to convince me to forgive and forget. After it, she never asked me again.

**Moment Three—*The Chart*.** Blocking the last bleak barrier from my mind, I walked toward the dining area, ready to confront the next drawback. A grievance, escalating in my mind for days leading to the event, now came glaringly into view. Slowly, I made my way to the front of the line, staring blankly at the large board. I had never been so fearful of finding my seat placement before. My eyes, watering, staggered back and forth, searching for a name I knew would be missing.

> *The Mathew family, only three listed? This chart is wrong. There are four of us! Dad, where's your name?*

My irrational and inescapable, grief-stricken thought process swirled and spiraled. Defeated and pierced a third time, my head reeled lower, plummeting from the pain caused by a cardboard sign. Noticing the trail of people behind me, I touched the tips of my fingers to my heart, released my father's name from my lips, and took my seat at the empty table inside.

**Moment Four—*The Table*.** I sat at the assigned table with my mother, brother, and our close family friends. The last time we all convened like this was during the forty-day prayer held for my father. The small talk began, but Dad was not mentioned. I intuited they felt helpless at the sight of my suffering. Even so, I never understood the intention of eliminating a deceased loved one from the griever's mind. That statement, *I didn't want to remind you of him*, has always created more mind-boggling pain than easing. If I am breathing, I am reminded of him—others add little to this equation. Honestly, nothing was more painful than knowing a vital person was missing and everyone turning a blind eye. But our society heals in this way, deflecting or forgetting. I decided that if nobody wanted to talk about my father, I did not want to speak to anyone. For the remainder of the night, I exercised my right to remain silent.

**Moment Five—*The Festivities*.** I was sure now that a wedding was the absolute worst first event a griever can attend. Every tradition, speech, person, drink, food item, and any other aspect of the union exacerbated my grief to the millionth degree, reminding me of the great love I had lost. I do not remember which word, sound, or syllable provoked me, but once I was triggered, there was no going back. Turning away from my tablemates, I had no choice but to allow the rushing water cascade to the floor. A server stopped to reassure me, as strangers move to comfort us more quickly than our own: *Don't cry, this is a happy time, not a sad time.* I could not blame her for trying; she did not know every ounce of my happiness had died four months earlier. Sobbing heavier, an aunty sitting nearby came to my rescue, and in an attempt to console me, she disclosed, *We are all missing him dearly. We are all thinking of him today.*

The sheer gratitude of finally hearing one person—*just one person*—say the words out loud caused me to lose my bearings. My soft-spoken, quiet nature splintered. Releasing an explosion of tears, I ran out of the room with no intention of returning.

**Moment Six—*The Aftermath*.** The car ride home revealed how broken the three of us were. My brother, unable to contain his emotions, released his grief by venting his frustration; I cried the whole way home, devastated by my dealings; and my mother said nothing, allowing both to happen. *No one will truly understand our pain*, was the consensus. Of course, whispers arose around my emotional outburst, how I should have stayed home if I was distressed. They did not see the bouldering strength it took me to get there—how I dragged my soul to appease them. Unfortunately, our first community function brought forward the opposite effect of having a community in the first place.

Not only at this wedding, but socially interacting throughout our bereavement, time and time again, left us wanting. We craved a solid support system where our pain would be welcomed, nourished, and healed. People would listen to us, but not for too long. People would visit us, but only if the elephant in the room was removed. One visitor came to *our* house during *our* mourning period and assertively stated, *We can't talk about death. I can't handle depressing topics.* Irate, the intense rage of grief furiously boiled as I brooded, *it must be nice to have the privilege to opt out.*

In death, the struggles accompanying the child of two immigrant parents and the extensive sacrifices they made became clearer—what my parents left behind was transparent. Suddenly, I longed to feel secure and surrounded by my blood-related relatives, those who carried the pain of losing my father as deeply as I did. For them, I was *Moncychayande priyapettu mol—Our older brother Moncy's beloved daughter.* They empathized with the real reason behind my acute sorrow more easily. The takeaway from this evening then was that at the core of one's grief, when all else has shattered and the sheltering dynamic dismantles, the bonding element of one's family is everything.

After this night, my decision turned drastic. I rejected community gatherings, limited social interactions, and isolated myself, staying confined within the walls of my apartment. And no one came to look for me either; our culture's grief-avoidant behavior unveiled. After bearing my broken heart for everyone to see, not one call or text came through to check on me. Officially, my sorrow transformed into intense shame. Carrying this feeling forward, I took my father's death and placed our story in a sacred box, opening the lid only for those who understood the turmoil of prolonged mourning and demonstrated compassion for my relentless suffering. This was the only option I had left to protect my complicated grief—diminishing his death altogether.

While submerged in the *dark night of grief*, my discernment grew. I started to dissect and analyze the cultural context in which I was forced to grieve. As a second-generation Canadian, my parents were the only link I had to a closer cultural circle, and with my father's demise, my ties were severing. Typically, the tone of most conversations conveys that our lives are easy, but the children of immigrants have their own struggles, often having to prove themselves on both sides of the coin. To westerners, I was not *Canadian* enough. And to easterners, I was not *Indian* enough. Neither end of the spectrum wanted to fully claim me as their own. No matter how hard I worked to find a proper place among my people, my unbearable loss reminded me I was all alone. Yet, when I belonged to no one, I belonged to God. And with no strings attached to the world around me, I had free rein to reach another level of consciousness, one that was prejudiced free. Here, the *invisible hand* reached forward and lifted my eyes to a destiny I had already committed to fulfill.

To advance our knowledge of grief, contextually, being mashed in the middle had its advantages. I was in the perfect position to compare and contrast eastern mourning traditions to those of the west and vice versa. Using a multicultural lens, I expanded my understanding of how various cultures actively and effectively grieve—an underdeveloped concept in modern western societies. Therefore, enduring a night of intolerable interactions presented an opportunity to dive deeper into the frequent challenges of the grieving community, adding an illustration of my own. As I sat with others who had similar experiences, I realized I was being called to address a more complex problem than an autoethnography study. Spiritually, I felt summoned to fill in those gaps in humanity, the grim spaces and places where we still struggle to uphold each other out of the shadows—herein lies the motive behind my books, to illuminate the darkness and make grief visible.

At my wedding, I can set an example, reaching out to those who may be in their own swirl of grief. *To make myself better*, consciously choosing to include lost members of the community within my rituals and traditions, honoring those guests attending in spirit. To approach all celebrations moving forward with empathy and compassion, healing the wounds of others at all times, as we are meant to do. Perhaps this is my true purpose, to use my suffering to soothe the suffering of others. When I set fire to this knowledge, a single spark brought my grief to its knees.

After the reception, I felt ashamed at how I handled the evening, at my inability to *stay strong* in front of others. In the early onset of my grief, I wished I could have done better—been better. But looking back now, I see that I surpassed my goal. No other person would have coped better than me because no other person has lost a father like mine.

**Figure 39**
*Sisters*

# 39

## The First Support Group

As June ended, so did my duties as a schoolteacher. Returning home, I collapsed in my chair and contemplated the timeline of 2017. The last six months saw my father's death, his funeral and burial, a trip to India, my return to work, and now, all at once, *nothing*. For the first time since he died, I was free from all external interruptions and intentional distractions, turning me solely inward. My mind, muddled with mourning, had two months to process his tragic demise.

All through my first summer holiday without him, the full force of grief knocked me off my feet. And once I sat down, I was unable to get back up. I became severely depressed and uncontrollably anxious, rendering my physical body useless. When the sun rose, recurring images from the hospital exploded as intrusive memories, and when the sun set, the same visuals wove my nightmares. Powerless to the present moment, I could not function long enough to carry out daily routines or common tasks. I became fixated on my father's story, repeating the same broken version of his inconclusive death to anyone who listened, including strangers; my detachment soared as my social interactions plummeted to near nothing; my identity suffered as I estranged myself; and the yearning, longing, and incessant searching for my dad intensified with each passing day. In short, my mourning took a *complicated* turn. And as I rounded the corner, the ignorance of grief illiteracy jumped out and startled me.

Imitating my father's circumstances when he died, I was not that young, but not that old either. I was thirty-one and belonged to an age group where most of my friends still had their parents seated beside them. Unintentionally, their comments and suggestions were not only irrelevant but often hurtful, harmful, and insensitive to the true nature of what loss through death entails. Death was a choiceless event, an ill-mannered guest that thrust its way through our door, sat at the head of our table, and devoured all of our stored resources and supplies for the winter, decreasing our chances of survival. And unless the other person was a member of my household, the catastrophic consequences brought on by the invasion of grief carried little to no significance to them. Thus, minimizing my suffering by being told to *let him go* by a person whose plate was still full, only salted my wounds further. *How do I move on from my father?* He was not a short-lived romance from whom I had separated and would eventually find someone else. This was the man from whom my cells were created, with each molecule desperately reaching for him still. As others attempted to navigate my loss, the power of language became evident. Their limited vocabulary or stock phrases reverberated consequences throughout my system, and their platitudes plundered my psyche, magnetic, drawing the life force out of me. Even when their words stemmed from a heart filled with good intentions, their communication overran with a misinformed and uneducated approach to loss.

My pain was glaringly visible, a characteristic usually not transparent in my private life, so I know why people pushed me to move past him. I was no longer the upbeat personality that once lit a room; now, I was the sorrowful and despondent individual who darkened it. No favorable emotion was potent enough to pierce the thick cloud of grief hovering over me like a bad cliché. Hence, injecting myself into happy and healthy company had a downing effect on both parties. I struggled with pretending to be robotic and making small talk, and they scrambled to engage in meaningful conversations about my dad. Before he died, the extent to which I talked about him was labeled inspiring; afterward, when my discourse remained unchanged, they referred to it as *damaging*.

I often caught myself quietly observing the elated actions of others, envious of their ability to feel bliss and flash a casual smile across the room when my happiness had become obsolete. I avoided taking photos because my lips no longer curved upward, my reflection was unrecognizable, and I did not want to capture memories as a paper-thin, bereaved person. With my father's demise came the death of a selfie, a signature hallmark responsible for capturing joy at any event. And joy was an emotion I no longer sensed. At times, I judged the credibility of the suffering of others when they shared *devastating* news with me, pointing out it was, *in fact*, not devastating at all. The sting of my father's death overtook my ability to offer compassion for trivial annoyances and even moderate ones too, as death became the ultimate marker for determining the validity of a person's anguish. Seeing how many avoided my suffering, I began returning the favor. My grief brought forward an intense apathy for the problems of others, leaving both me and the person seeking my comfort surprised by my actions.

As time went on, I felt I was making progress, using techniques like tapping my sternum to slow my breathing, keeping the chest pains and heart palpitations at bay. Yet, whenever a social interaction took place, the façade fell through. The ability to hide my sorrow had long since left me, and the more seeable my grief was, the more it translated into a direct sign of weakness, leaving room for others to comment on my prominent struggles. They saw a woman incapable of adjusting and resuming a life that no longer pertained to me. What could not be seen was the enormous strength it took to wake each morning and try living once more without him. Those heartrending moments where I could not locate the tiniest sliver or spark of desire to go on but surrendered to a colorless life anyway. Sincerely, I was trying my best to recover, but the reactions to the best of my grief responses shocked me. *How long is this going to take? It's been four months. You should be over this by now.* Frozen, the chill of my father's final fading breath caressed my shoulder once more.

Starting as the heroine, eventually, I was declared my own antagonist. *What happened to you? You seemed so strong before!* I often pondered their definition of strength, as a durable spirit does not form from a passive, submissive endurance of life's complexities. Emotionally charged and massively pained, I could not communicate an answer to a solution-less problem. Yet, the response in my mind rang loud and clear: *My father died! That's what happened*. But this was not a plausible enough reason for them. So, instead of working through this significant loss with me, I would be handed an endless list of outdated clichés to navigate and choose from to feel better.

*He's in heaven now, you should be at peace; you're lucky to have had him for this long, be grateful, some people don't even have a father; he would not want you to be sad, he would want you to be happy; we all have to go through this someday, the natural cycle of life, accept it;* and, my personal favorite, *time heals all wounds, it will get easier.*

Except, *it doesn't*—unless a person receives the space and support needed to engage in the necessary grief work. But though my *someday* had dawned, nobody seemed to be able to hold that space long enough for me to work through his death, so my symptoms kept worsening. I could not move past my inner ramblings on my own—from the inside, the doors were locked shut, and those who stood on the outside and could let me out chose to keep them closed. And the more I was subjected to the avoidance and insensitivity of others, the more distant I became.

Sincerely, I believed I had recruited an army of people to lead me to the other side of loss; however, at the pivotal point of the battle, sadly, the soldiers I selected had gone missing in action. My relationships became brittle. The pungent aroma of death encircled me, wafting a cry for help to those near me to soften my pain, and still, they ignored me. Most turned a blind eye to what his death did to me, how it rearranged my atoms and altered my core. In exchange, my eyes opened to what his death did to them, how it kept them the same and revealed their true nature.

First, I was told not to rely so heavily on others, to lower my expectations, and that grief was an independent endeavor—blind advice, wiping their hands clean of my suffering. Then, I was pressured to accept the rampant grief illiteracy running wild around me, a problem that need not be solved. Finally, I was coached to empathize with those who have not had the same lived experiences as me: *You can't blame them; they haven't lost someone like you have.* Others expected me to excuse their coldness and pretend like this is how we are supposed to treat each other. Yet, experiencing death does not set the bar for humaneness, kindness, or providing one another with the community required to heal from catastrophes. Thoughts and actions that exude from a higher heart, with an intuitive awareness around the needs of others, always renders compassion. But because death is uncomfortable, no one requires non-grievers to adjust their behavior; it is comfortable to let their actions slide, to deny death and strip away its honor. As a culture, we are so determined to avoid the soul-crushing repercussions of loss that we move too quickly to adapt to our flawed interactions, reinforcing the same backward, low-level thinking.

My father died in my arms, and I had to be more understanding toward them. Because he died, I became a social outcast.

Bereavement exposed me to the innate selfishness of humans, causing my selfless nature to draw back and hide. After my social interactions fell short, I concluded that living my life as a good, caring person had gone in vain as grief amplified what I did for others in their time of need and emphasized what was not being done for me in mine. That, my excessive kindness had consistently been taken advantage of—and after his death, transformed into a tragic case of unrequited love. This extreme imbalance of mutual friendship set me into a hypervigilance, still active in my interactions today. Moreover, my punishment doubled down when the heightened version of these attributes, which manifested while I was my *father's keeper*, returned and sought revenge.

Compassion fatigue and caregiver withdrawal formed out of my crippling heartache, diminishing my purpose, and thus, my will to live. Since my father was the only person who reciprocated the warmth of my efforts, without him, life was now meaningless. And as my support dwindled and I moved further into the dark woods, I frequently sat with a question provoked by his loss, *What's the point of living without him?* When the lowest of the low arrived, and the pitchfork in the road appeared, so did my father in a dream visitation, with a message, crisp and clear: *When it is time, I will come and get you, don't try to come before that.* Maybe my mind created the counsel it needed to survive. Regardless, the dream gave me the tenacity to hold on, and contrary to the beliefs of those who labeled me as weak, the true extent of my fortitude and toughness of spirit was the sole reason I pushed past the barriers and limitations of a mindset riddled with grief. To them, I was broken and did not fit the constructs of a resilient person. Even grief literature supports this view, as I often read that those who adjust well immediately after a loss are considered *resilient grievers*.[24] However, for me, a resilient person is someone who experienced the level of suffering that I did and found a way to remain alive anyway.

---

24  *Grief Counseling and Grief Therapy: A Handbook for the Mental Health Practitioner*. W. Worden. (2018). Springer Publishing Company, LLC.

The intensity of my sorrow directly correlated with an overflow of gratitude I felt for having a father like mine in the first place. Yet, others mistook my prolonged grief as my inability to accept the biological progression of human life and my incapability to move past my father's death because of this. My struggle was not in letting go of his identity; my challenges grew around relearning *mine* separate from him. Still, some continuously urged me to surrender to the *circle of life*, as though *The Lion King* was their only benchmark for losing a father. I was not trying to fix the death of my father. I tried to immerse in his loss, embrace his demise, and come to terms with our tragedy. It was others who could not find a sense of hospitality for the unwelcome guest now seated at my table.

Their non-acceptance of the severity of my misfortune left my father's death compared to a laundry list of ultimate sorrows, having absolutely nothing to do with us. Our culture was armed and ready with a hierarchy of grief, deaths considered more tragic, weighed and measured from bearable to insufferable, placed in some illusory and predetermined order:

> *At least you didn't lose a spouse, that's the worst type of loss; at least you didn't lose a child, that's a real painful loss; at least it wasn't your mom, losing her would be harder; at least you're not a dependent, financially, you weren't relying on him; at least you have a brother, imagine being an only child; at least it wasn't a violent death, he died peacefully; at least he lived a full life, especially after the heart surgery; at least you got to say goodbye, some don't even get that chance; at least it wasn't what happened to that other family, that was terrible; at least it wasn't the other way around, he wouldn't survive your loss; at least it wasn't completely unexpected, he was sick for a while.*

To an extent, death is always unexpected; loss births shock. Albeit, even if I had found myself in any of those other crises, the ranked order in the eyes of outsiders merely adjusts accordingly. Death is tragic, no matter what circumstance; death is *still* painful no matter what external label the relationship wears; and the grief that arises from loss through death pierces larger holes in the spirit, incomparable to other losses.

As a grief researcher, I am sure the type, way, and natural order of loss are all contributing factors that play a crucial role in one's ability to process and reconcile with the death of a loved one. Though, I am equally sure that the suffering I experienced when my father died reached a *once-in-a-lifetime* level of pain, and to coerce me to think otherwise would be a betrayal of this truth. As Gabor Maté concluded: *Trauma is not what happens to you; trauma is what happens inside you.*[25] Therefore, my father may be but one person to the world, but to me, he was my whole world. Dad may not have been my spouse or child, but he was my father. He was the one person in my life—*for the rest of my life*—that knew me intuitively from my first inhaled breath and kept me at the front of his mind until his exhaled last. My grief thrived from the root of our relationship, solidified on the sprouts of our bond, and multiplied from the fruits of our labor—from the love he left me *before* he left me.

Craving this irreplaceable and irreplicable bond has turned me into a wanderer. I will walk the rest of my time on earth searching for him in the love of others, knowing I will emerge empty-handed each time. A sinking feeling will depress my chest at the mention of his death, and the deep-seated loneliness that formed because of his loss will never leave me. The tears retrieved from this endless ocean are justified, and any person who bore witness to our time together would not argue otherwise. But herein lies the real problem, our unrelenting desire to compare and contrast relationships without grasping the whole picture.

As a teacher, I have reinforced among my students to never compare their injuries to another's—this is society's way of avoiding the actual emotional depth of a situation. Pain will always be subjective to the individual; it is a feeling created through the layers of experience their mind has endured. My pain is not *lessened* by greatening the pain of another. And their ache will not be *greatened* by reducing my own. To compare one person's loss to another is of no use at all; only the person creating the sorrow remains shackled by it.

As I matured through traumatic grief, I wanted to address the root of my affliction, even though everyone else wanted to tiptoe around it—including the doctor. Because of my father's heart condition and the increased risk of cardiovascular disease in female grievers, when my ferocious chest pains worsened, I went to find out if I was suffer-

---

25 *How Childhood Trauma Leads to Addiction – Gabor Maté*. After Skool. (2021). YouTube [video].

ing from the initial stages of a heart attack—a paranoia stirred from complicated mourning. When the electrocardiogram revealed I was healthy, the doctor diagnosed me with having *psychosomatic* sensations, stress-induced physical pain. She suggested I take antidepressant drugs as a remedy, the popular allopathic solution to most modern problems. But I was not depressed, I was bereaved, and pills would not process the loss of my father. Hence, I declined, wanting to avoid the route of medication.

Naturally, the physician questioned my decision. Before my father's death, I had already encountered two separate major traumas, a physical assault through robbery at age seventeen and my father's heart attack and critical open-heart surgery at nineteen. Since I was a teenager, I purposely avoided dealing with the emotional aftermath, burying both in my subconscious mind. Ten years later, the trauma resurfaced. The repercussions of not handling a situation *when* it was handed to me materialized in the form of acute insomnia. Eventually, a trusted psychologist dug deeper and discovered the source of my sleep issues. Using EMDR therapy, we traveled back in time and processed both unfortunate circumstances, alleviating my distress, and returning me to a full night's rest. Explaining my mental health history to the doctor, I added,

> *If I take this medication now, maybe the grief will subside, or maybe it won't. But I still wouldn't be addressing the issue of my dad's death. I would be dulling my grief, and that is not a wise choice for me. I know that if I use antidepressants to numb the pain, it will result in one of two outcomes—either I will have to stay on them for the rest of my life, as many grievers end up doing, or my grief will return and hit me full force at a greater depth when I stop the medication. My pain does not stem from a biological imbalance but an emotional one, and I know what the cause is—my father's death. Let me work through his loss and process it now so that I don't have to prolong the inevitable and wake up ten years later, still traumatized.*

The doctor agreed. Because of the debilitating effects of my grief, I had already researched multiple avenues of healing, including medication. But what I learned from compiling the real-life experiences of others and the advice read in books, the only way through grief is to go through it, and the interplay in our society that encourages otherwise needs to shift. If I had chosen any route other than working through my loss's raw, debilitating agony, these stories might have stayed hidden or the richness of the writing removed.

Grieving was an insurmountable obstacle that required every last ounce of my energy, guzzling my vigor and vitality, leaving me drained and depleted. At times, close friends did reach out and invite me to gatherings, but I did not have the stamina to get dressed, go to them, and endure an evening of simulated socializing. Moreover, our tradition of fasting from celebrations did not always bode well with my circle of friends. Even when the affair was intimate and simple, I declined, deterred by the fact that I would have to explain my visible, unsettling responses to his death. Thus, I did push people and places away, those I could no longer establish common ground with. I stepped back and vanished into the thick air of my soul's entanglement with loss.

The easiest interactions were with those who made an effort to come to me. And the few that did, witnessed my deterioration, how fragile and broken I had become, how difficult it was for me to carry a conversation about anything other than my father's death. Approaching my grief with persistence and patience was key, but not everyone accepted the length of my bereavement, and most visits were a one-off agreement. To heal, I needed to seek out a community that would support my chosen path of mourning without comparisons and with the understanding that *pain* is *pain*. So, when the new school year started, I actively sought compassionate companionship from grievers who lived the trials and tribulations of a loved one's death; I surrounded myself with those living a similar experience as me. Through the encouragement of my colleagues, I found an adult–parent loss support group offered by a local grief counseling center. I did not know then how the experience would change me.

Only a few seats were empty in the twenty-person gathering. Timidly, I scanned the room to see where I would feel the most comfortable. Left and center, a woman's energy drew me toward the vacant spot beside her. She exuded an aura that was warm and inviting, so I chose to sit next to her. Because of my shyness and inability to annunciate over the detriment of my grief, I sat down in silence. We did not talk for the first few sessions; however, *kismet* had plans, assigning us to snack duty on the third.

The relevancy of these sessions struck instantaneously, as the first task was designed to face our grief head-on. Sitting in an open circle, one by one, we were asked to acknowledge our loved ones and their fate: *My dad's name is Eapen Mathew, and he died.* A seemingly simple phrase would not leave my lips without a rumble. Within seconds of the first person's attempt, the room filled with sobbing adults nervously awaiting their turn. At last, when each person walked through the fire, the ice in the room was broken.

Throughout the meetings, I listened intently to the stories of each member as they spoke of their upsetting encounters with the grief-illiterate actions of others. I even grew awareness of my own misconceptions of what painful loss entails. After losing my father, I experienced a phenomenon I dub the *rage of age*—an unfair perception surfaced toward those who had had their parents longer than me. Yet, listening to an older woman's inability to find sincere compassion for her grief after losing a mother of nearly seventy years proved unbearable for me to justify my suffering regarding our respective timelines. In her words, she mustered: *They look at me like I am ungrateful. They don't realize the pain of loving someone for that much longer.* I contemplated two junctures, the possible loss of my father when I was 19 in contrast to his actual loss at 31. The *rage of age* vanished, and my feelings of injustice faded. I learned that I did not lack empathy; I overflowed with envy.

Each survivor talked through their tears and justified their sorrow as if needing to convince us of the realness of their wounds. To witness similar problems shared by an entire group of grievers reinforced my perspective that reform was essential and that I was far from an anomaly. Thankfully, those who attended did not have to prove whether they were *close* enough, had the relationship *long* enough, or were *aged* enough to be exempt from the genuine hardship of loss. Illness was not an automatic rationale for a loved one dying because: *Well, he was sick for a while now, wasn't he?* Members of the grieving community knew that *loss* is *loss*.

At the end of the third evening, a group of four of us left together. Walking at a synchronized pace, we openly discussed the value of attending these sessions and the benefits of having this community. During a break in the conversation, I used the opportunity to thank the woman for bringing her share of snacks, and as the other two ladies exited through the side doors, we turned left and headed out the main entrance.

Alone, she turned to me and spoke gently,

> *I just wanted to let you know that I'm here for you. When you talk about your dad, I can hear the pain in your voice, and your relationship reminds me a lot of the one I had with my mom. If you need anything, I am here.*

Perhaps it had been so long since someone witnessed my heartache emphatically, without trying to deflect or excuse my distress, or maybe it had been too long since someone offered to help. Whatever the reason was, I was touched. Stepping out of my comfort zone, I grabbed onto the helping hand of the stranger standing in front of me, *Maybe we can go for a coffee sometime?*

Kindly, she smiled and nodded as I took out my cellphone to save her number.

Outside, the atmosphere shifted. We were the last two cars in the parking lot, and the harvest moon painted a supernormal picture above us. The *invisible hand* was beside me, poking me to introduce her to my father. So, I turned my phone around and beamed proudly, *This is my dad.* The beautiful background displaying our father–daughter duo was the same photo I hung in his hospital room, known for evoking emotion. Still, I was not expecting the sentiment that arose in the woman standing next to me. Instantly, she overflowed with grief as the words she was attempting to formulate stayed stuck in the back of her throat.

Fearing I had upset her or reminded her of the mother she recently lost, I quickly apologized, *I'm sorry, I just wanted to show you what he looked like.*

She regained her composure. Then, the following words escaped her, *I knew your dad.*

My eyes widened as my mind stretched to comprehend her statement. I stood staring at her in disbelief, searching for the words to continue.

*What? What do you mean?*

Slowly, the woman—whose energy magnetized me from the very first night—explained, *From Toastmasters, we were in Toastmasters together. I didn't even know he died!* I froze, wonderstruck. The mere mention of the public speaking club my father regularly attended solidified she was telling the truth. Tears streamed down her face as she came to terms with yet another layer added to her compounding grief. Exhaling the pain, she continued,

> Your dad was one of the first people I met when I came to this country, and he welcomed me with open arms. I can't believe he died. I can't believe I'm standing here with Eapen's daughter!

My heart fell, losing equilibrium. In three sentences, she managed to compliment my father and me simultaneously. Out of all the people I chose to acquaint myself with, I sat beside the *one* woman in the room who knew my dad. Reeling from shock, I called my mother and cried the rest of the drive home. Truthfully, we could have gone the whole six sessions without ever coming to this realization.

But this night was set aside for us—my father's will.

The support group I found sustained me as the *Rule of Thirds* had eliminated most people from my life. Unfortunately, not even *a third of a third* of my friends stayed to support me past the initial heroic phase of mourning. My suffering was swept under the rug or passed off to the next person, leaving me out of sight and presumably, out of mind. And when these human ghosts eventually returned, their excuses were divided into two categories: the unaccountable, *I was going to reach out to you, but I assumed you had so many people supporting you already*; and the inexcusable, *I was going to reach out to you, but I didn't know what to say, so I didn't say anything at all.* That phrase—*I was going to reach out to you, but*—should be removed from our conversations altogether. If not, *the truth is you didn't reach out, for your own selfish reasons, to protect yourself, not me*—should be the standard answer.

Solitude is needed to heal, but abandonment is not. At the high point of my life, I imagined my friends would form a long line to support me upon learning my dad had died. But, when the day came, my assumption was wrong, and the line, itself, was a mirage. Everyone assumed by relying heavily on an imaginary other that, in the end, no one showed at all. To be clear, showing up and witnessing the loss of a friend is not the same as doing one's due diligence following a death. And since I did not want to impose or burden others with my sorrow, I vocalized my disappointment and disappeared from the social scene altogether.

\*\*\*

*My best friend and her daughter popped into the room in time for Dad's hourly vitals.*

*The nurse, noticing the vibrancy of the child, inquired, "Who's this young lady?"*

*With ease, my father replied, "My granddaughter."*

*I looked over at my friend, who was like a daughter to my father, and saw her emotion well at my father's expression of love and belonging toward them. My heart expanded for two reasons that day—knowing he loved them as his own and hearing him embody the affection of a grandfather, at least once, before he left.*

\*\*\*

Death strengthens and softens a person concurrently, and when it comes to grief interactions, they are narrowed down based on quality, not quantity. The lethargy and loneliness of grief kept me locked away in my apartment for most of my bereavement. But I did manage to form social connections with other grievers. I did learn how to resurrect compassion and infuse it into areas that mattered, such as helping others cope with grief and loss. And I did have in my possession one excellent friend made of superior quality.

Over the past thirty years, she has been like a *sister* to me, like a *daughter* to my father. Without asking, she visited Dad in the hospital twice a day daily. Apart from my immediate family, she was the last person to spend time with him before he died, and this in itself is the greatest gift a person could give me. My best friend never felt the need to create solutions for my grief. Instead, she sat unmoved beside me, bracing me as I stumbled through it. She allowed me to deconstruct, put back together, and process my story of loss *over* and *over* until reconciliation became possible. She let me—without interference, without domineering control—grieve fully. Alone or with others, she tells stories of my father, belly laughing over the funny things he did to entertain us. She talks about him openly, without fearing it as *unhealthy*, understanding for me—he is my *vitality*. She reflects on the unconditional kindness he showed her during her own trying times when others had abandoned her. And she cried. For an entire year, every night, she wept with me. Last, she extended her love and care to my mother, staying in regular contact with her and visiting her on weekends simply to spend time with her. When we felt forgotten, she made sure we were not.

She is proof we can be an exception to the rule—we *can* companion grief effectively without having to experience a primary loss ourselves.

Before becoming a part of the grieving community, I was under the impression that everyone operated in a highly compassionate fashion. But the truth is only a few people went above and beyond to reach into the dark pit of grief and lend me their hand to pull me out. The rest were misled to believe they would fall in with me if they stayed too long. To truly intervene in our handling of grief, empathy must surpass sympathy—the *higher* self must rise above the *lower*. And when the brooding and pensive nature of mourning turned to mindful contemplation, I saw the strength of my sorrow.

Grief was the only emotion brave enough to ask me to step out of the skin I mistook as protective, shedding the layers of people and places that would not lead me to my destiny. It was the only force adamantly loving my father more deeply after his death. Grasping this, a glimmer of gratitude rose from my grief. Weaving all of my interactions together as one cord, first, I silently observed how grief illiteracy *slithered* its way through society. Then, when the time was right, I used a strand of education to *strangle* the snake.

**Figure 40**
*Releasing and Reconciling*

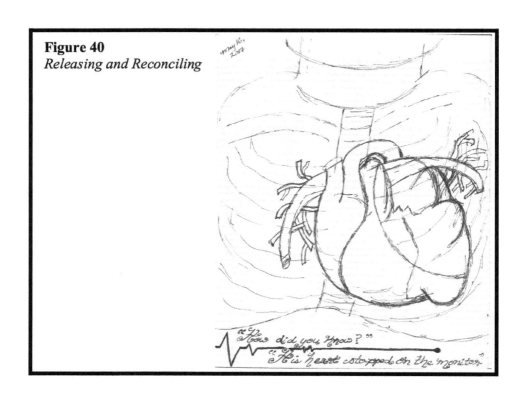

# 40

## The First Year of Mourning

*When I was six years old, two child celebrities from my favorite television show were touring through Calgary. I was so excited! My parents knew how much this meant to me and took me to watch the parade. Although we arrived early, large masses of people had already lined both sides of the street. Everyone was waiting to catch a glimpse of the stars, soon passing by on a float, traveling down the center lane. And when the pop personalities finally emerged, the number of people had doubled, blocking them from my view. Standing to the side, my father, watching me struggle, moved toward me. Grabbing my arms, he hoisted me onto his shoulders. My face illuminated, positioned overtop of the others.*

*Perched on my father's shoulders, I was always one step ahead of everyone else. With his help, I saw everything clearly.*

\*\*\*

My grief was thick and tangled, uncovering all sorts of knots inside and outside of me. By the end of the first year of mourning, fourteen visible truths, as narrated throughout these stories, descended in the form of revelations. Each reality summarizes the wisdom I gained through my encounter with death, grief, loss, trauma, reconciliation, and healing.

## A Summary of Revelations

***Revelation 1: Large Gaps Exist in Our Culture.*** The inaccurate perceptions of death and vague expressions of mourning used to counter my bereavement drove a wedge between me and my surrounding society. As I endured these thoughtless words and actions, the illiteracy of non-grievers translated to apathy. An underdeveloped grasp of a *language of loss* was evident, and this lack of compassionate preciseness was damaging, inhibiting my reconciliation.

The words we use to navigate, companion, and process grief are limited, leaving us unable to communicate the impact of death and verbalize its aftermath. Instead, we resort to empty sentiments, hoping this will be enough to soothe one's spirit. But our current condolences barely scrape the surface; to rekindle the soul, we must travel deeper, beneath the layers of tough skin. We must stand inside the heart of the griever. Thus, moving inward, plummeting into my pain, and putting pen to paper, I attempted to construct a language for loss through these stories. I sifted through my vocabulary and searched for thicker descriptions, evoking the emotions from my experiences. And the more I deconstructed my suffering—writing, rewriting, and revising—the closer I got to defining the intimate aspects of grief, aligning intense feelings to expression. As I sharpened the language of loss, the rougher facets of prolonged mourning softened. Finding the articulation to shape my story was challenging and still needs sharpening. But that is what we collectively need, *sharpening*.

***Revelation 2: One Year is Not Enough.*** By the end of the first year, I sensed those around me expected an agreement to be signed, sealed, and delivered. That, the allotted timestamp for closing my bereavement came with the responsibility to *sign* the contract that terminates my grieving, *seal* the envelope that closes my father's life, and *deliver* the news that my healing was complete and my previous life restored. One year later, he was officially dead. As much as I tried to adhere to the unspoken societal laws of death and grieving, it was not possible to *shut off* my grief. I could still feel the weight of an empty chair, the volume of my mother's silence, the heaviness of my brother's sighs, and my own tumultuous turmoil as we continued to bear the repercussions, adjusting to the presence of my father's absence. The second revelation demonstrated that our culture's interpretation of grieving and the true nature of grief differed.

Although the traditional time for mourning had closed—in both eastern and western hemispheres—my grief did not abide. My first year was exhausted by overcoming the shock of demise, trying my best to survive the *year of firsts*, and coming to terms with secondary losses—a plethora of invisible, subtle aggressions. And though hard to perceive before death occurs, an endless list of slight and not-so-slight alterations stung me:

> The first time I dialed my father's number and realized he would not answer; the first time I entered our home and understood his chair was permanently empty, that his belongings had no owner; the first time I was excited to share good news with him and was met with devastation.

> The first time I went to purchase a gift for him and realized this was no longer necessary; the first time I finished a book and could not hand the knowledge over; the first time I cooked his favorite meal, and food was left untouched; the first time I saw a trailer for a movie, and the film went unwatched.

> The first time I had to remove him as my beneficiary and delete him from my emergency contacts, and the layers of my loss unraveled; the first time I noticed another attached to his cell number, a number I had gifted him, and felt a stranger's betrayal; the first time someone else near to me fell ill and I riddled with anxiety.

> The first time one of his plants died, and I felt his death all over again.

The center of my sorrow was unaffected during the first year of losses. I simply dipped my toes in, felt the chilling water, and ran back to the safe shore. Despite what many believe, the second year of grieving was more difficult—once the shock subsided, the pain was rawer, scalding, and more real. My father's death had set in, and the grueling grief work began. In the third year of active mourning, my wounds started to mend. Finally, in the fourth year, I felt my spirit return. Grief does not take to the shape of our square box because we do not set out to cure our losses—we set an intention to heal our sorrow. And to heal effectively, our walls must lower, and our timelines abolished.

***Revelation 3: Marking the Anniversary is Important.*** Each year our family has a long road of signature signposts to cross before rounding my father's death anniversary—my parents' wedding anniversary, Christmas Day, New Year's Day, Dad's birthday, and then only January 14. This festive bombardment carries heavy reminders of what he endured in the hospital, forever changing our happy holidays and darkening our golden memories. And even though the anticipation of each occasion spiked my reactions and responses to his first death anniversary, some form of safeguarding took place when the actual day arrived. The *invisible hand* swaddled me with grace, and the cultural traditions in place to auspiciously guide the day cushioned and comforted all three of us.

We marked his death day using ritualistic prayers, remembrance announcements in India, and a luncheon for our church's congregation in Canada. And observing the anniversary of his last day on earth, through small acts or large, continues to be a valuable asset of healing. To pause and collect the heaviness of his death, breaking and releasing bits of the boulder, mattered. Rituals then voiced our private feelings—we remain as four, and he lives through us.

***Revelation 4: Restructuring Identity.*** I am no longer the person I once was; the depth of my loss has changed me. While the first year of mourning consisted of searching for my father—in pictures, belongings, and faces in a crowd—the second year involved searching for *myself*, collecting fragments of an identity that had dispersed and shattered.

My reflection was different, unrecognizable, showcasing a tinge in my eyes that revealed my life story had tainted me. Others often commented how *I looked so much happier in older photos, like a different person altogether*—because I was. I disconnected from those around me, was forgiven of past transgressions, and understood happiness as elusive. The qualities that made me human had slipped away. Moreover, grief did not feed off my inability to accept my father's death; it thrived off my incapability to relinquish that which died within me.

The more I fought against the changing nature of my identity, succumbing to the ego and lower self—*the part of me that wanted to suffer*—the more I resisted my spiritual evolution, draining my life force further. I was obstinate, trying to find her, rescue her, and bring her back. But the pain in my eyes spoke volumes; like my father, she could not be resuscitated. Brought to my knees in despair, I prayed for a solution—hearing the call of the higher, I surrendered to restructuring my identity and reworking my spirit. I awoke to the knowledge that *two* people died in the room that night. Then, I laid her to rest alongside my dad and embodied my rebirth through relearning and rebuilding. Consciously, I engaged with the *Dark Night of the Soul* [26] and gave the force permission to transform me.

As I crossed the threshold to my destiny, my father's revelations appeared and flowing with the current, not against, my grief significantly lessened. I was empowered to walk the earth confident in the knowledge that my father's hand rested where his soul exhaled—on my right shoulder.

***Revelation 5: Grief is My Soul's Reflection.*** Dad's last breath chiseled my heart, cracking it open, spilling my enormous love for him, drowning the people around me. Others could not imitate or reciprocate the strength of this love—the material was too thick and potent, infinite and uncontainable. Yet, if they had managed to barricade or stunt the force of my affection, the intensity of my grief, I would not have been able to continue a bond with my father. I would not have aligned with my greater purpose. Since I could no longer indulge in the lackluster company of others, I learned to familiarize myself with the new reflection life painted me. I sat alone at a table where only my grief was courageous enough to join me. And, after endless hours spent in each other's company, we became acquainted, formed a friendship, and became one.

Bereavement is not a journey best walked alone—that is an excuse created by others—but in the end, my grief was the only energy that loved my father as much as I did. Because of this, my whole heart returned, admiring the fierceness of my soul's reflection.

***Revelation 6: Grievers Unite and Join Forces.*** Although my supposed support system fell, a new structure rose in unexpected places. Slowly, a resurgence of old acquaintances reached out to cross paths with mine to revive me. Members of the grieving community emerged through

---

[26] *Dark Nights of the Soul*. T. Moore. (2004). Gotham Books.

colleagues, reiki clients, and mutual contacts who gladly stepped up to the plate, offering their hearts and hands for encouragement. They had lived through the difficulty of finding authentic grief support, so they broke unhealthy cycles. Whether they made short visits to my home, gifted me with symbolic father–daughter items, or provided me with journals to actively grieve, their small gestures turned into great sources of comfort. They knew that sitting unmoved in stillness and silence did not require *words*. Joining forces, they banded together and threw down a rope into my well of darkness. And, bit by bit, the grieving villagers pulled together and brought me out. Now, to show my gratitude, I place my hand on the cord and pay this kindness forward.

***Revelation 7: Grief Holds up a Mirror of Death.*** Death lurks in the shadows. But when my father died, he brought a universal truth to light—nothing is permanent. Hence, the dark times that befell our household reminded neighboring houses that no one evades losing a loved one, which became an underlying reason why I could not forge and sustain connections with those outside the grieving community. To come to terms with the impermanence of their loved ones, or themselves, was inconceivable, and the intensity of my grief made them uncomfortable, fearing something similar would happen to them.

Astutely, C.S. Lewis equated the feeling of grief with *fear*,[27] and fear, I noticed, traveled both ways. The phrases, *I can't imagine what you are going through*, or *I don't know how you do it*, were internal reflections of, *I don't want to imagine; I won't be able to do it*. The unthinkable then created situations where I would be left comforting others for the loss of my father as they contemplated the *possible* loss of theirs. Or I was forced to witness them take their parents for granted while living and breathing air still.

This spectrum ran deep, from listening to others complain about their fathers, refusing to mend the issues, and seeking my advice, to consoling a married woman who could not bear *not* having had her father walk her down the aisle. As mind-boggling as these exchanges were, they only reinforced the need to expand our education on death, companioning grief, and improving our social grief etiquette toward one another.

---

[27] *A Grief Observed*. C. Lewis. (1961). Bantam Books.

***Revelation 8: Grief Oscillates.***[28] Outdated, misunderstood theories have taught us that grief passes through set stages or linear phases, but those who grieve know nothing is straightforward about sorrowing. Grief is not a mixture of independent emotions; profoundly, it stands alone, a sensation that came to life only after my father was pronounced dead. No matter how inevitable death seemed, his actual death was what locked my understanding of his loss in place.

When I am honest with myself, I know I never fully believed he would die—my hope was far greater than I had imagined. So, when he did die, terror took over, and an anticipatory feeling radically shifted into the solid shape of grief. Endless hope layered with utter disbelief and my high attachment to my father became the building blocks of my complicated mourning.

My grief rose and fell in waves—external factors determined the height, and internal factors determined the depth. I judged myself harshly for not having done enough or not having spent more time with him, without realizing that this, too, was grief taking wing. These ripples, tides, and tsunamis were not bringing me to a destination; instead, they took me along on a sacred wandering, where I learned grief oscillates, swaying back and forth in a calculated manner.

If I were to have felt the full force of my father's death all at once, I would not have survived. Therefore, grief, though relentless, was fair, offering breaks to adapt to my mind's needs. First, the crest of the waves sharpened along the edge of my consciousness, keeping me in tune with its demands. Then, the synergy between my body, mind, and spirit ensured the troughs pulled me under only when I was strong enough to swim. Methodically, the healing waters reached for the shore and receded, creating a natural, intentional rhythm.

***Revelation 9: Right-brained Activities Release Grief.*** The trauma of loss significantly affected the functioning of the left side of my brain, decreasing my ability to reckon with logic, language, and reasoning. Instead, an explosion of energy burst from the right hemisphere, expanding my intuition, emotion, and creativity.[29] Grief researchers have shown that creative endeavors have a positive impact on bereavement.

---

28 "The dual process model of coping with bereavement: A decade on," by M. Stroebe & H. Schut, 2010, *OMEGA - Journal of Death and Dying*, 61(4), 273–289.
29 *The Body Keeps the Score: Brain, Mind, and Body in the Healing of Trauma*. B. Van der Kolk. (2014). Penguin Books.

Dancing, singing, sculpting, painting, art-making, enacting, and scrapbooking help us explore our loss and process painful emotions through movement.[30] Hence, by immersing myself in creative, arts-based activities that engaged my grief in calming ways, I released pent-up, unsettled energy that triggered my overactive nervous system.

Visually, I created picture projects through albums, slideshows, and framed montages. Expressively, I penned beautiful poetry, crafting metaphors describing the magnitude of my loss. Auditorily, I learned how to play the sitar, channeling my sadness into the spiritual sounds of an Indian instrument. Lastly, I used art to sketch my recurring, intrusive thoughts, such as—*his heart stopped on the monitor*. Instinctually, I knew that by drawing out the painful memories, my mind would process the trauma and leave my system, which it did. The images dissolved, and the disturbance left me. Thus, right-brained activities gave me an outlet to harness my grief, and then, using creative shifts, I found release.

***Revelation 10: Writing Saved Me.*** At the tender age of four, my father sat me at his typewriter and instructed me to write as though he saw what my future held in store. I remember him placing my hands on the keys and teaching me to construct proper sentences, as though he knew beautiful words were a part of my destiny. Before I entered primary school, I was seated in his classroom. Daily, he assigned me pages from the dictionary, testing me on various spellings and definitions; I learned shorthand, taking diction as he spoke, training to sift through the clutter; and I completed his self-made grammar sheets, ensuring my editing skills were on par with his.

After I became an English teacher, *like him*, I often reflected on his training, laughing and thinking about how he purposely aligned my path with teaching. But after he died, the true aim of his lessons unfolded. To ease the suffering of his loss, organically, he had left me the right tools. My paralyzing grief found refuge in words through journaling, letter writing, and storytelling. And using the continuous writing motion of my hands, movement in the rest of my limbs restored. Therefore, writing saved me, swaying life into a lifeless soul. By constructing these coherent plots, shifting perspectives, find-

---

[30] *Grief and the Expressive Arts: Practices for Creating Meaning.* R. Neimeyer & B. Thompson. (2014). Routledge, Taylor & Francis Group.

ing benefit, becoming an overall better person,[31] and including the four cornerstones of grief stories (relationship building, designing a blueprint of grief, strengthening spiritual health, and leaving a lasting footprint)[32]—expressive storytelling transformed my grief from a weighted boulder to a quill feather.

**Revelation 11: *My New Identity is His Old Identity*.** When my father's flame burnt out, my spark dimmed. My interests and hobbies took a backseat while his pastimes grabbed the steering wheel, driving my desires. I spent my days engaged in activities that he liked to do. Sometimes, I walked around garden centers because his presence was profound in his frequented spaces—one houseplant grew to a dozen within the first few months of his loss. Often, I browsed his vast book titles, quickly noting we had a similar collection. And from time to time, I caught myself mimicking his mannerisms, or his *dad jokes* surprisingly found a way into my dialogue. Without noticing, my new identity shaped around who he was, and our sameness brought irrefutable comfort.

But gradually, I watched my old joys slip away. I lost my ability to laugh, to smile, to use *exclamation marks* in my correspondence. I refused to go to our restaurant, buy unnecessary things, or listen to music that once brought me joy. All earthly pleasures and material wealth were removed and kept at a distance from me; my grief transformed me into a practicing ascetic. Burned and bruised from the hurt, I no longer sought new friendships or relationships, as the idea of being close to someone and then losing them frightened me. I had decided not another drop of pain would survive me.

For the most part, I accepted the changes happening—the blandness, the quarantine, the deprivation. But one secondary loss injured me more than the others: *I had stopped dancing.* I learned Indian classical dance as a young child, and my spirit evolved through rhythm, transforming dance into a potent elixir. I performed at multicultural and civic functions, created workshops, and promoted my culture at post-secondary events. When I became a teacher, I passed this love on to my students, encouraging their self-expression through movement.

---

[31] *Opening Up by Writing It Down: How Expressive Writing Improves Health and Eases Emotional Pain.* J. Pennebaker & J. Smyth. (2016). The Guilford Press.
[32] *Life: To Be Given Back Again to Whence It Came.* L. Mathew. (2022). DIO Press Inc.

And since my father attended my last performance at my school's cultural function—it became my final performance. The innate joy that once glided through my body stiffened; his last breath blew out my fire. Yet, the more I consciously work through my grief, the more my body sways alongside the music again. Certainly, the last piece of healing, maturing my grief, will solidify the day I wear my *chilanka* (musical anklets) and embrace the art of dance once more.

**Revelation 12: Holistic Healing is Essential.** Death tore my soul. The lacerations from his loss left long-lasting impressions across the landscape of my well-being, ensuring grief affected my whole self. My reactions and responses to his demise triggered physical, social, psychological, behavioral, and spiritual repercussions. Hence, to uphold the weaving of the *invisible hand*, stitching and suturing my wounds, I had to think outside the box. And since multidimensional aspects of my health were at risk, I took a multifaceted approach to heal.

To secure a functional grief care regime, I sought advice from medical doctors, naturopaths, nutritionists, Ayurvedic practitioners, grief counselors, psychologists, psychiatrists, social workers, spiritual leaders, and healers. I attended educational sessions, retreats, workshops, and conventions, discussing the nature of trauma, grief, loss, and healing. I read books, watched documentaries, listened to podcasts, and engaged in conversations with other grievers. I mourned through ritualistic traditions and ceremonies, transmuting pain into action, which allowed meaningful motions to ease my suffering. I used therapeutic writing techniques to consciously record, organize, interpret, analyze, and release my sorrow. I pursued grief work in a dignified fashion—conscientiously, deliberately, actively. But, most importantly, I permitted myself to take breaks from feeling the constant horror of loss. Else, I may not have survived. To move through grief effectively, I had to stop and rest, absorbing the ointments I applied and allowing time for my wounds to repair and mend.

As a griever, I walked through the dark passage of mourning alone, and no light could be seen at the end of the tunnel—but eventually, flickers seeped through the cracked holes of the walls, punctured by a potent mourning process, guiding me toward brilliance. Death is a wound that never closes; the sadness of losing him is irreparable. The sutures held me in place to survive my father's loss, but the loss itself will never leave me. Yet, as I actively mourn and reconstruct meaning in the dynamics of my life,[33] my suffering heals as promised: *Blessed are those who mourn, for they will be comforted.*[34] Though the soul is torn, the spirit's material outlasts calamity. And though sewn scars do not fade—the cicatrix illustrates our individual, resilient path, mapping our trek out of the wilderness of grief.

**Revelation 13: *The Site of Loss is Sacred Ground.*** A year after my father's death, my mother was hospitalized. Even though the issue would be non-life-threatening, returning to the hospital where our father died left my brother and me in shambles. I received the call, and I panicked, *I will never go back there*. Then, when she was admitted, I drove down the eerie strip of road, and my statement shifted, *I will never walk past that corridor*. Next, I twisted and turned to avoid that wing of the hospital, *I will never go to the ICU*. Finally, as I sat in a chair, watching my mother rest peacefully, I became still and silent, and a higher perspective emerged, interweaving our circumstances with a powerful opportunity. A full circle action awaited me—I only had to complete it.

Heading to the cafeteria, I stealthily slipped around the corner of the staircase, *still* dodging the critical care facility. My humanness lagged, so the *invisible hand* brought me to a halt. Surprisingly, I stopped, turned, and moved upward. Without conscious knowledge, somehow, I stood in front of the long, white-walled strip of tiles I had once fearfully wheeled my father down on a stretcher. A child, terror-filled, I inched my way down the haunted hallway. I sat in those same chairs where I received heart-shattering news, stared at those same doors I longed to see my father return alive through, and peered into the same visiting room where our family was declared broken. Unmoved, I sat for two minutes. Everything was as I had left it, except the spaces were much smaller than I remembered. *One hundred eighty seconds later*, my stomach started twisting. I placed my hand on the holy ground where my father's soul departed, made a sign of the cross, and hastily ran back to my mother.

Initially, my brother could not comprehend my actions. But af-

---

33 *Meaning Reconstruction & the Experience of Loss*. R. Neimeyer. (2001). [Kindle version].
34 *Matthew 5:4*. New International Version Bible. (1973). New International Version Bible Online.

ter hearing my explanation—*I just needed to face my fears while I was already here because if I didn't do this now, I would never come back and revisit them later*—he decided he should face his demons too. And once both of us made the invisible visible, a playfulness returned. For the first time in a long time, we laughed. My mother's hospitalization was not about reexperiencing a separate tragedy but about revisiting the same one. And by revisiting the sacred site of loss, our family's suffering became a lot lighter.

**Revelation 14: Acquiring an Angel.** When guided by an ethereal hand, a personal angel known dearly, life moves with grace and ease. Ever since my father crossed over to a place where he can see me, though I cannot see him, my days overflow with serendipitous and blessed occurrences. Gifts arrived for all three of us in unimaginable ways that only my father would understand were important. And as an array of opportunities aligned perfectly on my path, I often stopped to wonder if Dad's hand turned the handles on doors that could only be opened from *the other side*. Some regard these acts as coincidences or flukes, but small showers of love continue to rain down on me from someone who has an intimate knowledge of me, wholly and entirely. Whether in the form of *extraordinary experiences*[35] or simply receiving that little bit of help I needed to succeed, Dad has proved time and time again to have taken a more permanent seat in my life as my guardian angel. My father kept his promise—spiritually, he surrounds me. This book, if anything, is proof of that.

---

[35] *Gifts from the Unknown: Using Extraordinary Experiences to Cope with Loss & Change.* L. LaGrand. (2001). Authors Choice Press.

# ~Epilogue~

*Death is nothing at all.*
*It does not count.*
*I have only slipped away into the next room.*
*Nothing has happened.*

*Everything remains exactly as it was.*
*I am I, and you are you,*
*and the old life that we lived so fondly together is untouched, unchanged.*
*Whatever we were to each other, that we are still.*

*Call me by the old familiar name.*
*Speak of me in the easy way which you always used.*
*Put no difference into your tone.*
*Wear no forced air of solemnity or sorrow.*

*Laugh as we always laughed at the little jokes that we enjoyed together.*
*Play, smile, think of me, pray for me.*
*Let my name be ever the household word that it always was.*
*Let it be spoken without an effort, without the ghost of a shadow upon it.*

*Life means all that it ever meant.*
*It is the same as it ever was.*
*There is absolute and unbroken continuity.*
*What is this death but a negligible accident?*

The Revelations of Eapen

*Why should I be out of mind because I am out of sight?*
*I am but waiting for you, for an interval,*
*somewhere very near,*
*just round the corner.*

*All is well.*
*Nothing is hurt; nothing is lost.*
*One brief moment and all will be as it was before.*
*How we shall laugh at the trouble of parting when we meet again!*

—Henry Scott Holland

**Figure 41**
*My Great Love Story*

# 41

## The First Request

### Continuing Bonds With My Father

*After his death, I began searching. Without conscious effort, I became overwhelmed by a profound urge to search for my father everywhere. My mother and brother could not comprehend my behavior and often commented that they did not feel the need to scour through his things. But I wasn't searching for things—I was searching, specifically, for him. My identity imploded, my suffering intensified, and the only advice I craved to hear was his. Sincerely, I believed that he left clues behind, hidden for me to find, and these puzzle pieces would help me locate him again.*

*Riled by their accusatory tone, I took advantage of a day when no one was home. Hurriedly, I ransacked my father's closet, grabbed a suitcase, and brought the treasure chest back to my apartment to look through with ease. But regrettably, upon lifting the lid, I realized the briefcase belonged to my mother. Dejected, I threw my hands in the air and sat on the floor on the verge of tears. Before hurling myself further into my pit of grief, I sensed an inkling, a nudge, a whisper—look through it anyway, Linita, something is waiting for you. At once, I remembered mistakes are a mirage and that nothing is accidental.*

*Shuffling through the mountain of old bills, suddenly, in clear sight, a gift surfaced. A set of old letters my mother kept, written to her while she took care of her ailing mother in India, floated to the top of the pile. Stapled together were three layers of messages—one from me, my brother, and last, my father. Romantic displays of affection between my parents were rare, but now, out of nowhere, a love letter appeared. Scanning my father's words, his personality popped off the page and lay in my hands once more. For me, this was enough, but what I stumbled on was much more. Knowing my mother was grieving the loss of her dad, my father wrote a poem to give her spiritual sustenance as interpreted through a dream visitation:*

> I had another encounter with the deceased… guess who? Since it is a private conversation, I am not supposed to reveal it directly. Hence, I have to paraphrase it in the following verse. It is not anything mundane, but universal and eternal. I hope it will be my contribution to his eternal memory.
>
> 'Life
> For Most of us it passes – day by day;
> Sometimes in pain,
> All too rarely with joy,
> But mostly it just passes.
> Until one day
> Our precarious hold slips, is joggled,
> and oh-so-nearly falls from our grasp
> Then we know, if it's not too late,
> That each new day is too precious
> Just to let pass.
> It is instead a fresh gift given,
> To be savoured, whether in pain
> Or with joy,
> But always to be lived and somehow
> To be given back again to whence it came'[36]

*My father's arms stretched off the page and wrapped around me. Understanding that my mother was struggling then, he wrote this poem to comfort her. And knowing that I was suffering now, he brought his counsel forward to heal me. Awestruck, an explosion of tears moved me.*

*My searching had yielded unimagined results. Because of an untameable ache, I fully engaged in my first reciprocal experience of continuing bonds with my father.*

\*\*\*

---

[36] *E. Mathew. (July 6, 1992). Personal Communication.*

## The First Request

Shortly after he died, a profound sense of yearning collapsed me to the floor. Caving in, this would be the first time I completely lost my breath to grief. The oxygen in my lungs refused to release into a world where my father did not exist; instead, the air stayed trapped in my heart, where he remained *alive* and *well*. I would not have survived this tragedy had I not found a way to continue my relationship with him—and, at the opportune time, guidance delivered me.

Emulating my father's energy, I closed my eyes, and drained of all sensation, the *invisible hand* drew me inward. Inside this poignant silence, woven within the threads of my soul, a message awaited me.

> *If you are as close to your father as you claim to be, then the true nature of your relationship starts now.*

The words were crisp and clear, and attached to them was a request from him—prove you can continue our rare bond, *do not let my death deter you.*

I am my father's daughter, every cell of mine infuses with the knowledge and love of him, and our connection far surpasses the limitations of the physical realm. If any two people *could* master continuing a bond past death, the bold example is us. A higher power had challenged me, fully knowing that when it comes to finding ways to express my love for my father—I stay victorious.

With an extensive background in spiritual literacy, I already knew how to read the signs around me—earth stars pointing us in the right direction. As a healer, my intuitive ability rests on the foundation that I am highly-sensitive, fully empathic, and keenly observational. Therefore, stepping into the unknown was not daunting for me. Finding light in the dark was innate and organic, and paying attention to non-verbal cues was embedded in my way of life, rooted in our father-daughter relationship.

As I worked more closely with grieving populations, our commonalities of extraordinary experiences struck me. Listening to their stories, I learned that continuing a relationship with a deceased loved one did not necessarily stem from having a specific cultural, spiritual, or religious background. Any person can lay down the panels, bridging a bond with their beloved if they are willing. And though not a requirement, in my case, having a firm grasp on transcendent and metaphysical concepts before loss eased the reciprocity permitted from the other side because a solid spiritual connection was already intact. Like all other life skills, reinforcement leads to mastery.

Keen to master this spiritual phenomenon, I continued having conversations with grievers from all walks of life, read more books on sixth-sense occurrences, and listened to podcasts of well-known public figures who had broached their own encounters with the deceased.

> *My father and I were so close, and because of the way he died, [I felt] that he had never left me....When I got the Nobel prize...all of a sudden, I looked up and I saw my father in the hall...I couldn't speak. I couldn't open my mouth. It took me, I think, one or two or three long endless minutes for me—to start talking. I couldn't talk.*[37]

I stumbled upon this interview while sinking in the sadness of milestones my father will miss—Holocaust survivor *Elie Wiesel's* experience, offering me relief. By comparing and contrasting the extraordinaries of others against my extrasensory perceptions, clearer patterns emerged. Using multiple layers of information, I formulated a guided approach to Continuing Bonds[38] to support others seeking ways to engage with this grief model and strengthen their ties post-loss. My thorough exploration and vivid insights into the magical elements of death, dying, and grieving helped me narrow and identify *five golden keys* that unlocked and opened the door to find my father once more.

## The Five Keys of Continuing Bonds

The *first key* is to sharpen the art of making astute observations. To initiate the process, I had to agree on items I knew my father would place on my path: *daffodils, butterflies,* and the number *14*. Sure enough, when I need his instruction or blessing, either individually or in combination, one of these three items cleverly delivers a wink of reassurance. And the more I recognized the spiritual constellation, the more the universal design unraveled, showering me with grief gifts at precisely the right time.

For instance, on my third trip to India after his death, I lived through a natural disaster—the worst flood Kerala had seen in over

---

37 *Elie Wiesel: Living with an Open Heart*. (2018). In Oprah's Super Soul Conversations [audio]. Apple Podcasts.
38 *Continuing Bonds in Bereavement: New Directions for Research and Practice*. D. Klass & E. Steffen. (2018). Routledge, Taylor & Francis Group.

a century. Since the airport submerged under water, my mother and brother's flight was canceled. Distraught by the state-wide emergency, feeling fearful and trapped, I sank in my chair as the panic and loneliness of the situation set in. Right then, out of the corner of my eye, a plaque on the wall tugged at me. My eyes fixated on the numbers at the bottom 41:10—a numerical anagram of my father's death day. Hastily, I asked my cousin to read the *Vattezhuthu* (rounded script) out loud. And before I knew it, a message appeared:

> *Fear not, for I am with you;*
> *Be not dismayed, for I am your God.*
> *I will strengthen you,*
> *Yes, I will help you,*
> *I will uphold you with My righteous right hand.*[39]

The comfort of my father's presence overcame me, driving the fear out of my circumstances. When I trained my mind to pay attention to everything, even the invisible became visible.

The *second key* is to embrace the unknown by immersing in life's mysteries and merging with them. As humans, if we continuously engage with a fixed mindset, we do not maximize our brainpower; thus, I consciously reinforce neural pathways that encourage me to grow out of my comfort zone. By limiting the doubts, disbelief, and disillusionment that arose from interacting with the magical elements of death and dying, I increased my trust in these spiritual exchanges and the frequency in which I received them. Steadily, my reaction to timely coincidences shifted from *curiosity* to *certainty*.

Influenced by my cultural heritage, which nourishes these encounters, I created new routines that enabled me to keep my father's role intact—such as touching his grave instead of his feet to acquire his blessings. By willingly embracing these new habits, I was not tricking myself into thinking he was present; I embodied a confidence that knew he was. I participated in these practices daily as though he had attended to auspicious matters. Hence to hold my father still, I had to seek ways to embrace his new form.

---

[39] *Isaiah 41:10.* New King James Version. (1982). Bible Gateway Online.

The *third key* is to surrender to one's sixth sense, a crucial skill to engage when connecting with spirit is concerned. My father raised me engulfed in his warmth—I know him well. So, sensing his presence and being sure of him is instinctual. I can *feel* when he enters a room. A peaceful wave emerges, my spine chills, my hair stands to greet him, and a warm sensation of *being home* springs forward. Even those who entered my apartment or tuned into my stories often raised their arms to display their own reception of goosebumps while hearing me talk of my father—a sense beyond the primary five bridged us to a sliver of his world.

Retreating to India so soon after he died immersed me in the spiritual, maternal energy of the country. A mother's instinct for present *and* lost children replicated, as in Kerala, visitations from the deceased were welcomed, openly discussed, and viewed as propitious. I shared my experiences with my relatives without judgment, which, in turn, strengthened my spiritual health and abilities. Moving through the motherland, when crucial matters arose, my father's favorite song spun in the background, counseling my decisions through lyrical guidance. And when I returned home, the same song managed to follow me the first night itself, providing continued comfort. When my despondency grew, my questioning of my role as an effective caregiver lingered, the lyrics rang vibrant: *Neerumen praanalil nee aasha than thenozhukki— You poured soothing, hopeful honey over my suffering soul.*

These sixth-sensory experiences emboldened me. I became good at decoding the language of spirit, sheltering me. And as I learned to adapt my life in larger ways, the avenues he used to communicate with me spread. His words of wisdom or distinguishable sayings traveled through well-timed, third-party sources. Or his conversations would spark telepathically. Like a chinook wind on a cold day, Dad's advice would brush past and warm me. Slowly, I saw his continued involvement in my decision-making processes.

I also had to differentiate between having a dream and receiving a visitation. After he died, I dreamt of him nightly. At first, we were transported back to the hospital, where he remained gravely ill. I knew these were merely dreams because our interactions were casual, we engaged in repetitive behaviors, and the visuals depicted me heavily resisting the matter of his death, a strong indicator of psychological distress.[40] But as I continued to process my grief, his ailing condition concurrently improved, and my dreams became a valid measure of my healing.

*Dream visitations*, on the other hand, differed. They were sparse and infrequent, occurring at desperate lows, during intervals when I was not awake but not in a deep sleep either. A meditative, spiritual, subconscious space opened, and a lucid opportunity to rekindle our relationship transpired. A *figure* or *form* materialized; I could not see his face or physical features clearly—only a simple outline of energy remained. I would have to choose to move toward him. And when I did, an all-too-familiar scenario ensued.

> *Carrying out my routine, I ran upstairs toward Dad's room, eager to see him. Intrusively, my mind spoke, "He won't be there, Linita. He died." Keeping my conscience at bay, I climbed the long staircase anyway. Finally, I reached the top of the hurdle and turned left toward his bedroom. A feeling of fear and excitement mingled into one. Entering, I found him standing in front of me, waiting for me.*
>
> *His form was not the same as before, it had transformed, almost abstract, but I knew it was him—his energy exuded. Dad looked healthier, fuller, and lighter than he had ever looked in his physical form. He took my arm and sat me next to him, placing my head on the rise of his belly, like before. Patting my head, my father comforted me, his universal sign to let me know all was well. We spoke no words between us.*
>
> *Suddenly, I drew to the condition of his feet. I had spent a good portion of my life putting diabetic lotion on his legs, so I knew the shape and state of his feet better than anyone. But now, they were soft and glowing; not a single crack defined his skin. Amazed, I reached down to touch them, to make sure of what I saw—that he was real. Barely brushing past the edge of his toe, my brain fired a signal, waking me instantaneously. Our extraordinary experience had come to an end.*

My fragile mind, unable to handle those brief interactions, shocked me awake. However, as I continued to permit contact with my sixth-sense perceptions, my fear vanished, and our visits comfortably resumed. I eagerly await these dreams, feeling refreshed and rejuvenated, as I did after our visits when he lived.

---

40 "Comforting versus distressing dreams of the deceased: Relations to grief, trauma, attachment, continuing bonds, and post-dream reactions," J. Black, et al. (2020). *OMEGA - Journal of Death and Dying, 84*(2), 525–550.

The *fourth key* is to discern and silence the naysayers. Continuing a bond with a person who has died is an unusual practice in modern western societies, which will attract unsolicited advice and judgment. Especially since this theory is only now gaining momentum as a healthy part of the mourning process. Yet, the silver lining that arose from spending so much time alone is that I stopped valuing the opinions of others, specifically in handling my grief. When my suffering should have mattered, *they were silent*, and so when my coping strategies should make no difference, *they are not consulted*. Purposely, I cut off the interference that tried to inhibit my regenerating connection with my father. Instead, I focused on cultivating my understanding of leading a spiritual life in the human body.

Early in my grieving, I reminded myself that an ongoing relationship with my father was between *me* and *my father*, and the overstepping comments that I should *detach from him* were pushed out of my mind. They did not feel me craving a dad's touch, the solid suffering of my eyes, or the overflow of love I carried with no coinciding tributary to pool. And if the balm I applied on my wounds soothed my gashes, the end justified the means. Nevertheless, to shield myself from others, I created a mantra to solidify my stance through sacred sounds:

*I inhale, –*
*And you are there.*
*I exhale, –*
*And you are also there.*

*Those who assume we must separate,*
*Must not know the value of air.*

Mantras are effective because they fortify the habits we seek to gain. Death diminishes the physical, but the spiritual, emotional, and psychological impact of the person lives on. By reciting these phrases daily, I took control over my mourning and my right to continue the beautiful relationship I had with my father. And those who encouraged using extraordinary experiences to heal helped me transition more smoothly into reconciliation. Therefore, if those surrounding the griever are not fully encouraging the magical elements of death and dying while surviving loss—perhaps one's relationship with the deceased is not the one that needs letting go.

The last, most vital, *fifth key* is to remember the relationship is reciprocal. As much as I needed to feel my father's presence reaching out to me, he needed to feel mine reaching out to him. All healthy relationships flourish through intentional reciprocity.

Apart from our cultural practice of adorning Dad's image with symbolic gestures, our family developed our own rituals, extending our interactions with him. For special anniversaries, birthdays, and holidays, we meet with him graveside, greeting the head of our household with flowers and spending the first few minutes of the occasion with him. Our cards to each other still bear his name, emphasizing death did not remove him from our family. And since my father was an avid gardener, proud of his indoor and outdoor pots, we maintain his hobbies for him. Although our participation in tending his land may have been mandatory in the past—now, on our own accord, we buy his favorite blooms and spend May's long weekend getting his garden ready for the growing season. And whenever a tomato or apple appears, my mother places the fruit of his labor on the mantle next to his picture, ensuring he reaps the rewards of his hard work from previous years.

Once, through a dream visitation, my father appeared to me and said: *My heart is still beating—it is beating through you.* Holding this truth above all other certainties in my life, I wake each morning knowing my physical steps match the spiritual dance of his soul.

At the break of dawn, I brew a fresh cup of black coffee and place it near his picture while I get ready for the day ahead. His ring and necklace finalize any outfit, adding a layer of protection to my attire. Drinking the coffee, I stand in front of his picture and take his blessings before stepping out of my home. And if a challenging task comes forward, I visit his grave and kneel at his headstone before making any major decisions. As the sun sets, his playlist of songs softly airs while cooking his signature dishes. Then, wrapping myself in his shawl, I sit on the floor and pray the same way we used to. Before heading to bed, I light the candle beside his picture and recap my day, penning letters to him. Continuing a bond with a loved one does not have to be an extravagant, mystical, otherworldly affair. An eternal relationship can grow from simple gestures found in the daily rounds of living—routines that reach forward and greet the ones we love.

Accordingly, I am confident in proclaiming our bond prevailed past his death. Leaning into the omnipresent feel of his *invisible hands*, now resting on my shoulders, a deeper, more meaningful, more vibrant connection has thrived, flowing through the very center of my life.

*When butterflies flit or daffodils bloom,*
*I know this must be you.*
*When the number 14 appears, and it always does,*
*I know this must be you.*
*When your loving touch resumes, transported through dreams,*
*I know this must be you.*
*When those who enter my home feel a spark of your soul,*
*I know this must be you.*

*When I ask a difficult question and receive a simple answer,*
*I know this must be you.*
*When your lovable quotes and catchphrases materialize,*
*I know this must be you.*
*When all at once, I'm clever like you,*
*I know this must be you.*
*When your laughter rumbles or your voice echoes through,*
*I know this must be you.*

*When grief collapsed me to the floor, and I lifted to my feet,*
*I know this must be you.*
*When our last conversation intervenes and rings true,*
*I know this must be you.*
*When the sun showers your grave through an obsidian sky,*
*I know this must be you.*
*When I could not survive without you*
*and learned I would not have to,*
*I know this must be you.*

*When these revelations flowed effortlessly,*
*renewing the lost purpose of these hands,*
*I know this must be you.*

# The First Request

*As I exit the darkest night of my soul,*
*I see a light—*
*And I know, indeed, it is you.*

My father trained me to establish a keen eye for the beauty in my surroundings: *A thing of beauty is a joy forever,*[41] *Linita.* I know now his revelations along the way were merely teaching me how to continue our bond once he was gone—to find him in the simple pleasures of life. My father does not appear in large, visible gestures here and there. Instead, I discover him in small subtleties that cross my path every day.

Eapen Mathew was revolutionary, conquering gender, racial, and spiritual biases beyond his time. He was a great man who—as *Mahatma Gandhi* suggested—shook the world in a gentle way. He was devout and faithful, obedient to his Creator, meditating on divinity; he was brilliant and exceptional, an endless vessel of knowledge, continuously striving to learn more; he was compassionate and warm-hearted, emphatic to those around him, offering an unwavering helping hand; he was still and silent, surrendering to life's challenges, accepting the larger plan; and he was a father beyond measure, bearing his losses wholeheartedly for the center of his universe—his children.

Quietly and invisibly, my father moved through this world, absorbing the joy found in modest treasures—reading, writing, walking, gardening, listening, praying, and engaging with the spirit around him. Freely, he passed his knowledge and wisdom onto others, requesting little to nothing in return.

When Mumtaz died, Shah Jahan built for her the Wonder of the Taj Mahal. And when my father died, I wrote for him these stories. Great love aspires to do great things. Within my words, evidenced in pages of masterful storytelling, lies the immeasurable worth of a stay-at-home father. He is my life's great love story.

Before he left, Dad gifted me the words, *The beauty of a daughter belongs to her father.* At last, concluding *The Revelations of Eapen,* I can present him with my response that, truly: *The beauty of a father belongs to his daughter.*

---

[41] *Endymion, Book 1.* J. Keats. (1818). Poetryfoundation.org.

# References

*A mari usque ad mare | The Canadian Encyclopedia.* (n.d.). Retrieved December 18, 2021, from https://www.thecanadianencyclopedia.ca/en/article/a-mari-usque-ad-mare

After Skool. (2021, January 19). *How childhood trauma leads to addiction – Gabor Maté* [Video]. YouTube. https://www.youtube.com/watch?v=BVg2bfqblGI

*Al Scalpone.* (n.d.). Oxford Reference. Retrieved April 20, 2021, from https://www.oxfordreference.com/view/10.1093/acref/9780191826719.001.0001/q-oro-ed4-00016647

Attig, T. (2011). *How we grieve: Relearning the world* (Rev. ed). Oxford University Press.

Attig, T. (2019). *Catching your breath in grief: -- And grace will lead you home.* Breath of Life Publishing.

*Bible gateway passage: Isaiah 41:10 - New King James Version.* (n.d.). Bible Gateway. Retrieved March 21, 2022, from https://www.biblegateway.com/passage/?search=Isaiah%2041%3A10&version=NKJV

Black, J., Belicki, K., Piro, R., & Hughes, H. (2020). Comforting versus distressing dreams of the deceased: Relations to grief, trauma, attachment, continuing bonds, and post-dream reactions. *OMEGA - Journal of Death and Dying, 84*(2) 525–550. https://doi.org/10.1177/0030222820903850

Breathing exercises: Three to try | 4-7-8 breath | Andrew Weil, m.d. (2016, October 28). *DrWeil.Com.* https://www.drweil.com/health-wellness/body-mind-spirit/stress-anxiety/breathing-three-exercises/

Brown, B. (2017). *Braving the wilderness: The quest for true belonging and the courage to stand alone* (First edition). Random House.

*Death is nothing at all by Henry Scott Holland, famous death poem.* (n.d.). Family Friend Poems. Retrieved January 13, 2021, from https://www.familyfriendpoems.com/poem/death-is-nothing-at-all-by-henry-scott-holland

Dickens, C., (2018). *A tale of two cities.* Alma Classics.

Foundation, P. (2022, July 15). *From Endymion by John Keats* [Text/html]. Poetry Foundation. https://www.poetryfoundation.org/poems/44469/endymion-56d2239287ca5

Foundation, P. (2020, November 15). *I wandered lonely as a cloud by William Wordsworth* [Text/html]. Poetry Foundation. https://www.poetryfoundation.org/poems/45521/i-wandered-lonely-as-a-cloud

Foundation, P. (2020, November 15). *The road not taken by Robert Frost* [Text/html]. Poetry Foundation. https://www.poetryfoundation.org/poems/44272/the-road-not-taken

*King James Bible.* (2020). King James Bible Online. https://www.kingjamesbibleonline.org (Original work published 1611).

Klass, D., & Steffen, E. (Eds.). (2018). *Continuing bonds in bereavement: New directions for research and practice.* Routledge, Taylor & Francis Group.

LaGrand, L. E. (2001). *Gifts from the unknown: Using extraordinary experiences to cope with loss & change.* Authors Choice Press.

Lewis, C. S. (1961). *A grief observed.* Bantam Books.

Lewis, T., Amini, F., & Lannon, R. (2001). *A general theory of love* (1. Vintage ed). Vintage.

Mathew, L. E. (2022). *Life: To be given back again to whence it came: Confronting grief illiteracy and healing loss using the art of storytelling.* DIO Press Inc.

Moore, T. (2004). *Dark nights of the soul: A guide to finding your way through life's ordeals.* Gotham Books.

Neimeyer, R. A. (2001). *Meaning reconstruction & the experience of loss* [Kindle version]. Retrieved from Amazon.com.

Neimeyer, R.A., & Thompson, B.E. (2014). *Grief and the expressive arts: Practices for creating meaning.* Routledge, Taylor & Francis Group.

*New International Version Bible—Read free online.* (n.d.). Biblestudytools.com. Retrieved November 15, 2020, from https://www.biblestudytools.com/niv/ (Original work published 1973).

Parkes, C. M., & Prigerson, H. G. (2010). *Bereavement: Studies of grief in adult life, fourth edition.* Penguin Books.

Pennebaker, J. W., & Smyth, J. M. (2016). *Opening up by writing it down: How expressive writing improves health and eases emotional pain* (Third edition). The Guilford Press.

*Serenity prayer.* (n.d.). Retrieved November 15, 2020, from https://www.beliefnet.com/prayers/protestant/addiction/serenity-prayer.aspx

Stroebe, M., & Schut, H. (2010). The dual process model of coping with bereavement: A decade on. *OMEGA - Journal of Death and Dying, 61*(4), 273–289.

Taylor, S. (2015). *The calm center: Reflections and meditations for spiritual awakening.* New World Library.

Van der Kolk, B. (2014). *The body keeps the score: Brain, mind, and body in the healing of trauma.* Penguin Books.

Weller, F. (2015). *The wild edge of sorrow: Rituals of renewal and the sacred work of grief.* North Atlantic Books.

Winfrey, Oprah (Host). (2018, September 18). Elie Wiesel: Living with an Open Heart [Audio podcast episode]. In Oprah's Super Soul Conversations. Apple Podcasts.

Wolfelt, A. (2003). *Understanding your grief: Ten essential touchstones for finding hope and healing your heart.* Companion Press.

Worden, J.W. (2018). *Grief counseling and grief therapy: A handbook for the mental health practitioner.* Springer Publishing Company, LLC.

# About the Author

**Linita Eapen Mathew**, Ed.D., M.Ed., B.Ed., B.A., is a secondary English Language Arts and mental health support teacher from Calgary, Alberta. She obtained her Doctor of Education from the University of Calgary, writing an autoethnographic dissertation that explored the effect of storytelling on bereavement. She received the Canadian Association of Teacher Education (2021) thesis and dissertation award for her work's contribution to teacher education. Using her skills and expertise for service, she created and led numerous Grief and Writing Through Grief workshops for educators and bereavement support centers across North America. The topic of her Master of Education (2014) focused on the benefit of embedding spirituality in education, bringing proactive mental health practices into the classroom to support student well-being. Her focus has always been to increase student achievement from the inside out—using targeted relationship building, spiritual dialogue, active listening, and compassionate writing exercises to reduce student suffering, which, in turn, raises self-esteem, resiliency, and grit toward successful goal completion and vocational alignment. Apart from being an educator, she is a writer at heart who has previously worked as a freelance writer and editor; and she is the symposium co-editor for the *British Journal of Guidance and Counselling*. After completing her Reiki Master training in 2016, she became the sole proprietor of PRANA, a thriving Reiki energy healing business based in Calgary, where she uses her understanding of spirituality to support the holistic healing of others.

CPSIA information can be obtained
at www.ICGtesting.com
Printed in the USA
BVHW090301171122
652161BV00003B/5